D0930434

Figures of Capable Imagination

Continuum Books by Harold Bloom

Kabbalah and Criticism (1975)
Figures of Capable Imagination

FIGURES OF CAPABLE IMAGINATION

HAROLD BLOOM

A CONTINUUM BOOK

The Seabury Press : New York

The Seabury Press, Inc.
815 Second Avenue
New York, N.Y. 10017

Printed in the United States of America

Acknowledgment is made to the publishers and editors of the following essays, in their first appearance and original form: 1) *Diacritics* and *New Perspectives on Wordsworth and Coleridge,* ed. G. Hartman (Columbia Univ. Press). 2) *Yale French Studies* and *Selected Writings of Walter Pater,* ed. H. Bloom (New American Library). 3) *Virginia Quarterly Review* and *Romanticism: Vistas, Continuities, Instances,* ed. G. Hartman and D. Thorburn (Cornell Univ. Press). 4) *Literary Theory and Structure,* ed. F. Brady, J. Palmer, and M. Price (Yale Univ, Press). 5) *Social Research* and *Death in American Experience,* ed. Arien Mack (Schocken Books). 6) *Prose* and Mr. Coburn Britton. 7) *Chicago Review.* 8) *Southern Review.* 9) *Salmagundi* and *American Poetry Since 1960,* ed. R. B. Shaw (Carcanet Press). 10) *Salmagundi* and *A. R. Ammons,* ed. E. Phillips (Wake Forest Univ. Press). 11) *Somewhere Is Such a Kingdom: Poems 1952–1971,* by Geoffrey Hill (Houghton, Mifflin). 12) *Commentary.* 13) *The Head of the Bed* by John Hollander (David Godine).

LIBRARY OF CONGRESS CATALOGING IN PUBLICATION DATA

Bloom, Harold.   Figures of capable imagination.

(A Continuum book)

1. American poetry—20th century—History and criticism. 2. Emerson, Ralph Waldo, 1803–1882—Criticism and interpretation. 3. English poetry—19th century—History and criticism. I. Title.

PS323.5.B6   811'.009   75-35826   ISBN 0–8164–9277–8

For J. Hillis Miller

I would not be hurried by any love of system, by any exaggeration of instincts, to underrate the Book. We all know, that as the human body can be nourished on any food, though it were boiled grass and the broth of shoes, so the human mind can be fed by any knowledge. And great and heroic men have existed who had almost no other information than by the printed page. I only would say that it needs a strong head to bear that diet. One must be an inventor to read well. As the proverb says, "He that would bring home the wealth of the Indies, must carry out the wealth of the Indies." There is then creative reading as well as creative writing. When the mind is braced by labor and invention, the page of whatever book we read becomes luminous with manifold allusion.

EMERSON, *The American Scholar*

Contents

Prefatory Note

These essays were written during a four-year period (1970–74) and were intended to illustrate, and be illustrated by, four short books I wrote in those years, *The Anxiety of Influence, A Map of Misreading, Kabbalah and Criticism,* and *Poetry and Repression,* all studies in poetic misprision. In a few of the essays, I have retained some short passages that are used in other contexts in the four tractates on influence.

Some of the essays have been revised since their original appearance. I have grouped them, but assert their "unity" only in association with a group of my writings that includes, in addition to the four short books on misprision, my full-length study, *Yeats,* and the later essays among those gathered in the collection, *The Ringers in the Tower.*

New Haven, Connecticut
December 8, 1974

Introduction

Borges has a story, *The Theologians,* that concerns the rivalry
of two learned Doctors of the Church, Aurelian of Aquileia
and John of Pannonia, who compete with one another in the
refutation of esoteric heresies. As Borges summarizes it:
"Both served in the same army, coveted the same guerdon,
warred against the same Enemy, but Aurelian did not write
a word which secretly did not strive to surpass John." When
Borges brings this tale to a climax, Aurelian has brought John
to the stake on a conviction of heresy, and then dies himself
in an Irish forest when a lightning bolt sets fire to surround-
ing trees. At the story's close, in the timeless kingdom of
Heaven, Aurelian learns that, for God, he and his rival John
"formed one single person." Like so much of Borges, this
reduces to a parable of literary influence, which is my obsessive subject.

All influence is dialectical, in that it involves both gain and
loss for both giver and recipient. And so all influence induces
anxiety, the dread that there will be not enough for oneself,
particularly of mental or spiritual space. The fear of there not
being enough left to do is probably the largest component in
the anxiety-of-influence, but even this fear, like most fears, is
a cover or mask for something else, the horror-of-origins that
seems to be one of the most basic of human anxieties. Freud
located this horror in our repressed sense of the Primal Scene
where our parents begat us, or alternatively in his more
fanciful Primal Scene of transgression in which a primal
horde of rival sons murdered a Sacred Father. The contemporary French philosopher Jacques Derrida has gone Father
Freud one better, by locating the Primal Trespass in what he

calls the Scene of Writing. I am attempting to go one stage beyond, by situating the anxiety-inducing transgression in what might be called the Primal Scene of Instruction, upon which all subsequent knowledge and individual relation to tradition depends. For each of us, however buried in the psyche, there hovers an obscure sense of a Scene of Instruction, by means of which there first came to us both a sense of the power that knowledge could bring us, and the guilt of indebtedness knowledge brought to us also.

Poets lie, both to themselves and to everyone else, about their indebtedness to one another, and most critics and literary scholars tend to follow poets by hopelessly idealizing all inter-poetic relations. Now that the tides of aggressive ignorance, or the counter-culture, are ebbing, many of the absurd hopes that the young and their middle-aged followers placed in an apocalypse of society are coming to rest in the arts, particularly literature, in the belief that there at least the repressed can return, a belief much encouraged by such false prophets as Marcuse and Norman O. Brown. But the dialectics of influence, if examined without over-idealizing, reveal that literature itself is founded upon rivalry, misinterpretation, repression, and even plain theft and savage misprision. And here, I think, is where I would seek to center the defence of my own studies. The splendor of literature is that it does show also the redemptive aspect of influence-anxiety, for the best poetry shows how the relation of any poet to his precursor is humanized into the greater themes of all human influence-relations which, as I say, include lust, envy, sexual jealousy, the horror and splendor of families, friendship, and the poet's reciprocal relation to his contemporaries, ultimately to all of his readers. To idealize imaginative literature is to repeat, albeit in a finer tone, those errors, however generous, that deranged our academies some five years ago. To see literature for what it is, the dark mirror of our egoism and our fallen condition, is to see ourselves again as perhaps eternity sees us, more like one another than we can bear to believe.

:I:

I

Coleridge

THE ANXIETY OF INFLUENCE

Coleridge observed that "psychologically, Consciousness is the problem," and he added somberly: "almost all is yet to be achieved." How much he achieved, Kathleen Coburn and others are showing us. My concern here is the sadder one of speculating yet again why he did not achieve more as a poet. Walter Jackson Bate has meditated, persuasively and recently, upon Coleridge's human and literary anxieties, particularly in regard to the burden of the past and its inhibiting poetic splendors. I swerve away from Mr. Bate to center the critical meditation upon what might be called the poetics of anxiety, the process of misprision by which any latecomer strong poet attempts to clear an imaginative space for himself. Coleridge could have been a strong poet, as strong as Blake or Wordsworth. He could have been another mighty antagonist for the Great Spectre Milton to engage and, yes, to overcome, but not without contests as titanic as *The Four Zoas* and *The Excursion,* and parental victories as equivocal as *Jerusalem* and *The Prelude.* But we have no such poems by Coleridge. When my path winds home at the end of this essay, I will speculate as to what these poems should have been. As critical fathers for my quest I invoke first, Oscar Wilde, with his glorious principle that the highest criticism sees the object as in itself it really is not, and second, Wilde's critical father, Walter Pater, whose essay of 1866 on "Coleridge's Writings" seems to me still the best short treatment of Coleridge, and this after a century of commentary. Pater, who knew his debt to Coleridge, knew also the anxiety Coleridge caused him, and Pater therefore came to a further and subtler knowing. In the Organic Analogue, against which the entire soul of the great Epicurean critic rebelled, Pater recognized the product of Coleridge's profound anxieties as a creator. I begin therefore with Pater on Coleridge, and then will move immediately deep into the Coleridgean interior, to look upon Coleridge's fierce refusal to take on the ferocity of the strong poet.

This ferocity, as both Coleridge and Pater well knew, expresses itself as a near-solipsism, an Egotistical Sublime, or Miltonic godlike stance. From 1795 on, Coleridge knew, loved, envied, was both cheered and darkened by the largest instance of that Sublime since Milton himself. He studied constantly, almost involuntarily, the glories of the truly modern strong poet, Wordsworth. Whether he gave Wordsworth rather more than he received, we cannot be certain; we know only that he wanted more from Wordsworth than he received, but then it was his endearing though exasperating weakness that he always needed more love than he could get, no matter how much he got: "To be beloved is all I need,/ And whom I love, I love indeed."

Pater understood what he called Coleridge's "peculiar charm," but he resisted it in the sacred name of what he called the "relative" spirit against Coleridge's archaizing "absolute" spirit. In gracious but equivocal tribute to Coleridge he observed:

> The literary life of Coleridge was a disinterested struggle against the application of the relative spirit to moral and religious questions. Everywhere he is restlessly scheming to apprehend the absolute; to affirm it effectively; to get it acknowledged. Coleridge failed in that attempt, happily even for him, for it was a struggle against the increasing life of the mind itself. . . . How did his choice of a controversial interest, his determination to affirm the absolute, weaken or modify his poetic gift?

To affirm the absolute, Pater says, or as we might say, to reject all dualisms except those sanctioned by orthodox

Christian thought, is not *materia poetica* for the start of the nineteenth century, and if we think of a poem like the "Hymn before Sunrise in the Vale of Chamouni," then we are likely to agree with Pater. We will agree also when he contrasts Wordsworth favorably with Coleridge, and even with Goethe, commending Wordsworth for "that flawless temperament . . . which keeps his conviction of a latent intelligence in nature within the limits of sentiment or instinct, and confines it to those delicate and subdued shades of expression which perfect art allows." Pater goes on to say that Coleridge's version of Wordsworth's instinct is a philosophical idea, which means that Coleridge's poetry had to be "more dramatic, more self-conscious" than Wordsworth's. But this in turn, Pater insists, means that for aesthetic success ideas must be held loosely, in the relative spirit. One idea that Coleridge did not hold loosely was the Organic Analogue, and it becomes clearer as we proceed in Pater's essay that the aesthetic critic is building toward a passionate assault upon the Organic principle. He quotes Coleridge's description of Shakespeare as "a nature humanized, a genial understanding, directing self-consciously a power and an implicit wisdom deeper even than our consciousness." "There," Pater comments, with bitter eloquence, " 'the absolute' has been affirmed in the sphere of art; and thought begins to congeal." With great dignity Pater adds that Coleridge has "obscured the true interest of art." By likening the work of art to a living organism, Coleridge does justice to the impression the work may give us, but he "does not express the process by which that work was produced."

M. H. Abrams, in his *The Mirror and the Lamp,* defends Coleridge against Pater by insisting that Coleridge knew his central problem "was to use analogy with organic growth to account for the spontaneous, the inspired, and the self-evolving in the psychology of invention, yet not to commit himself so far to the elected figure as to minimize the supervention of the antithetic qualities of foresight and choice." Though Abrams called Pater "short-sighted," I am afraid the critical palms remain with the relative spirit, for Pater's point was not that Coleridge had no awareness of the dangers of using the Organic Analogue, but rather that awareness, here as elsewhere, was no salvation for Coleridge. The issue is whether Coleridge, not Shakespeare, was able to direct "self-consciously a power and an implicit wisdom deeper than consciousness." Pater's complaint is valid because Coleridge, in describing Shakespeare, Dante, Milton, keeps repeating his absolute formula that poems grow from within themselves, that their "wholeness is not in vision or conception, but in an inner feeling of totality and absolute being." As Pater says, "that exaggerated inwardness is barren" because it "withdraws us too far from what we can see, hear, and feel," because it cheats the senses and the emotions of their triumph. I urge Pater's wisdom here not only against Coleridge, though I share Pater's love for Coleridge, but against the formalist criticism that continued in Coleridge's absolute spirit.

What is the imaginative source of Coleridge's disabling hunger for the Absolute? On August 9, 1831, about three years before he died, he wrote in his Notebook: "From my earliest recollection I have had a consciousness of Power without Strength—a perception, an experience, of more than ordinary power with an inward sense of Weakness. . . . More than ever do I feel this now, when all my fancies still in their integrity are, as it were, drawn *inward* and by their suppression and compression rendered a mock substitute for Strength." Here again is Pater's barren and exaggerated inwardness, but in a darker context than the Organic principle provided.

This context is Milton's "universe of death," where Coleridge apprehended death-in-life as being "the wretchedness of *division.*" If we stand in that universe, then "we think of ourselves as separated beings, and place nature in antithesis to the mind, as object to subject, thing to thought, death to life." To be so separated is to become, Coleridge says, "a soul-less fixed star, receiving no rays nor influences into my Being, *a Solitude which I so tremble at, that I cannot attribute it even to the Divine Nature.*" This, we can say, is

Coleridge's Counter-Sublime, his answer to the anxiety of influence in strong poets. The fear of solipsism is greater in him than the fear of not individuating his own imagination.

As with every other major Romantic, the prime precursor poet for Coleridge was Milton. There is a *proviso* to be entered here; for all these poets—Blake, Wordsworth, Shelley, Coleridge (only Keats is an exception)—there is a greater Sublime poetry behind Milton, but as its author is a people and not a single poet, and as it is far removed in time, its greatness does not inhibit a new imagination, not unless it is taken as the work of the Prime Precursor Himself, to whom all creation belongs. Only Coleridge acquired a doubly Sublime anxiety of influence, among these poets. Beyond the beauty that has terror in it of Milton was beauty more terrible. In a letter to Thelwall, December 17, 1796, Coleridge wrote: "Is not Milton a *sublimer* poet than Homer or Virgil? Are not his Personages more sublimely cloathed? And do you not know, that there is not perhaps *one* page in Milton's Paradise Lost, in which he has not borrowed his imagery from the *Scriptures?*—I allow, and rejoice that *Christ* appealed only to the understanding & the affections; but I affirm that, after reading Isaiah, or St. Paul's Epistle to the Hebrews, Homer & Virgil are disgustingly *tame* to me, & Milton himself barely tolerable." Yet these statements are rare in Coleridge. Frequently, Milton seems to blend with the ultimate Influence, which I think is a normal enough procedure. In 1796, Coleridge also says, in his review of Burke's *Letter to a Noble Lord:* "It is lucky for poetry, that Milton did not live in our days." Here Coleridge moves toward the center of his concern, and we should remember his formula: "Shakespeare was all men, potentially, except Milton." This leads to a more ambiguous formula, reported to us of a lecture that Coleridge gave on November 28, 1811: "Shakespeare became all things well into which he infused himself, while all forms, all things became Milton—the poet ever present to our minds and more than gratifying us for the loss of the distinct individuality of what he represents." Though Coleridge truly professes himself more than gratified, he admits loss. Milton's greatness is purchased at the cost of something dear to Coleridge, a principle of difference he knows may be flooded out by his monistic yearnings. For Milton, to Coleridge, is a mythic monad in himself. Commenting upon the apostrophe to light at the commencement of the third book of *Paradise Lost,* Coleridge notes: "In all modern poetry in Christendom there is an under consciousness of a sinful nature, a fleeting away of external things, the mind or subject greater than the object, the reflective character predominant. In the Paradise Lost the sublimest parts are the revelations of Milton's own mind, producing itself and evolving its own greatness; and this is truly so, that when that which is merely entertaining for its objective beauty is introduced, it at first seems a discord." This might be summarized as: where Milton is not, nature is barren, and its significance is that Milton is permitted just such a solitude as Coleridge trembles to imagine for the Divine Being.

Humphry House observed that "Coleridge was quite unbelievably modest about his own poems; and the modesty was of a curious kind, sometimes rather humble and overelaborate." As House adds, Coleridge "dreaded publication" of his poetry, and until 1828, when he was fifty-six, there was nothing like an adequate gathering of his verse. Wordsworth's attitude was no help, of course, and the Hutchinson girls and Dorothy no doubt followed Wordsworth in his judgments. There was Wordsworth, and before him there had been Milton. Coleridge presumably knew what "Tintern Abbey" owed to "Frost at Midnight," but this knowledge nowhere found expression. Must we resort to psychological speculation in order to see what inhibited Coleridge, or are there more reliable aids available?

In the *Biographia Literaria* Coleridge is not very kind to his pre-Wordsworthian poetry, and particularly to the "Religious Musings." Yet this is where we must seek what went wrong with Coleridge's ambitions, here, and if there were space, in "The Destiny of Nations" fragments (not its arbitrarily yoked-together form of 1817), and in the "Ode to the Departing Year" and "Monody on the Death of Chatterton" in its earlier versions. After Wordsworth had descended upon Coleridge, supposedly as a "know-thyself" admonition from heaven, but really rather more like a new form of the Miltonic blight, then Coleridge's poetic ambitions sustained another kind of inhibition. The Miltonic shadow needs to be studied first in early Coleridge, before a view can be obtained of his more mature struggles with influence.

With characteristic self-destructiveness, Coleridge gave "Religious Musings" the definitive subtitle: "A Desultory Poem, Written on the Christmas Eve of 1794." The root-meaning of "desultory" is "vaulting," and though Coleridge consciously meant that his poem skipped about and wavered, his imagination meant "vaulting," for "Religious Musings" is a wildly ambitious poem. "This is the time," it begins, in direct recall of Milton's "Nativity" Hymn, yet it follows not the Hymn but the most sublime moments of *Paradise Lost*, particularly the invocation to Book III. As with the 1802 "Hymn before Sunrise," its great fault as a poem is that it never stops whooping; in its final version I count well over one hundred exclamation-points in just over four hundred lines. Whether one finds this habit in Coleridge distressing or endearing hardly matters; he just never could stop doing it. He whoops because he vaults; he is a high-jumper of the Sublime, and psychologically he could not avoid this. I quote the poem's final passage, with relish and with puzzlement, for I am uncertain as to how good after all it may not be, though it does seem palpably awful. Yet its awfulness is at least Sublime; it is not the drab, flat awfulness of Wordsworth at *his* common worst in *The Excursion* or even (heresy to admit this!) in so many passages of *The Prelude* that we hastily skip by, with our zeal and relief in getting at the great moments. Having just shouted out his odd version of Berkeley, that "Life is a vision shadowy of truth," Coleridge sees "the veiling clouds retire" and God appears in a blaze upon His Throne. Raised to a pitch of delirium by this vision, Coleridge soars aloft to join it:

> *Contemplant Spirits! ye that hover o'er*
> *With untired gaze the immeasurable fount*
> *Ebullient with creative Deity!*

And ye of plastic power, that interfused
Roll through the grosser and material mass
In organizing surge! Holies of God!
(And what if Monads of the infinite mind?)
I haply journeying my immortal course
Shall sometime join your mystic choir! Till then
I discipline my young and novice thought
In ministeries of heart-stirring song,
And aye on Meditation's heaven-ward wing
Soaring aloft I breathe the empyreal air
Of Love, omnific, omnipresent Love,
Whose day-spring rises glorious in my soul
As the great Sun, when he his influence
Sheds on the frost-bound waters—The glad stream
Flows to the ray and warbles as it flows.

Scholars agree that this not terribly pellucid passage somehow combines an early Unitarianism with a later orthodox
overlay, as well as quantities of Berkeley, Hartley, Newton,
Neo-Platonism, and possibly more esoteric matter. A mere
reader will be reminded primarily of Milton, and will be in
the right, for Milton counts here and the rest do not. The
Spirits Coleridge invokes are Miltonic Angels, though their
functions seem to be more complicated. Coleridge confi-
dently assures himself and us that his course is immortal, that
he may end up as a Miltonic angel, and so perhaps also a
Monad of the infinite mind. In the meantime, he will study
Milton's "heart-stirring song." Otherwise, all he needs is
Love, which is literally the air he breathes, the sunrise radiat-
ing out of his soul in a stream of song, and the natural Sun
toward which he flows, a Sun that is not distinct from God.
If we reflect on how palpably sincere this is, how wholehearted, and consider what was to be Coleridge's actual poetic course, then we will be moved. Moved to what? Well,
perhaps to remember a remark of Coleridge's: "There are
many men, especially at the outset of life, who, in their too
eager desire for the end, overlook the difficulties in the way;
there is another class, who see nothing else. The first class

may sometimes fail; the latter rarely succeed." Whatever the truth of this for other men, no man becomes a strong poet unless he starts out with a certain obliviousness of the difficulties in the way. But soon enough he will meet those difficulties, and one of them will be that his precursor and inspirer threatens to subsume him, as Coleridge is subsumed by Milton in "Religious Musings" and his other pre-Wordsworthian poems. And here I shall digress massively, before returning to Coleridge's poetry, for I enter now upon the enchanted and baleful ground of poetic influence, through which I am learning to find my way by a singular light, which will bear a little explanation.

I do not believe that poetic influence is simply something that happens, that it is just the process by which ideas and images are transmitted from earlier to later poets. On that view, whether or not influence causes anxiety in the later poet is a matter of temperament and circumstance. Poetic influence thus reduces to source-study, of the kind performed upon Coleridge by Lowes and later scholars. Coleridge was properly scornful of such study, and I think most critics learn how barren an enterprise it turns out to be. I myself have no use for it as such, and what I mean by the study of poetic influence turns source-study inside out. The first principle of the proper study of poetic influence, as I conceive it, is that no strong poem has sources and no strong poem merely alludes to another poem. The meaning of a strong poem *is* another strong poem, a precursor's poem which is being misinterpreted, revised, corrected, evaded, twisted askew, made to suffer an inclination or bias which is the property of the later and not the earlier poet. Poetic influence, in this sense, is actually poetic misprision, a poet's taking or doing amiss of a parent-poem that keeps *finding* him, to use a Coleridgean turn-of-phrase. Yet even this misprision is only the first step that a new poet takes when he advances from the early phase where his precursor floods him, to a more Promethean phase where he quests for his own fire, which nevertheless must be stolen from his precursor.

I count some half-dozen steps in the life-cycle of the strong poet, as he attempts to convert his inheritance into what will aid him without inhibiting him by the anxiety of a failure in priority, a failure to have begotten himself. These steps are revisionary ratios, and for the convenience of shorthand, I find myself giving them arbitrary names, which are proving useful to me, and perhaps can be of use to others. I list them herewith, with descriptions but not examples, as this can only be a brief sketch, and I must get back to Coleridge's poetry, but I hope, with this list helpfully in hand, to find my examples in Coleridge.

1. *Clinamen*, which is poetic misprision proper; I take the word from Lucretius, where it means a "swerve" of the atoms so as to make change possible in the universe. The later poet swerves away from the precursor, by so reading the parent-poem as to execute a *clinamen* in relation to it. This appears as the corrective movement of his own poem, which implies that the precursor poem went accurately up to a certain point, but then should have swerved, precisely in the direction that the new poem moves.

2. *Tessera*, which is completion and antithesis; I take the word not from mosaic-making, where it is still used, but from the ancient Mystery-cults, where it meant a token of recognition, the fragment, say, of a small pot which with the other fragments would reconstitute the vessel. The later poet antithetically "completes" the precursor, by so reading the parent-poem as to retain its terms but to mean them in an opposite sense, as though the precursor had failed to go far enough.

3. *Kenosis*, which is a breaking-device similar to the defense mechanisms our psyches employ against repetition-compulsions; *kenosis*, then, is a movement toward discontinuity with the precursor. I take the word from St. Paul, where it means the humbling or emptying-out of Jesus by himself, when he accepts reduction from Divine to human status. The later poet, apparently emptying himself of his own afflatus, his imaginative godhood, seems to humble himself as though he ceased to be a poet, but this ebbing is so

performed in relation to a precursor's poem-of-ebbing that the precursor is emptied out also, and so the later poem of deflation is not as absolute as it seems.

4. *Daemonization,* or a movement toward a personalized Counter-Sublime, in reaction to the precursor's Sublime; I take the term from general Neo-Platonic usage, where an intermediary being, neither Divine nor human, enters into the adept to aid him. The later poet opens himself to what he believes to be a power in the parent-poem that does not belong to the parent proper, but to a range of being just beyond that precursor. He does this, in his poem, by so stationing its relation to the parent-poem as to generalize away the uniqueness of the earlier work.

5. *Askesis,* or a movement of self-purgation which intends the attainment of a state of solitude; I take the term, general as it is, particularly from the practice of pre-Socratic shamans like Empedocles. The later poet does not, as in *kenosis,* undergo a revisionary movement of emptying, but of curtailing; he yields up part of his own imaginative endowment, so as to separate himself from others, including the precursor, and he does this in his poem by so stationing it in regard to the parent-poem as to make that poem undergo an *askesis* also; the precursor's endowment is also truncated.

6. *Apophrades,* or the return of the dead; I take the word from the Athenian dismal or unlucky days upon which the dead returned to reinhabit the houses in which they had lived. The later poet, in his own final phase, already burdened by an imaginative solitude that is almost a solipsism, holds his own poem so open again to the precursor's work that at first we might believe the wheel has come full circle, and that we are back in the later poet's flooded apprenticeship, before his strength began to assert itself in the revisionary ratios of *clinamen* and the others. But the poem is now *held* open to the precursor, where once it *was* open, and the uncanny effect is that the new poem's achievement makes it seem to us, not as though the precursor were writing it, but as though the later poet himself had written the precursor's characteristic work.

These then are six revisionary ratios, and I think they can be observed, usually in cyclic appearance, in the life's work of every post-Enlightenment strong poet, which in English means, for practical purposes, every post-Miltonic strong poet. Coleridge, to return now where I began, had the potential of the strong poet, but declined the full process of developing into one, unlike Blake, Wordsworth, and the major poets after them down to Yeats and Stevens in our time. Yet his work, even in its fragmentary state, demonstrates this revisionary cycle in spite of himself. My ulterior purpose in this discussion is to use Coleridge as an instance because he is apparently so poor an example of the cycle I have sketched. But that makes him a sterner test for my theory of influence than any other poet I could have chosen.

I return to Coleridge's first mature poetry, and to its *clinamen* away from Milton, the Cowperizing turn that gave Coleridge the Conversation Poems, particularly "Frost at Midnight." Hazlitt quotes Coleridge as having said to him in the spring of 1798 that Cowper was the best modern poet, meaning the best since Milton, which was also Blake's judgment. Humphry House demonstrated the relation between "Frost at Midnight" and *The Task*, which is the happy one, causing no anxieties, where a stronger poet appropriates from a weaker one. Coleridge used Cowper as he used Bowles, Akenside, and Collins, finding in all of them hints that could help him escape the Miltonic influx that had drowned out "Religious Musings." "Frost at Midnight," like *The Task*, swerves away from Milton by softening him, by domesticating his style in a context that excludes all Sublime terrors. When Coleridge rises to his blessing of his infant son at the poem's conclusion he is in some sense poetically "misinterpreting" the beautiful declaration of Adam to Eve: "With thee conversing I forget all time," gentling the darker overtones of the infatuated Adam's declaration of love. Or, more simply, like Cowper he is not so much humanizing Milton—that will take the strenuous, head-on struggles of Blake, Wordsworth, Shelley, Keats—as he is making Milton more childlike, or perhaps better, reading Milton as though Milton loved in a more childlike way.

The revisionary step beyond this, an antithetical completion or *tessera*, is ventured by Coleridge only in a few pan-
theistic passages that sneaked past his orthodox censor, like
the later additions to "The Eolian Harp," or the veiled vision
at the end of the second verse paragraph of "This Lime-Tree
Bower My Prison." With his horror of division, his endless
quest for unity, Coleridge could not sustain any revisionary
impulse which involved his reversing Milton, or daring to
complete that sacred father.

But the next revisionary ratio, the *kenosis* or self-emptying, seems to me almost obsessive in Coleridge's poetry, for
what is the total situation of the Ancient Mariner but a
repetition-compulsion, which his poet breaks for himself
only by the writing of the poem, and then breaks only
momentarily. Coleridge had contemplated an Epic on the
Origin of Evil, but we may ask: where would Coleridge, if
pressed, have located the origin of evil in himself? His Mariner is neither depraved in will nor even disobedient, but is
merely ignorant, and the spiritual machinery his crime sets
into motion is so ambiguously presented as to be finally
beyond analysis. I would ask the question: what was
Coleridge trying (not necessarily consciously) to do for himself by writing the poem? and by this question I do not
mean Kenneth Burke's notion of trying to do something for
oneself as a person. Rather, what was Coleridge the poet
trying to do for himself as poet? To which I would answer:
trying to free himself from the inhibitions of Miltonic influence, by humbling his poetic self, and so humbling the Miltonic in the process. The Mariner does not empty himself
out; he starts empty and acquires a Primary Imagination
through his suffering. But, for Coleridge, the poem is a
kenosis, and what is being humbled is the Miltonic Sublime's account of the Origin of Evil. There is a reduction
from disobedience to ignorance, from the self-aggrandizing
consciousness of Eve to the painful awakening of a minimal
consciousness in the Mariner.

The next revisionary step in clearing an imaginative space
for a maturing strong poet is the Counter-Sublime, the attaining of which I have termed *daemonization*, and this I

take to be the relation of "Kubla Khan" and "Christabel" to *Paradise Lost.* Far more than "The Rime of the Ancient Mariner," these poems demonstrate a trafficking by Coleridge with powers that are daemonic, even though the "Rime" explicitly invokes Neo-Platonic daemons in its marginal glosses. Opium was the avenging daemon or *alastor* of Coleridge's life, his Dark or Fallen Angel, his experiential acquaintance with Milton's Satan. Opium was for him what wandering and moral taletelling became for the Mariner— the personal shape of repetition-compulsion. The lust for paradise in "Kubla Khan," Geraldine's lust for Christabel; these are manifestations of Coleridge's revisionary daemonization of Milton, these are Coleridge's Counter-Sublime. Poetic Genius, the genial spirit itself, Coleridge must see as daemonic when it is his own, rather than when it is Milton's.

It is at this point in the revisionary cycle that Coleridge begins to back away decisively from the ferocity necessary for the strong poet. He does not sustain his daemonization, closes his eyes in holy dread, stands outside the circumference of the daemonic agent, and is startled by his own sexual daring out of finishing "Christabel." He moves on to the revisionary ratio I have called *askesis,* or the purgation into solitude, the curtailing of some imaginative powers in the name of others. In doing so, he prophesies the pattern for Keats in *The Fall of Hyperion,* since in his *askesis* he struggles against the influence of a composite poetic father, Milton-Wordsworth. The great poems of this *askesis* are "Dejection: An Ode" and "To William Wordsworth," where criticism has demonstrated to us how acute the revision of Wordsworth's stance is, and how much of himself Coleridge purges away to make this revision justified. I would add only that both poems misread Milton as sensitively and desperately as they do Wordsworth; the meaning of "Dejection" is in its relation to "Lycidas" as much as in its relation to the "Intimations" Ode, even as the poem "To William Wordsworth" assimilates *The Prelude* to *Paradise Lost.* Trapped in his own involuntary dualisms, longing for a monistic wholeness such as he believes he is found by in Milton and Wordsworth, Coleridge in his *askesis* declines to see how much of his composite parent-poet he has purged away also.

After that, sadly enough, we have only a very few occasional poems of any quality by Coleridge, and they are mostly not the poems of a strong poet, that is, of a man vaulting into the Sublime. Having refused the full exercise of a strong poet's misprisions, Coleridge ceased to have poetic ambitions. But there is a significant exception, the late manuscript fragment "Limbo" and the evidently still-later fragment "Ne Plus Ultra." Here, and I think here only, Coleridge experiences the particular reward of the strong poet in his last phase, what I have called the *apophrades* or return of the dead, not a Counter-Sublime but a negative Sublime, like the *Last Poems* of Yeats or *The Rock* of Stevens. Indeed, negative sublimity is the mode of these Coleridgean fragments, and indicates to us what Coleridge might have become had he permitted himself enough of the perverse zeal that the great poet must exhibit in malforming his great precursor. "Limbo" and "Ne Plus Ultra" show that Coleridge could have become, at last, the poet of the Miltonic abyss, the bard of Demogorgon. Even as they stand, these fragments make us read Book II of *Paradise Lost* a little differently; they enable Coleridge to claim a corner of Milton's Chaos as his own.

Pater thought that Coleridge had succumbed to the Organic Analogue, because he hungered too intensely for eternity, as Lamb had said of his old school-friend. Pater also quoted De Quincey's summary of Coleridge: "he wanted better bread than can be made with wheat." I would add that Coleridge hungered also for an eternity of generosity between poets, as between people, a generosity that is not allowed in a world where each poet must struggle to individuate his own breath, and this at the expense of his forebears as much as his contemporaries. Perhaps also, to modify De Quincey, Coleridge wanted better poems than can be made without misprision.

I suggest then that the Organic Analogue, with all its pragmatic neglect of the processes by which poems have to be produced, appealed so overwhelmingly to Coleridge because it seemed to preclude the anxiety of influence, and to obviate the poet's necessity not just to unfold like a natural growth but to develop at the expense of others. Whatever the values of the Organic Analogue for literary criticism—and I believe, with Pater, that it does more harm than good—it provided Coleridge with a rationale for a dangerous evasion of inner steps he had to take for his own poetic development. As Blake might have said, Coleridge's imagination insisted upon slaying itself on the stems of generation, or to invoke another Blakean image, Coleridge lay down to sleep upon the Organic Analogue as though it were a Beulah-couch of soft, moony repose.

What was our loss in this? What poems might a stronger Coleridge have composed? The Notebooks list *The Origin of Evil, an Epic Poem, Hymns to the Sun, the Moon, and the Elements—six hymns,* and more fascinating even than these, a scheme for an epic on "the destruction of Jerusalem" by the Romans. Still more compelling is a March, 1802, entry in the Notebooks: "Milton, a Monody in the metres of Samson's Choruses—only with more rhymes/—poetical influences—political-moral-Dr. Johnson/" Consider the date of this entry, only a month before the first draft of "Dejection," and some sense of what *Milton, a Monody* might have been begins to be generated. In March, 1802, William Blake, in the midst of his sojourn at Hayley's Felpham, was deep in the composition of *Milton: A Poem in 2 Books, to Justify the Ways of God to Men.* In the brief, enigmatic notes for *Milton, a Monody* Coleridge sets down "—poetical influences—political-moral-Dr. Johnson," the last being, we can assume, a refutation of Johnson's vision of Milton in *The Lives of the Poets,* a refutation that Cowper and Blake would have endorsed. "Poetical influences," Coleridge says, and we may recall that this is one of the themes of Blake's *Milton,* where the Shadow of the Poet Milton is one with the Covering Cherub, the great blocking-agent who inhibits fresh human creativity by embodying in himself all the sinister beauty of tradition. Blake's *Milton* is a kind of monody in places, not as a mourning for

Milton, but as Milton's own, solitary utterance, as he goes down from a premature Eternity (where he is unhappy) to struggle again in fallen time and space. I take it though that *Milton, a Monody* would be modeled upon Coleridge's early "Monody on the Death of Chatterton," and so would have been Coleridge's lamentation for his Great Original. Whether, as Blake was doing at precisely the same time, Coleridge would have dared to identify Milton as the Covering Cherub, as the angel or daemon blocking Coleridge himself out from the poet's paradise, I cannot surmise. I wish deeply that Coleridge had written the poem.

It is ungrateful, I suppose, as the best of Coleridge's recent scholars keep telling us, to feel that Coleridge did not give us the poems he had it in him to write. Yet we have, all apology aside, only a double handful of marvelous poems by him. I close therefore by attempting a description of the kind of poem I believe Coleridge's genius owed us, and which we badly need, and always will need. I would maintain that the finest achievement of the High Romantic poets of England was their humanization of the Miltonic Sublime. But when we attend deeply to the works where this humanization is most strenuously accomplished—Blake's *Milton* and *Jerusalem, The Prelude, Prometheus Unbound,* the two *Hyperions,* even in a way *Don Juan*—we sense at last a quality lacking, in which Milton abounds, for all his severity. This quality, though not in itself a tenderness, made Milton's Eve possible, and we miss such a figure in all her Romantic descendants. More than the other five great Romantic poets, Coleridge was able, by temperament and by subtly shaded intellect, to have given us a High Romantic Eve, a total humanization of the tenderest and most appealing element in the Miltonic Sublime. Many anxieties blocked Coleridge from that rare accomplishment, and of these the anxiety of influence was not the least.

2

Walter Pater

> . . . . *What is this song or picture, this engaging*
> *personality presented in life or in a book, to* me?
> *What effect does it really produce on me? Does it*
> *give me pleasure? and if so, what sort or degree of*
> *pleasure? How is my nature modified by its pres-*
> *ence, and under its influence?*
>
> P A T E R ("Preface" to *The Renaissance*)

> . . . *Why should a poem not change in sense*
> *when there is a fluctuation of the whole of appear-*
> *ance? Or why should it not change when we real-*
> *ize that the indifferent experience of life is the*
> *unique experience, the item of ecstasy which we*
> *have been isolating and reserving for another time*
> *and place, loftier and more secluded.*
>
> S T E V E N S ("Two or Three Ideas")

* * *

I • ''AESTHETIC'' CRITICISM

Pater is a great critic of a kind common enough in the nineteenth century—Coleridge, Lamb, Hazlitt, De Quincey,
above all Ruskin—but scarcely to be found in the twentieth.
Difficult to define, this sort of critic possesses one salient
characteristic. His value inheres neither in his accuracy at
the direct interpretation of meaning in texts nor in his judgments of relative eminence of works and authors. Rather, he
gives us a vision of art through his own unique sensibility, and

so his own writings obscure the supposed distinction between criticism and creation. "Supposed," because who can
convince us of that distinction? To adapt Shelley's idea of the
relation between poetry and the universe, let us say that
criticism creates the poem anew, after the poem has been
annihilated in our minds by the recurrence of impressions
blunted by reiteration. Ruskin's or Pater's criticism tends to
create anew not so much a particular work of art but rather
the precisely appropriate consciousness of the perceptive
reader or viewer. This does not mean that these great critics
are monuments to the Affective Fallacy, or that literary his-
torians with formalist tendencies are justified in naming Ruskin and Pater as critical Impressionists. Oscar Wilde, who
brilliantly vulgarized both his prime precursors, insisted that
their work treated "the work of art simply as a starting-point
for a new creation." Matthew Arnold had asserted that the
"aim of criticism is to see the object as in itself it really is."
A few years later, implicitly invoking Ruskin against Arnold,
Pater slyly added that "the first step towards seeing one's
object as it really is, is to know one's impression as it really
is, to discriminate it, to realise it distinctly." Wilde, attempting to complete his master, charmingly amended this to the
grand statement that "the primary aim of the critic is to see
the object as in itself it really is not." Between Arnold's self-
deception and Wilde's wit comes Pater's hesitant and skeptical emphasis upon a peculiar kind of vision, with which he
identifies all aesthetic experience.

We owe to Pater our characteristic modern use of "aesthetic," for he emancipated the word from its bondage to
philosophy, both when he spoke of the "aesthetic critic" in
his "Preface" to *The Renaissance,* and when he named the
work of Morris and Rossetti as the "aesthetic poetry" in *Appreciations.* Vulgarized again by his ebullient disciple Wilde,
and by the parodies of Wilde as Bunthorne in Gilbert and
Sullivan's *Patience,* and of Pater himself as Mr. Rose in W. H.
Mallock's *The New Republic,* Pater had to endure the de-
basement of "aesthete" as a term, and we endure it still.
Pater meant us always to remember what mostly we have

forgotten: that "aesthete" is from the Greek *aisthetes,* "one who perceives." So the "aesthetic critic" is simply the perceptive critic, or literary critic proper, and "aesthetic poetry" is precisely the contemporary poetry that is most perceptive, that is, in one's judgment most truly poetry.

Pater's key terms as a critic are "perception" and "sensation," which is response to perception. "Vision" for Pater, as for Blake, is a synonym for Coleridge's or Wordsworth's "Imagination," and Pater further emulated Blake by questing after the "spiritual form" of phenomena as against "corporeal form." This is the "form" that: "Every moment . . . grows perfect in hand or face," according to the almost preternaturally eloquent "Conclusion" to *The Renaissance.* In the marvelous "Postscript" on "Romanticism" to *Appreciations,* Pater traces the genesis of form:

> . . . there are the born romanticists, who start with an original, untried *matter,* still in fusion; who conceive this vividly, and hold by it as the essence of their work; who, by the very vividness and heat of their conception, purge away, sooner or later, all that is not organically appropriate to it, till the whole effect adjusts itself in clear, orderly, proportionate form; which form, after a very little time, becomes classical in its turn.

Vividness and *heat* purge away from the Romantic idea all that is not form, and form is the reward of the aesthete or perceptive man, if he has the strength to persist in his purgation. "In the end, the aesthetic is completely crushed and destroyed by the inability of the observer who has himself been crushed to have any feeling for it left." That dark observation is by Wallace Stevens, an heir (unwilling) of Pater's aestheticism. A more accurate observation of the aesthete's defeat comes from as great an heir, more conscious and willing, who attributed to Pater's influence his poetic generation's doomed attempt "to walk upon a rope, tightly stretched through serene air." Yeats nevertheless got across to the other side of the Nineties, and carried Pater alive into our century in *Per Amica Silentia Lunae* (1917) and *A Vision* (1925, 1937). Pater's vision of form culminates in Yeat's Phase 15: "Now contemplation and desire, united into one, inhabit a world where every beloved image has bodily form, and every bodily form is loved." Pater, for whom the attained form demanded purgation, an *askesis* (to which I shall return), hesitantly held back from this Yeatsian version of a High Romantic Absolute.

To know Pater, and to apprehend his influence not only on Stevens and Yeats, but on Joyce, Eliot, Pound and many other writers of our century, we need to place Pater in his Oedipal context in the cultural situation of his own time. The pleasures of reading Pater are intense, to me, but the importance of Pater transcends those pleasures, and finally is quite out of proportion to Pater's literary achievement, fairly large as that was. Pater is the heir of a tradition already too wealthy to have required much extension or variation when it reached him. He revised that tradition, turning the Victorian continuation of High Romanticism into the Late Romanticism or "Decadence" that prolonged itself as what variously might be called Modernism, Post-Romanticism, or, self-deceivingly, anti-Romanticism, the art of Pound's Vortex. Though Pater compares oddly, perhaps not wholly adequately, with the great Victorian prose prophets, he did what Carlyle, Ruskin, Newman, Arnold could not do: he fathered the future. Wistful and elaborately reserved, renouncing even his own strength, he became the most widely diffused (though more and more hidden) literary influence of the later nineteenth upon the twentieth century. In its diffusion, particularly in America, the Paterian influence was assimilated to strikingly similar elements in Nietzsche and Emerson, a process as indubitable as it is still largely unstudied. When Yeats proclaimed the "profane perfection of mankind" or Pound or Stevens their images of the poet as a crystal man they combined Pater with Nietzsche and Emerson (both of whom he seems to have neglected). "Just take one step farther," Nietzsche urged, and "love yourself through Grace; then you are no longer in need of your God, and the whole drama of fall and redemption is acted out in yourself." "In the highest moments, we are a vision," is the antinomian counsel of Emerson. Pater's first essay, "Diaphaneite," read to an Oxford literary group in 1864, presented the artist as a transparent or crystal image of more-than-human perfection, an Apollonian hero. How often, in Modern poetry, we have heard these strains mingled, until by now our latest poets alternately intoxicate and eradicate themselves in the inhuman effort that might sustain a vision so exalted. Pater, though a theorist of the Dionysian, evaded the heroic vitalism of a Nietzsche or the quasi-divine self-reliance of an Emerson, declining to present himself either as prophet or as orator. Yet his baroque meditations upon art, hieratic and subdued, touch as firmly upon the ruinous strength of our major Modern poets as any other precursor of our sensibility does.

II · PRIVILEGED MOMENTS

Pater's context begins with his only begetter, Ruskin, whose effect can be read, frequently through negation, throughout Pater's work. Believing, as he says in "Style," that imaginative prose largely took the place of poetry in the modern world, Pater necessarily assumed, consciously I think, the characteristic malady of post-Enlightenment poetry, the new creator's anxiety-of-influence in regard to his precursor's priority, which becomes a menacing spiritual authority, in a direct transference from the natural to the imaginative world. Ruskin, despite his irrelevant mania for ferocious moralizing, is the major "aesthetic critic," in Pater's sense, of the nineteenth century. Stylistically, Pater owed more to Swinburne, but stance rather than style is the crucial indebtedness of a poet or imaginative prose writer. This is Swinburne, *sounds* like Pater, yet menaced him not at all:

> All mysteries of good and evil, all wonders of life and death, lie in their hands or at their feet. They have known the causes of things, and are not too happy. The

fatal labour of the world, the clamour and hunger of the
open-mouthed all-summoning grave, all fears and hopes
of ephemeral men, are indeed made subject to them,
and trodden by them underfoot; but the sorrow and
strangeness of things are not lessened because to one or
two their secret springs have been laid bare and the
courses of their tides made known; refluent evil and
good, alternate grief and joy, life inextricable from
death, change inevitable and insuperable fate.

Swinburne is speaking of Michelangelo, Aeschylus,
Shakespeare; masters of the Sublime, whose mastery does
not lessen "sorrow and strangeness." The accent here
becomes Pater's (Cecil Lang surmises that Gautier's prose is
behind Swinburne's, and Gautier also affected the early
Pater) but the attitude, superficially akin to Pater's, is profoundly alien to the Epicurean visionary. Swinburne broods
on knowledge and powerlessness, but Pater cared only
about perception, about seeing again what Michelangelo,
Aeschylus, Shakespeare *saw*. Ruskin's Biblical style was no
burden to the Hellenizing Pater, but Ruskin's critical stance
was at once initial release yet ultimate burden to his disciple. For this is Pater's Gospel, but it is Ruskin's manifesto:
". . . the greatest thing a human soul ever does in this world
is to see something, and tell what it saw in a plain way.
Hundreds of people can talk for one who can think, but
thousands can think for one who can see. To see clearly is
poetry, prophecy and religion all in one." Pater was not
concerned to tell what he saw in a plain way, but he was
kindled by this exaltation of seeing.

Ruskin himself, though uniquely intense as a prophet of
the eye, belonged to the Spirit of the Age in his emphasis, as
Pater well knew. The primal source of later Romantic seeing
in England was Wordsworth, who feared the tyranny of the
eye, yet who handed on to his disciples not his fear of the
visual, nor (until much later) his Sublime visionary sense, but
his program for renovation through renewed encounters
with visible nature. Carlyle, a necessary link between Words-

worth and Ruskin, equated the heroism of the poet with "the seeing eye." But a trouble, already always present in Wordsworth and Coleridge, developed fully in Ruskin's broodings upon vision. *Modern Painters III* (1856) distinguishes "the difference between the ordinary, proper, and true appearances of things to us; and the extraordinary, or false appearances, when we are under the influence of emotion, or contemplative fancy; false appearances, I say, as being entirely unconnected with any real power or character in the object, and only imputed to it by us." This imputation of life to the object-world Ruskin called the "pathetic fallacy" and judged as "a falseness in all our impressions of external things." The greatest order of poets, the "Creative" (Shakespeare, Homer, Dante), Ruskin declared free of the pathetic fallacy, finding it endemic in the second order of poets, the "Reflective or Perceptive" (Wordsworth, Keats, Tennyson). Himself a thorough Wordsworthian, Ruskin did not mean to deprecate his Reflective (or Romantic) grouping, but rather to indicate its necessary limitation. Like Pater after him, Ruskin was haunted throughout his life and writings by Wordsworth's "Intimations" Ode, which objectified for both critics their terrible sense of bereavement, of estrangement from the imaginative powers they possessed (or believed themselves to have possessed) as children. Both Ruskin and Pater began as Wordsworthian poets, and turned to imaginative prose partly because of the anxiety-of-influence induced in them by Wordsworth.

Ruskin's formulation of the pathetic fallacy protests the human loss involved in Wordsworth's compensatory imagination. As such, Ruskin's critique prophesies the winter vision of Wallace Stevens, from "The Snow Man" through to "The Course of a Particular." When Stevens reduces to what he calls the First Idea, he returns to "the ordinary, proper, and true appearances of things to us," but then finds it dehumanizing to live only with these appearances. So the later Ruskin found also, in his own elaborate mythicizings in *Sesame and Lilies* and related books, and in the Wordsworthian autobiography *Praeterita* that closed his work.

What Wordsworth called "spots of time," periods of particular splendor or privileged moments testifying to the mind's power over the eye, Ruskin had turned from earlier, as being dubious triumphs of the pathetic fallacy. Pater, who subverted Ruskin by going back to their common ancestor, Wordsworth, may be said to have founded his criticism upon privileged moments of vision, or "epiphanies" as Joyce's Stephen, another Paterian disciple, was to term them.

The "epiphany," for us, has been much reduced, yet still prevails as our poets' starting-point for moving from sensation to mastery, or at least to self-acceptance:

> *Perhaps there are times of inherent excellence,*
> . . . .
> *Perhaps there are moments of awakening,*
> *Extreme, fortuitous, personal, in which*
> *We more than awaken. . . .*

But Stevens' good moments, as here in *Notes Toward a Supreme Fiction,* have receded even from the modified Wordsworthianism that Pater offered as privileged moments, or pathetic fallacies raised to triumphs of perception. For Ruskin's "Perceptive" poets are Pater's "Aesthetic" poets, not a second order but the only poets possible in the universe of death, the Romantic world we have come to inhabit. Joyce's Stephen, recording epiphanies as "the most delicate and evanescent of moments," is recollecting Pater's difficult ecstasy that flares forth "for that moment only." The neo-orthodox, from Hopkins through Eliot to Auden, vainly attempted to restore Pater's "moments" to the religious sphere, yet gave us only what Eliot insisted his poetry would not give, instances of "the intense moment / Isolated, with no before and after," the actual art (such as it is) of *Four Quartets* even as it was of *The Waste Land.* Pater remains the most honest recorder of epiphanies, by asking so little of them, as here in the essay on the poet Joachim Du Bellay in *The Renaissance:*

> A sudden light transfigures a trivial thing, a weather-
> vane, a windmill, a winnowing flail, the dust in the barn
> door; a moment—and the thing has vanished, because
> it was pure effect; but it leaves a relish behind it, a
> longing that the accident may happen again.

"He had studied the nostalgias," like his descendant in
Stevens' more qualified vision, and he did not pretend we
could be renovated by happy accidents. Yet he offered a
program more genuinely purgative than High Romanticism
had ventured:

> . . . painting and poetry . . . can accomplish their
> function in the choice and development of some special
> situation, which lifts or glorifies a character, in itself not
> poetical. To realise this situation, to define, in a chill and
> empty atmosphere, the focus where rays, in themselves
> pale and impotent, unite and begin to burn . . .

This, from the early essay on "Winckelmann," presents the
embryo of a Paterian epiphany. Here is such an epiphany at
its most central, in the crucial chapter, "The Will as Vision,"
of *Marius the Epicurean:*

> Through some accident to the trappings of his horse
> at the inn where he rested, Marius had an unexpected
> delay. He sat down in an olive garden, and, all around
> him and within still turning to reverie. . . . A bird came
> and sang among the wattled hedgeroses: an animal
> feeding crept nearer: the child who kept it was gazing
> quietly: and the scene and the hours still conspiring, he
> passed from that mere fantasy of a self not himself, be-
> side him in his coming and going, to those divinations
> of a living and companionable spirit at work in all
> things. . . .
> In this peculiar and privileged hour, his bodily frame,
> as he could recognize, although just then, in the whole
> sum of its capacities, so entirely possessed by him—Nay!
> actually his very self—was yet determined by a far-
> reaching system of material forces external to it. . . . And

might not the intellectual frame also, still more inti-
mately himself as in truth it was, after the analogy of the
bodily life, be a moment only, an impulse or series of
impulses, a single process . . . ? How often had the
thought of their brevity spoiled for him the most natural
pleasures of life . . . —To-day at least, in the peculiar
clearness of one privileged hour, he seemed to have
apprehended . . . an abiding place. . . .

Himself—his sensations and ideas—never fell again
precisely into focus as on that day, yet he was the richer
by its experience . . . It gave him a definitely ascertained
measure of his moral or intellectual need, of the demand his soul must make upon the powers, whatsoever
they might be, which had brought him, as he was, into
the world at all . . .

All of Pater is in this passage. Wordsworth lamented the
loss of an earlier glory, ultimately because such glory was
equal to an actual sense of immortality. He celebrated "spots
of time," not because they restored that saving sense, but in
the hope they testified to his spirit's strength over a phe-
nomenal world of decay, and so modestly hinted at some
mode of survival. Ruskin, until he weakened (on his own
terms), insisted on the Homeric strength of gazing upon
ocean, and seeing no emblem of continuity but only pure
physical nature: "Black or clear, monstrous or violet-
coloured, cold salt water it is always, and nothing but that."
Pater's Marius has been found by a skeptical but comforting
compromise between the natural visions of Wordsworth and
Ruskin. "Peculiar and privileged," or "extreme, fortuitous,
personal" as Stevens was to call it, the time of reverie abides
in Ruskin's "pure physical nature," yet holds together in
continuity not only past and present but what was only potential in the past to a sublimity still possible in the future.
The self still knows that it reduces to "sensations and ideas"
(the subtitle of *Marius the Epicurean*), still knows the brevity
of its expectation, knows even more strongly it is joined to no
immortal soul, yet now believes also that its own integrity
can be at one with the system of forces outside it. Pater's

strange achievement is to have assimilated Wordsworth to Lucretius, to have compounded an idealistic naturalism with a corrective materialism. By de-idealizing the epiphany, he makes it available to the coming age, when the mind will know neither itself nor the object but only the dumbfounding abyss that comes between.

III • H I S T O R I C I S M S   *Renaissance and Romanticism*

Pater began to read Ruskin in 1858, when he was just nineteen, eight years before he wrote his first important essay, "Winckelmann." From then until the posthumously published writings, Pater suffered under Ruskin's influence, though from the start he maintained a revisionary stance in regard to his precursor. In place of Ruskin's full, prophetic, even overwhelming rhetoric, Pater evolved a partial, hesitant, insinuating rhetoric, yet the result is a style quite as elaborate as his master's. The overt influence, Pater buried deep. He mentioned Ruskin just once in his letters, and then to claim priority over Ruskin by two years as the English discoverer of Botticelli (as late as 1883, Ruskin still insisted otherwise, but wrongly). Ruskin is ignored, by name, in the books and essays, yet he hovers everywhere in them, and nowhere more strongly than in *The Renaissance* (1873), for Pater's first book is primarily an answer to *The Stones of Venice* (1851, 1853) and to the five volumes of *Modern Painters* (1843–1860). Where Ruskin had deplored the Renaissance (and located it in Italy, between the fourteenth and sixteenth centuries), elevating instead the High Middle Ages, Pater emulated the main movement of English Romanticism by exalting the Renaissance (and then anticipated later studies by locating its origins in twelfth century France). Yet the polemic against Ruskin, here as elsewhere, remains implicit. One of Pater's friends reported that once, when talking of Ruskin's strength of perception, Pater burst out: "I cannot believe that Ruskin saw more in the church of St. Mark than I do." Pater's ultimate bitterness, in this area, came in 1885, when Ruskin resigned as Slade Professor of Fine Art at Ox-

ford. Pater offered himself for the professorship, but it went
to one Hubert Von Herkomer, and not to the author of the
notorious book on the Renaissance, whose largest departure
from Ruskin was in opposing a darker and hedonistic humanism to the overtly moral humanism of his aesthetic precursor.

The vision of Pater's *Renaissance* centers upon the hope
of what Yeats was to call Unity of Being. Drawing his epigraph from the Book of Psalms, Pater hints at the aesthetic
man's salvation from the potsherds of English Christianity in
the 1860s: "Though ye have lain among the pots, yet shall ye
be as the wings of a dove covered with silver, and her feath-
ers with yellow gold" (Psalms 68:13). The aesthetic man, sur-
rounded by the decaying absolutes inherited from Coler-
idge-as-theologian, accepts the truths of solipsism and isolation, of mortality and the flux of sensations, and glories in the
singularity of his own peculiar kind of contemplative temperament. Pater would teach this man self-reconcilement
and self-acceptance, and so Unity of Being. In the great
figures of the Renaissance—particularly Botticelli, Michelangelo, Leonardo—Pater presents images of this Unity of aesthetic contemplation. Ruskin, a greater critic than Pater, did
not over-idealize the possibilities of aesthetic contemplation,
not even in books as phantasmagoric as *The Queen of the Air*.
Pater's desperation, both to go beyond Ruskin and to receive
more from art, is at once his defining weakness in comparison
to Ruskin, and his greater importance for what was to come,
not just in the 1880s and 1890s, but throughout our century.

In his vision of the Renaissance, Pater inherits the particular historicism of English Romanticism, which had found its
own origins in the English Renaissance, and believed itself a
renaissance of that Renaissance. Between the High Romantics and Pater many losses were felt, and of these Darwin
compelled the largest. *The Renaissance* is already a Dar-
winian book, rather in the same way that *The Stones of Venice* was still a Coleridgean book. Pater's moral tentativeness
necessarily reflected his own profound repressions, including
his aversion to heterosexuality, and the very clear strain of
sadomasochism in his psyche. But the intellectual sanction of

Pater's skeptical Epicureanism was provided by the preva-
lent skepticism even of religious apologias in the age of Newman and the Oxford Movement. Evolution, whether as presented by Christian historicisms or by Darwin himself, gave
the self-divided Pater a justification for projecting his temperament into a general vision of his age's dilemmas. His
later work, considered further on in this essay, found a governing dialectic for his skepticism in the pre-Socratics and
Plato, but in *The Renaissance* the personal projection is more
direct, and proved more immediately influential.

The "Preface" to *The Renaissance* outlines a cycle in the
concept of renaissance, which goes from an early freshness
with "the charm of *ascesis,* of the austere and serious girding
of the loins in youth" to "that subtle and delicate sweetness
which belongs to a refined and comely decadence." The
Greek word *ascesis* (or *askesis*) originally referred to athleti-
cism, but easily transferred itself, even in ancient time, to an
exercise in spiritualizing purgation. Paterian *askesis* is less a
sublimation (as it seems when first used in the "Preface")
than it is an aesthetic self-curtailment, a giving-up of certain
powers so as to help achieve more originality in one's self-
mastery. An Epicurean or hedonistic *askesis* is only superficially a paradox, since it is central in the Lucretian vision that
Pater labored to attain. For Lucretius, truth is always in appearances, the mind is a flow of sensory patterns, and moral
good is always related directly to pleasurable sensations. But
intense pleasure, as Epicurus taught, is grossly inferior to
possessing a tranquil temperament. Pater's Epicureanism, in
The Renaissance, was more radical, and hesitates subtly at
exalting a quasi-homosexual and hedonistic humanism, particularly in the essays on Leonardo and on Winckelmann.

In the essay on "Two Early French Stories," Pater identifies his "medieval Renaissance" with "its antinomianism, its
spirit of rebellion and revolt against the moral and religious
ideas of the time." Pater's own antinomianism is the unifying
element in his great first book, as he elaborately intimates "a
strange idolatry, a strange rival religion" in opposition to the
Evangelical faith of Ruskin and the revived orthodoxies of

the Oxford Movement. The extraordinary essay on Botticelli,
a triumphant prose poem, sees in his Madonna "one of those
who are neither for Jehovah nor for His enemies," and hints
at a sadomasochistic sadness with which Botticelli conceives
the universe of pleasure he has chosen. In the essay on Leonardo, which may be Pater's finest poem, the visionary center
is reached in the notorious (and wholly magnificent) passage
on *La Gioconda,* which Yeats brilliantly judged to be the first
Modern poem, but which he proceeded to butcher by print-
ing in verse form as the first poem in *The Oxford Book of
Modern Verse* (1936). Yeats, in his "Introduction," asked an
insightful and largely rhetorical question: "Did Pater fore-
shadow a poetry, a philosophy, where the individual is nothing, the flux of *The Cantos* of Ezra Pound, objects without
contour . . . , human experience no longer shut into brief
lives, . . . the flux . . . that within our minds enriches itself,
redreams itself . . . ?"

Freud, in his study of Leonardo, found in the Mona Lisa
the child's defence against excessive love for his mother, by
means of identifying with her and so proceeding to love boys
in his own image, even as he had been loved. In one of his
most troubling insights, Freud went on to a theory of the
sexual origins of all thought, a theory offering only two ways
out for the gifted; either a compulsive, endless brooding in
which all intellectual curiosity remains sexual, or a successful
sublimation, in which thought, to some extent, is liberated
from its sexual past. Is Pater, throughout *The Renaissance,*
and particularly in the "Leonardo" and the "Conclusion,"
merely a fascinating, compulsive brooder, or has he freed his
thought from his own over-determined sexual nature? Some
recent studies reduce Pater only to the former possibility,
but this is to underestimate an immensely subtle mind. Here
is the crucial passage, not a purple patch but a paean to the
mind's mastery over its own compulsiveness:

> The presence that rose thus so strangely beside the
> waters, is expressive of what in the ways of a thousand
> years men had come to desire. Hers is the head upon

which all "the ends of the world are come," and the eyelids are a little weary. It is a beauty wrought out from within upon the flesh, the deposit, little cell by cell, of strange thoughts and fantastic reveries and exquisite passions. Set it for a moment beside one of those white Greek goddesses or beautiful women of antiquity, and how would they be troubled by this beauty, into which the soul with all its maladies has passed! All the thoughts and experience of the world have etched and moulded there, in that which they have of power to refine and make expressive the outward form, the animalism of Greece, the lust of Rome, the mysticism of the middle age with its spiritual ambition and imaginative loves, the return of the Pagan world, the sins of the Borgias. She is older than the rocks among which she sits; like the vampire, she has been dead many times, and learned the secrets of the grave; and has been a diver in deep seas, and keeps their fallen day about her; and trafficked for strange webs with Eastern merchants, and, as Leda, was the mother of Helen of Troy, and, as Saint Anne, the mother of Mary; and all this has been to her but as the sound of lyres and flutes, and lives only in the delicacy with which it has moulded the changing lineaments, and tinged the eyelids and the hands. The fancy of a perpetual life, sweeping together ten thousand experiences, is an old one; and modern philosophy has conceived the idea of humanity as wrought upon by, and summing up in itself, all modes of thought and life. Certainly Lady Lisa might stand as the embodiment of the old fancy, the symbol of the modern idea.

Most broadly, this is Pater's comprehensive vision of an equivocal goddess whom Blake called "the Female Will" and the ancient Orphics named *Ananke,* meaning "Necessity." Pater dreads and desires her, or perhaps desires her precisely through his dread. Desire dominates here, for the sight of her is a privileged moment, an epiphany of the only divinity Pater truly worshipped. In the essay following, on "The School of Giorgione," Pater speaks of "profoundly significant and animated instants, a mere gesture, a look, a smile, perhaps—some brief and wholly concrete moment—into which, however, all the motives, all the interests and effects of a long history, have condensed themselves, and which seem to absorb past and future in an intense consciousness of the present." The Lady Lisa, as an inevitable object of the quest for all which we have lost, is herself a process moving towards a final entropy, summing up all the estrangements we have suffered from the object-world we once held close, whether as children, or in history. She incarnates too much, both for her own good and for ours. The cycles of civilization, the burden our consciousness bears, renders us latecomers, but the Lady Lisa perpetually carries the seal of a terrible priority. Unity of Being she certainly possesses, yet she seems to mock the rewards Pater hoped for in such Unity. A powerful juxtaposition, of the ancient dream of a literal immortality, of living all lives, and of Darwinianism ("modern philosophy") ends the passage with an astonishing conceptual image. The Lady Lisa, as no human could hope to do, stands forth as a body risen from death, and also as symbol of modern acceptance of Necessity, the nondivine evolution of our species. She exposes, as Pater is well aware, the hopelessness of the vision sought by *The Renaissance,* and by all Romantic and post-Romantic art.

Yet, with that hopelessness, comes the curious reward of the supreme Paterian epiphany. Rilke remarked of the landscape behind the Madonna Lisa that "it is Nature which came into existence . . . something distant and foreign, something remote and without allure, something entirely self-contained. . . ." Following Rilke, the psychologist J. H. Van den Berg associates this estrangement of an outer landscape with the growth of a more inward, alienated self than mankind had known before:

> The inner life was like a haunted house. But what else could it be? It contained everything. Everything extraneous had been put into it. The entire history of the individual. Everything that had previously belonged to everybody, everything that had been collective prop-

erty and had existed in the world in which everyone
lived, had to be contained by the individual. It could not
be expected that things would be quiet in the inner self.

In his way, Van den Berg, like Rilke, sides with Ruskin and
not with Pater, for the implicit argument here is that the
Romantic inner self cost too much in solipsistic estrangement. But Pater was a divided man, humanly wiser than he
could let himself show as a Late Romantic moralist-critic. His
vision of the Mona Lisa is as much a warning as it is an ideal.
This, he says, is our Muse, mistress of Unity-of-Being. The
poets of the Nineties, including the young Yeats, chose to see
the ideal and not to heed the warning. The further work of
Pater, after *The Renaissance,* shows the Aesthetic Critic accepting his own hint, and turning away from self-destruction.

One cannot leave the "Conclusion" to *The Renaissance*
without acknowledging the power which that handful of
pages seems to possess even today, a hundred years after
their composition. In their own generation, their pungency
was overwhelming; not only did Pater withdraw them in the
second edition, because he too was alarmed at their effect,
but he toned them down when they were restored in the
third edition. The skeptical eloquence of the "Conclusion"
cost Pater considerable preferment at Oxford. There is a
splendidly instructive letter from John Wordsworth (clerical
grandnephew of the poet) to Pater, written in 1873, indig-
nantly summing up the "Conclusion" as asserting "that no
fixed principles either of religion or morality can be regarded
as certain, that the only thing worth living for is momentary
enjoyment and that probably or certainly the soul dissolves
at death into elements which are destined never to reunite."
One can oppose to this very minor Wordsworth a reported
murmur of Pater's: "I wish they would not call me a hedonist.
It gives such a wrong impression to those who do not know
Greek."

Early Pater, in all high seriousness, attains a climax in those
wonderful pages on the flux-of-sensations and the necessity
of dying with a faith in art that conclude *The Renaissance.*

Written in 1868, they came initially out of a review of William Morris' poetry that became the suppressed essay on "Aesthetic Poetry." They gave Pater himself the problem of how he was to write up to so fierce a demand-of-self: "To burn always with this hard, gemlike flame, to maintain this ecstasy, is success in life."

IV · FICTIVE SELVES

Pater's own life, by his early standards, was only ambiguously a success. His work, after *The Renaissance,* is of three kinds, all of them already present in his first book. One is "imaginary portraits," a curious mixed genre, of which the novel *Marius the Epicurean* is the most important, and of which the best examples are the semi-autobiographical "The Child in the House" and the book called *Imaginary Portraits.* Another grouping of Pater's work, critical essays, were mostly gathered in *Appreciations.* The last group, classical studies proper, stand a little apart from the rest of his work and will be considered at the close of this essay.

"Imaginary portraits," in Pater's sense, are an almost indescribable genre. Behind them stand the monologues of Browning and of Rossetti, the *Imaginary Conversations* of Landor, perhaps Sainte-Beuve's *Portraits contemporains.* Like *The Renaissance* and *Appreciations,* they are essays or quasi-essays; like "The Child in the House" they are semi-autobiographical; yet it hardly helps to see "Sebastian Van Storck," or "Denys L'Auxerrois" or "Hippolytus Veiled" as being essays or veiled confessions. Nor are they romance-fragments, though closer to that than to short stories. It may be best to call them what Yeats called his Paterian stories, "Mythologies," or "Romantic Mythologies." Or, more commonly, they could be called simply "reveries," for even at their most marmoreal and baroque they are highly disciplined reveries, and even the lengthy *Marius the Epicurean* is more a historicizing reverie than it is a historical novel. "Reverie" comes from the French *rever,* "to dream," and is already used in music to describe an instrumental composition of a dream-like character. The power and precariousness alike of Pater's reveries are related to their hovering near the thresholds of wish-fulfillment. I suspect that Pater's nearest ancestor here is Browning, even as Ruskin looms always behind Pater's aesthetic criticism. Just as Browning made fictive selves, to escape his earlier strain of Shelleyan subjectivity in the verse-romances *Pauline, Paracelsus* and *Sordello,* so Pater turned to "imaginary portraits" to escape the subjective confession that wells up in his "Leonardo da Vinci" and "Conclusion" to *The Renaissance.* On this view, *The Renaissance* is Pater's version of Shelley's "Alastor" or Keats' "Endymion": it is a prose-poem of highly personal Romantic quest after the image of desire, visualized by Pater in the Mona Lisa. Turning from so deep a self-exposure, Pater arrives at his kind of less personal reverie, a consciously fictive kind.

Pater had no gifts for narrative, or drama, or psychological portrayal, and he knew this well enough. Unlike Browning, he could not make a half-world, let alone the full world of a mythopoeic master like Blake. Pater, who intensely admired both poets, oriented his portraits with more specific reference to the most inescapable of Romantic poets, Wordsworth, concerning whom he wrote the best of his essays in strictly literary criticism. In the nearly-as-distinguished essay on "Coleridge," Pater justly praises Wordsworth as a more instinctual poet than Coleridge. Wordsworth is praised for "that flawless temperament . . . which keeps his conviction of a latent intelligence in nature within the limits of sentiment or instinct, and confines it to those delicate and subdued shades of expression which perfect art allows." Pater, too consciously, seeks in his portraits to be instinctual rather than intellectual, hoping that thus he can avoid drama and self-consciousness. Unfortunately, he cannot sustain the Wordsworthian comparison, as again he knew, for though he shared Wordsworth's early naturalism, he lacked the primordial, Tolstoyan power that sustains poems like "The Ruined Cottage," "Michael," "The Old Cumberland Beggar." Yet he yearned for such power, and would have been a Wordsworthian novelist, like George Eliot and Hardy, if he had found the requisite strength. But this yearning, poignantly felt all through the beautiful Wordsworth essay, was a desperate desire for his opposite. Wordsworth lived in nature, Pater in a dream. Longing for the sanctities of earth, Pater found his true brothers in Rossetti and Morris, poets of phantasmagoria, and his true children in Yeats and the Tragic Generation. The "imaginary portraits" are crucial to our understanding of Pater, but as art they are equivocal achievements, noble but divided against themselves.

V · SORROWS OF INFLUENCE

My own favorite among Pater's books is *Appreciations.* Pater is not the greatest critic English Romanticism produced—Coleridge and Ruskin vie for that eminence—but he is certainly the most underrated major nineteenth-century critic, in our own time. He is superior to his older rival, Arnold, and to his disciple, Wilde, both of whom receive more approval at this moment. Yet even as a literary critic, he is evasive, and remains more a master of reverie than of description, let alone analysis, which is alien to him. This becomes a curious critical strength in him, which requires both description and analysis to be apprehended.

Appreciations begins with the extraordinary essay on "Style," which is Pater's *credo* as a literary critic. As the essay urges awareness of the root-meanings of words, we need to remember that "style" originally meant an ancient instrument for writing on a waxed tablet, and having one pointed end for incising words, and one blunt end for rubbing out writing, and smoothing the tablet down. We might also remember that "appreciations" originally meant "appraisals." Before appraising Wordsworth, Coleridge, Rossetti, Morris, Lamb, and others, Pater offers us a vision of his stylistic attitude, incisive but also ascetic. Ian Fletcher, Pater's best scholar, reminds us that Pater's idea of style is "as a mode of perception, a total responsive gesture of the whole personality." Since Pater's own style is the most highly colored and self-conscious of all critics who have written in English, there is a puzzle here. Pater attempted to write criticism as though he were style's martyr, another Flaubert, and his insistence upon *askesis*, the exercise of self-curtailment, hardly seems compatible with a whole personality's total response. We do not believe that the style is the man when we read Pater, and a glance at his letters, which are incredibly dull and non-relevatory, confirms our disbelief. Pater's style, as befits the master of Wilde and Yeats, is a mask, and so Pater's idea of style and his actual style are irreconcilable. As always, Pater anticipates us in knowing this, and the essay "Style" centers upon this division.

Prose, according to Pater, is both music's opposite and capable of transformation into the condition of music, where form and matter seem to dissolve into one another. Pater's subject is always the mystery of utter individuality in the artistic personality; his style strives extravagantly to award himself such individuality. Whether in matter or style, Pater has therefore a necessary horror of literary influence, for to so desperate a quester after individuality *all* influence is over-influence. Pater's subject matter is also Ruskin's and Arnold's; his style is also Swinburne's, or rather one of Swinburne's styles. Unlike Emerson and Nietzsche, who refused to see themselves as latecomers, Pater's entire vision is that of a latecomer longing for a renaissance, a rebirth into imaginative earliness. The hidden subject of *Appreciations* is the anxiety of influence, for which Pater's remedy is primarily his idea of *askesis*. "Style" urges self-restraint and renunciation, which it calls an economy of means but which in Pater's actual style seems more an economy of ends. Ruskin, threatening precursor, was profuse in means and ends, master of emphasis and of a daemonic, Sublime style, which in his case *was* the man. Swerving from Ruskin, Pater turns to Flaubert in "Style," seeking to invent a father to replace a dominant and dangerous aesthetic parent. But guilt prevails, and Pater's anxiety emerges in the essay's long concluding paragraph, which astonishingly seems to repeal the special emphasis of everything that has come before. "Good art, but not necessarily great art," Pater sadly murmurs, suddenly assuring us that greatness depends not upon style but on the matter, and then listing Dante, Milton, the King James Bible, and Hugo's *Les Misérables,* which seems rather exposed in this sublime company, and hardly rivals Flaubert in its concern with form. By the test of finding a place in the structure of human life, Hugo will receive the palm before Flaubert, Ruskin before Pater, Tennyson (secretly despised by Pater) before Rossetti and Morris. The final *askesis* of the champion of style is to abnegate himself before the burden of the common life he himself cannot bear.

In the essay "Wordsworth," Pater has the happiness of being able to touch the commonal through the greatest mediating presence of nineteenth-century poetry. The essays on Wordsworth of Arnold and, *contra* Arnold, of A. C. Bradley, have been profoundly influential on rival schools of modern Wordsworthian interpretation, and Pater has not, but a reading of the three essays side by side will show Pater's superiority. His Wordsworth is neither Arnold's poet of Nature nor Bradley's poet of the Sublime, but rather a poet of instinctual pagan religion. Wordsworth would have been outraged by Pater's essay, and most modern scholars agree that Pater's Wordsworth is too much Pater's Marius and too little Wordsworth. Against which, here is Pater's account of Wordsworth's actual religion, *as a poet:*

> Religious sentiment, consecrating the affections and natural regrets of the human heart, above all, that pitiful awe and care for the perishing human clay, of which relic-worship is but the corruption, has always had much to do with localities, with the thoughts which attach themselves to actual scenes and places. Now what is true of it everywhere, is truest of it in those secluded valleys where one generation after another maintains the same abiding place; and it was on this side, that Wordsworth apprehended religion most strongly. Consisting, as it did so much, in the recognition of local sanctities, in the habit of connecting the stones and trees of a particular spot of earth with the great events

> of life, till the low walls, the green mounds, the half-obliterated epitaphs seemed full of voices, and a sort of natural oracles, the very religion of those people of the dales, appeared but as another link between them and the earth, and was literally a religion of nature.

What is most meaningful for Pater are those voices coming from low walls, green mounds, tombstones. These things remain *things* in Wordsworth, yet wholly other than ourselves, but we are deeply affected by what emanates from them. Pater was converted by them to the only religion he ever sincerely held, "literally a religion of nature." Just as the spots of time gave Wordsworth not a sense of the Divine, but precise knowledge to what point and how his own mind displayed a mastery over outward sense, so for Pater the spots of time he located in works of art gave a precise knowledge of the limited efficacy of the great Romantic program for renovation. The Romantics, as Pater understood and Arnold did not, were not nature-poets, but rather exemplars of the power of the mind, a power exerted against the object-world, or mere universe of death. Like Ruskin, and like Yeats and Stevens, Pater is a Romantic critic of Romanticism. Whether Pater writes on Giorgione or Winckelmann, the myth of Dionysus or Plato and the Doctrine of Change, Rossetti or Wilde, he writes as a conscious post-Wordsworthian, and his true subject is the partial and therefore tragic (because momentary) victory that art wins over the flux of sensations. The step beyond Pater is the one taken by his disciple, Yeats, who insists on the tragic joy of art's defeat, and who in his savage last phase celebrates the flux, exulting in his own doctrine of change.

Pater, withdrawing in *Appreciations* as in *Marius* from hailing the Heraclitean flux, is most moved by Wordsworth's quiet and primordial strength, the instinctual power of "impassioned contemplation." The eloquent and compassionate essay on "Coleridge" begins from Pater's recognition that Coleridge lacked this strength, and goes on to reject Coleridge's theological reliance upon out-

worn Absolutes. More strikingly, Pater pioneers in rejecting the Organic Analogue that Coleridge popularized.
The motto of Pater's essay on Coleridge might well come
from Nietzsche: "But do I bid thee be either plant or
phantom?" Coleridge, Pater suggests, bid us be both, and
so "obscured the true interest of art," which is to celebrate and lament our intolerably glorious condition of
being mortal gods.

Beyond his steady defence of art's dignity against metaphysical and religious absolutes, Pater's nobility and uniqueness as a nineteenth-century literary critic stem from his
insistence that the later nineteenth-century poet "make it
new," even as that poet (like Pater himself) remains fully
conscious of the inescapable sorrows of influence. Such a poet
wanders in the half-lights of being a latecomer, trailing after
the massive, fresh legacy of Goethe, Wordsworth, Blake,
Hugo, Keats, Shelley, Baudelaire, Browning, even as Pater
trailed after De Quincey, Lamb, Hazlitt, Coleridge, Arnold
and the inescapable Ruskin, quite aside from Swinburne and
the unmentioned Emerson and Nietzsche. Pater is still the
best critic pre-Raphaelite poetry has had, largely because he
understood so well the anxiety of influence consciously present in Rossetti and unconsciously at work in Morris. The
great essay on Morris, "Aesthetic Poetry," properly close to
the "Conclusion" to *The Renaissance* which he quarried
from it, presents Pater's most unguarded vision of poetic
experience, so that Pater inevitably suppressed it:

> . . . exotic flowers of sentiment expand, among people
> of a remote and unaccustomed beauty, somnambulistic,
> frail, androgynous, the light almost shining through
> them. . . . The colouring is intricate and delirious, as of
> "scarlet lilies." The influence of summer is like a poison
> in one's blood, with a sudden bewildered sickening of
> life and all things. . . . A passion of which the outlets are
> sealed, begets a tension of nerve, in which the sensible
> world comes to one with a reinforced brilliancy and
> relief—all redness is turned into blood, all water into

> tears. . . . One characteristic of the pagan spirit the
> aesthetic poetry has . . .—the sense of death and the
> desire of beauty: the desire of beauty quickened by the
> sense of death . . .

Remarkably hinting that sadomasochistic yearnings and
the anxiety of being a late representative of a tradition are
closely related, Pater implies also that the heightened intensity of Morris and Rossetti (and of Pater) compensates for a
destructively excessive sexual self-consciousness. The sensible world becomes phantasmagoria because one's own nature is baffled. A critic who understands the dialectic of style,
as Pater magnificently did, is in no need of psychoanalytic
reduction, as these essays on Morris and Rossetti show. *Appreciations,* which influenced Wilde and Yeats, Joyce and
Pound, and more covertly Santayana and Stevens, has had
little influence upon modern academic criticism, but one can
prophesy that such influence will yet come. In a letter (8
January 1888) to the young poet Arthur Symons, Pater recalled the marvelous dictum of Rossetti: "Conception, my
boy FUNDAMENTAL BRAINWORK, that is what makes the difference in all art." Pater's apt purpose in this recall was to
urge Symons, and the poets of his generation—Yeats, Dow-
son, Lionel Johnson—to make it new again through the fundamental brainwork necessary to overcome anxieties-of-
influence. Here is the prophecy, addressed to the Paterian
poets of the Tragic Generation, which Pound and his Mod-
ernists attempted to fulfill:

> I think the present age an unfavourable one to poets,
> at least in England. The young poet comes into a gener-
> ation which has produced a large amount of first-rate
> poetry, and an enormous amount of good secondary
> poetry. You know I give a high place to the literature of
> prose as a fine art, and therefore hope you won't think
> me brutal in saying that the admirable qualities of your
> verse are those also of imaginative prose; as I think is the
> case also with much of Browning's finest verse.

The Poundian dictum, that verse was to be as well written as prose, initially meant Browningesque verse and Paterian prose, as Pound's early verse and prose show. That literary Modernism ever journeyed too far from its Paterian origins we may doubt increasingly, and we may wonder also whether modern criticism as yet has caught up with Pater.

VI · CENTRIFUGAL AND CENTRIPETAL

In the important essay on Romanticism that he made the "Postscript" to *Appreciations*, Pater insisted that: "Material for the artist, motives of inspiration, are not yet exhausted..." yet he wondered how "to induce order upon the contorted, proportionless accumulation of our knowledge and experience, our science and history, our hopes and disillusion..." To help induce such an order seems to be the motive for *Plato and Platonism* (1893) and the posthumously published *Greek Studies* (1895). The Plato of Walter Pater is Montaigne's Plato (and probably Shelley's), a skeptical evader of systems, including his supposed own, whose idea of order is the dialectic: "Just there, lies the validity of the method—in a dialogue, an endless dialogue, with one's self." Clearly this is Pater more than Plato, and we need not wonder why Pater favored this above his other books. In the chapter, "The Genius of Plato," Pater gives us another reverie, an idealized imaginary portrait of what he would have liked the mind of Pater to be. A comparison with Emerson's Plato (also influenced by Montaigne) is instructive, for the Plato of *Representative Men* is criticized for lacking "contact," an Emersonian quality not far removed from "freedom" or wildness. Unlike Plato the author of the *Dialogues*, Walter Pater's visionary indeed lacks "contact," even as Pater severely made certain he himself lacked it.

Pater gives us the author of *The Republic* as "a seer who has a sort of sensuous love of the unseen," and whose mythological power brings the unseen closer to the seen. This Plato is possible and possibly even more than marginal, yet he does seem more Ficino or Pico della Mirandola than he was Plato, for he is more a poet of ideas than a metaphysician, and more of a solipsistic Realist than an Idealist. Above all, he is Pater's "crystal man," a model for Yeats' vision of an *antithetical* savior, a greater-than-Oedipus who would replace Christ, and herald a greater Renaissance than European man had known.

From reading both Hegel and Darwin, Pater had evolved a curious dialectic of history, expounded more thoroughly in *Greek Studies,* using the terms "centripetal" and "centrifugal" as the thesis and antithesis of a process always stopping short of synthesis:

> All through Greek history we may trace, in every sphere of the activity of the Greek mind, the action of these two opposing tendencies—the centrifugal and centripetal . . . There is the centrifugal, the Ionian, the Asiatic tendency, flying from the centre . . . throwing itself forth in endless play of undirected imagination; delighting in brightness and colour, in beautiful material, in changeful form everywhere, in poetry, in philosophy . . . its restless versatility drives it towards . . . the development of the individual in that which is most peculiar and individual in him . . . It is this centrifugal tendency which Plato is desirous to cure, by maintaining, over against it, the Dorian influence of a severe simplification everywhere, in society, in culture . . .

The centrifugal is the vision of Heraclitus, the centripetal of Parmenides, or in Pater's more traditional terms from the "Postscript" to *Appreciations,* the centrifugal is the Romantic, and the centripetal the Classic. Pater rather nervously praises his Plato for Classic correctiveness, for a conservative centripetal impulse against his own Heraclitean Romanticism. Reductively, this is still Pater reacting against the excesses of *The Renaissance,* and we do not believe him when he presents himself as a centripetal man, though Yeats was partially persuaded, and relied upon Pater's dialectic when he created his own version of an aesthetic historicism in *A Vision.*

Pater, in his last phase, continued to rationalize his semi-withdrawal from his own earlier vision, but we can doubt that even he trusted his own hesitant rationalizations. We remember him, and read him, as the maker of critical reveries who yielded up the great societal and religious hopes of the major Victorian prose-prophets, and urged us to abide in the mortal truths of perception and sensation. His great achievement, in conjunction with Swinburne and the pre-Raphaelites, was to empty Ruskin's aestheticism of its moral bias, and so to purify a critical stance appropriate for the apprehension of Romantic art. More than Swinburne, Morris, Rossetti, he became the father of Anglo-American Aestheticism, and subsequently the direct precursor of a Modernism that vainly attempted to be post-Romantic. I venture the prophecy that he will prove also to be the valued precursor of a post-Modernism still fated to be another Last Romanticism, another intoxication of belatedness. We can judge, finally, this ancestor of our own sensibility as he himself judged Plato:

> His aptitude for things visible, with the gift of words, empowers him to express, as if for the eyes, what except to the eye of the mind is strictly invisible, what an acquired asceticism induces him to rank above, and sometimes, in terms of harshest dualism, oppose to, the sensible world. Plato is to be interpreted not merely by his antecedents, by the influence upon him of those who preceded him, but by his successors, by the temper, the intellectual alliances, of those who directly or indirectly have been sympathetic with him.

3

Emerson

THE SELF-RELIANCE OF

AMERICAN ROMANTICISM

"Evil Tendencies Cancel" is the title of a tough little poem by Robert Frost, in which the blight fails to end the chestnut, which goes on growing, while waiting for another parasite, which "shall come to end the blight." I choose to read this as the governing fable of our American Romanticism, which means of Emersonianism, our true and glorious, if also disastrous, literary tradition. It keeps on sending up shoots, it keeps on catching the blight, and one blight keeps on slaying another, but the old chestnut lives. Emerson lives, because we are still alive, and all the exorcisers—Eliot, Winters, and their ilk—could not dissolve this brave ghostly father.

An American student of British Romanticism, when he turns to the study of the domestic variety, soon finds himself obsessed with, lost in, dazed by—Emerson. Otherwise, he can't hope to find himself at all. Emerson is appalling and peculiar—at first. Then he is—simply—ourselves, perhaps for worse. But—a certain way into him—he is what Matthew Arnold asserted him to be—the friend and the aider of anyone whatsoever who would live in the spirit.

"Whose spirit is this?" Stevens asked, listening to his singing girl at Key West, knowing that it was the spirit that he sought, but skeptical as to the spirit's sanction, its autonomy as against the world of wind and wave. Whose spirit is the spirit that Emerson perpetually invokes? What is the authority that he so beautifully and yet so arbitrarily assumes, nearly every day of his writing life? Aged twenty-seven, he writes this in his Journal as his first great declaration of self-reliance:

> Every man has his own voice, manner, eloquence,
> and, just as much, his own sort of love and grief and
> imagination and action. Let him scorn to imitate any
> being, let him scorn to be a secondary man, let him fully
> trust his own share of God's goodness, that, correctly
> used, it will lead him on to perfection which has no type
> yet in the universe, save only in the Divine Mind.

Very few among us are going to offer our neighbors that
Emersonian admonition. I won't, even though I am haunted
by Stevens' line in which he calls Narcissus: "Prince of the
secondary men." I get scared—sensibly so—when my students start fully trusting in their own share of God's goodness, and start acting as though that share will lead them on
to a "perfection which has no type yet in the universe, save
only in the Divine Mind." Why then should I be moved
rather than skeptical when Emerson urges me to scorn being
a secondary man, which means that I mustn't imitate any
other being whatsoever? Am I then only another armchair
Emersonian, like the voice in "The Man with the Blue Guitar" that cries out:

> *Am I a man that is dead*
>
> *At a table on which the food is cold?*
> *Is my thought a memory, not alive?*
>
> *Is the spot on the floor, there, wine or blood*
> *And whichever it may be, is it mine?*

The Emersonian way of answering such dreadful questions
is to ask a much happier one, a rather more rhetorical one.
Here he is five years further on, writing in his Journal, aged
thirty-two:

> Far off, no doubt, is the perfectibility; so far off as to
> be ridiculous to all but a few. Yet wrote I once that, God
> keeping a private door to each soul, nothing transcends
> the bounds of reasonable expectation from a man. Now
> what imperfect tadpoles we are! an arm or a leg, an eye

> or an antenna, is unfolded,—all the rest is yet in the
> chrysalis. Who does not feel in him budding the powers
> of a Persuasion that by and by will be irresistible?

This, the vision proper of the earlier Emerson, sees in the universe primarily the possibility for an original relation to the universe on the part of everyone, again whosoever. Whether this sees the universe at all, in whole or in part, is dubious; Emerson dwelt in possibility, a fairer house than prose. Through its more numerous windows, its superior number of doors, he saw, and he knew, and he became a kind of liberating god. But what did he see, what did he know, and what kind of man-godhood was this? What bread did he eat, what wine did he drink, to find in himself the real presence of a kind of giant of the imagination?

In his little book or manifesto, misentitled "Nature," Emerson writes: "of that ineffable essence which we call Spirit, he that thinks most, will say least." Emerson fortunately did not stop there, at saying least, but ventured the following giant formula:

> The ruin or the blank that we see when we look at
> nature, is in our own eye. The axis of vision is not coinci-
> dent with the axis of things and so they appear not
> transparent but opaque.

That is the more-than-Coleridgean formula, beautiful and extreme, which made possible the Romantic poem in America, down to this present day. Not the Romantic poem of Bryant or of Poe or of Longfellow, but of Thoreau, Whitman, Dickinson, Melville, Robinson, Frost, Stevens, Williams, Hart Crane, Roethke, and all their followers. For, if our own eye contains the ruin or blank we see in nature, then it contains also the joy and color we see there. And, in that ecstasy when the axis of vision and the axis of things coincide, and we see into the life of things, we behold a transparency that is also ourselves. The Emersonian or American Sublime is a wildness or holistic freedom in which the spirit, transparent to itself, knows its own splendor, and by knowing that knows again all things. This is not a mystical reverie that I am describing, but a rather sober, even matter-of-fact state. Perhaps it is the most American of states-of-mind, since it is the most impatient. Mysticism, according to one famous definition, has not the patience to wait for God's revelation of Himself. Emersonianism has not the patience to wait for mysticism. Let us, without delay, examine the Emersonian impatience at its most sublime and most notorious, by chanting the great epiphany from his "Nature":

> Crossing a bare common, in snow puddles, at twilight, under a clouded sky, without having in my thoughts any occurrence of special good fortune, I have enjoyed a perfect exhilaration. I am glad to the brink of fear. . . . Standing on the bare ground,—my head bathed by the blithe air and uplifted into infinite space,—all mean egotism vanishes. I become a transparent eyeball; I am nothing; I see all; the currents of the Universal Being circulate through me; I am part or parcel of God. The name of the nearest friend sounds then foreign and accidental: to be brothers, to be acquaintance, master or servant, is then a trifle and a disturbance. I am the lover of uncontained and immortal beauty.

To sandbag this rapture would be disgusting, if one sought the origins of such ecstasy only to reduce it. But the journal entry Emerson builds upon is so strikingly different, and so moving, that a contrast should help us to a vision of the Emersonian impatience. Listen for the plangency of loss in this, and you may hear a deeper sorrow than Emerson himself intended:

> As I walked in the woods I felt what I often feel—that nothing can befall me in life, no calamity, no disgrace (leaving me my eyes), to which Nature will not offer a sweet consolation. Standing on the bare ground with my head bathed by the blithe air, and uplifted into the infinite space, I become happy in my universal relations.

> The name of the nearest friend sounds then foreign and
> accidental. I am the heir of uncontained beauty and
> power. And if then I walk with a companion, he should
> speak from his Reason to my Reason; that is, both from
> God. To be brothers, to be acquaintances, master or
> servant, is then a trifle too insignificant for remem-
> brance. O, keep this humor (which in your lifetime may
> not come to you twice), as the apple of your eye. Set a
> lamp before it in your memory which shall never be
> extinguished.

Though even this journal entry is in a mode of what I will
describe as divination, I hear no impatience in it, whether
impatience with natural continuities or with human limitations. Though Emerson centers on his eyes, he *sees* nothing,
but inherits beauty and power. He is joyous because he is
wholly taken up into what Wordsworth called "Reason in her
most exalted mood." He speaks and hears as God, and in this
humor possesses as he would be possessed. At the climax of
his greatest poem Stevens proclaims: "I have not but I am,
and as I am I am." Beauty is not in things seen, not even by
seeing into the life of things, but is the recognition of self, and
power is one with self. But this humor is very rare; the walker
in the woods is thirty-two, the age at which his master Wordsworth wrote "Resolution and Independence" and the first
four stanzas of the "Intimations" ode. The fear that this humor may never return creates the extraordinary image of the
transparent eyeball, an image impatient with all possibility of
loss, indeed less an image than a promise of perpetual repetition. As he rewrites the journal entry into the passage of
"Nature," Emerson raises himself from the mere exercise of
a Divine faculty to being a part or particle of God Himself.
This raising is not at all akin to that muscular exertion by
which Whitman, according to the young Henry James, en-
deavoured to wrestle himself into poetry. The Emersonian
elevation authentically is shamanistic—it bears all the splendid and barbarous stigmata that E. R. Dodds, in his study of
the Greeks and the irrational, comprehensively located in

the Siberian shamans who had descended into Thrace, and whose egregious raptures lurk in the dark abysses from which Western poetic tradition emerged. Emerson—as we ought never to be surprised to realize—is at once our sweetest and most civilized writer and our wildest and most primitivistic. The spirit that speaks in and through him has the true Pythagorean and Orphic stink. Compared to Emerson, poor Allen Ginsberg is a pallid academic impostor, a gentle donkey masquerading as an enraged water-buffalo. The ministerial Emerson, who lived to sit on the Harvard Board of Overseers and to cast his vote there for compulsory chapel attendance, is full brother to the Dionysiac adept who may have torn living flesh with his inspired teeth.

The late Yvor Winters, who was not very fond of Emerson, attempted to dismiss our dialectically shamanistic ancestor by accusing him of what might be called rhetorical hypocrisy. I quote from Winters at his most morally passionate best:

> [Emerson] . . . was able to present the anarchic and anti-moral doctrines of European Romanticism in a language which for two hundred years had been capable of arousing the most intense and the most obscure emotions of the American people. He could speak of matter as if it were God; of the flesh as if it were spirit; of emotion as if it were Divine Grace; of impulse as if it were conscience; and of automatism as if it were the mystical experience. And he was addressing an audience which, like himself, had been so conditioned by two hundred years of Calvinistic discipline, that the doctrines confused nothing, at the outset, except the mind: Emerson and his contemporaries, in surrendering to what they took for impulse, were governed by New England habit; they mistook second nature for nature. They were moral parasites upon a Christian doctrine which they were endeavoring to destroy.

With so directly moral a critic as Winters (whose judiciousness resembled Dr. Johnson's about as closely as an avocado resembles a potato) I always like to cope by juxtaposition rather than direct attack, because it is not much fun just to say "You're another," in that you are a moral parasite upon a Romantic doctrine which you are endeavoring to destroy. Emerson did not allow himself much irony, ever, as he had far too many imprisoned truths that he rightly felt only he could set free. But—against the Winters vision I set Emerson in an uncharacteristic but wholly apposite ferocity, anticipating and to my mind wholly thawing out the Winters vision. In the great essay "Circles," to which I shall circle back later, Emerson attains a height from which all moral virtue is seen to fall away, until at last he can declare:

> There is no virtue which is final; all are initial. The virtues of society are vices of the saint. The terror of reform is the discovery that we must cast away our virtues, or what we have always esteemed such, into the same pit that has consumed our grosser vices. . . .

Emerson's eloquence gives us that grand phrase, "the terror of reform," but hardly tells us how we are to interpret "reform" or distinguish it from mere unamiable antinomianism, whose true enemy is never only "the virtues of society," but frequently approximates any principle of coherence whatsoever. Emerson—as Winters never saw—demands very close reading, for his prose is as evasive and vacillating as Pater's or Yeats', though instead of their elaborate, marmoreal hesitation he seems to offer us the rhapsode's impatient rushes, divine moments in which known truths take on overwhelming immediacy. This is his power over us—his rhetorical authority—but not a power he possesses over himself, as he is all too aware. For, in "Circles," he goes on to meditate upon the phenomenon of his afflatus, and its tendency to abolish remorse, in the manner of Blake and Shelley. Emerson reverses the process, as he reverses so many Romantic influxes. In him, the sweetness flows in, and the effect is the abolition of all remorse. "It is the highest power of divine moments," he writes, "that they abolish our contrition also. I accuse myself of sloth and unprofitableness day by day; but when these waves of God flow into me I no longer reckon lost time. I no longer poorly compute my possible achievement by what remains to me of the month or the year; for these moments confer a sort of omnipresence and omnipotence which asks nothing of duration, but sees that the energy of the mind is commensurate with the work to be done, without time."

We can begin by noting that the axis of vision suddenly has been made coincident with the axis of things, so that Emerson stands in his radiance of transparency, without time. But —for this once—the transparent eyeball darts out a balefully ironic light, as the American rhapsode responds to his version of that grand Blakean character, the Idiot Questioner, here the precursor of our recently departed sage of Stanford. Listen to the following, and wonder what any Emersonian could add to this uncharacteristic but wholly central outburst, this astonishingly formidable irony:

> And thus, O circular philosopher, I hear some reader exclaim, you have arrived at a fine Pyrrhonism, at an equivalence and indifferency of all actions, and would fain teach us that *if we are true,* forsooth, our crimes may be lively stones out of which we shall construct the temple of the true God!
>
> I am not careful to justify myself. I own I am gladdened by seeing the predominance of the saccharine principle throughout vegetable nature, and not less by beholding in morals that unrestrained inundation of the principle of good into every chink and hole that selfishness has left open, yea into selfishness and sin itself; so that no evil is pure, nor hell itself without its extreme satisfactions. . . .

When I encounter this mode of irony in Blake or Nietzsche, or even muted in Pater or Yeats, I know how to read it, but not when it rises against me from the pages of Emerson. For he is not an apocalyptic, Rabelaisian satirist, like Blake, nor a heroic vitalist like his admirer Nietzsche, nor an uneasy naturalizer of the psychic flux like Pater, nor a pseudo-apocalyptic charlatan and necromancer like the still indubitably great Yeats. "Circles" read closely, as Emily Dickinson clearly read it, is a genuinely shocking and unsettling essay, but unlike "The Marriage of Heaven and Hell," "Beyond Good and Evil," or some of the "Imaginary Portraits" or the drama "Purgatory," it does not intend to startle us into reconceptualizations by its rhetorical dissociations. What then is our circular philosopher up to, why does he so blandly tell us that he unsettles all things and simply experiments, an endless seeker with no past at his back? He has, as he well knew, and as Perry Miller and others have shown, Jonathan Edwards at his back, which is a formidable enough past for any man, even an American. Why does Emerson disown perpetually what he takes such ferocious pride in owning, the influx of power, the election as theorist of the poem of the mind in the act of finding what will suffice, the exhilaration of becoming a liberating god?

At the close of "Circles," Emerson speaks for the perpetual quest of virtually every American artist or person of sensibility when he declares that: "The one thing which we seek with insatiable desire is to forget ourselves, to be surprised out of our propriety, to lose our sempiternal memory and to do something without knowing how or why; in short to draw a new circle." Let us read closely: circumference can be widened only by self-forgetfulness, surprise, loss of memory and—most crucially—by doing something—(does he mean anything, just anything?)—something without knowing how we do it or why it is done. A motiveless act is one thing; we do much that is not malignant, much indeed positively benign, knowing not what we do and these may be—as Wordsworth said—the best portions of a good man's life. But to act without knowing *how* we act—at its best this may be Yeats' celebratory kind of *sprezzatura* (as derived from Castiglione) but more usually we meet this in Swift's dreadful and dreaded "Mechanical operation of the spirit." I suppose that Emerson—always a more-than-Platonic-Idealist—really means here what earlier he had oddly called Self-Reliance, a principle whose closest twentieth-century equivalent formula is Freud's "Where It was, there I shall be," or the progressive displacement of the id by the maturing ego. Yet that cannot be wholly what Emerson means. Freud, like one strain in Pre-Socratic thought, is telling us that a person's character is his fate. Emerson, like quite another strain in the Pre-Socratics, a shamanistic one, is telling us—as Yeats did—that the daemon is our destiny. Our longing for the wider circumference is daemonic, and belongs to personality as against character, to use an Emersonian dialectic which Yeats inherited from that brilliant rhetorician, his own father. The daemon knows how we do it or why it is done; we are along for the glory, and the sorrows, of the ride.

I divide the remainder of this essay equally between the glory and the sorrows of the Emersonian daemonic. The glory I take to be Emerson's beautiful self-confidence as to his own spiritual authority; the sorrows I shall invoke all belong to the great Serpent *Ananke*, Necessity, upon whose altars Emerson was to sacrifice the joy of his authority. What is a poet's or sage's authority? Vico gives us the certain answer: authority is precisely property, the author's sole possession, his commerce as granted him by Hermes, god of ownership and of thievery. Authority was at first titanic, belonging to such giants of the imagination as Prometheus, but then became divine, by Jove's expropriation, in Vico's account. Authority or property is power of divination, not only in the sense of augury but in the sense of gaining immortality, in becoming a god. The making that is poetry is god-making and even the ephebe or starting-poet is already as much daemon as man or woman. Emerson quotes Empedocles in this context, as approvingly as Yeats does, but with a little more self-referential irony. Yet the whole quotation, which Emerson does not give, must have alarmed him, for the daemonic in the shamanistic Empedocles is much starker than in Emerson's favorite Neoplatonic visionary, Proclus, whose daemons are benign interpreters between gods and men. But the same Empedocles who proudly says, "I go about among you an immortal god, no mortal now, honored . . . crowned with . . . flowery garlands," is also the tormented consciousness of the great fragment 115, which I shall quote entire, to show the large range of sorrow upon which Emerson had opened:

> There is an oracle of Necessity, an ancient ordinance of the gods, eternal and sealed fast by broad oaths, that whenever one of the daemons, whose portion is length of days, has sinfully polluted his hands with blood, or followed strife and forsworn himself, he must wander thrice ten thousand seasons from the abodes of the blessed, being born throughout the time in all manners of mortal forms, changing one toilsome path of life for another. For the mighty Air drives him into the Sea, and the Sea spews him forth on the dry Earth; Earth tosses him into the beams of the blazing Sun, and he flings him back to the eddies of Air. One takes him from the other, and all reject him. One of these I now am, an exile and a wanderer from the gods, for that I put my *trust* in insensate strife.

The actual Empedocles is thus already an authentic High Romantic ruined quester, closer to Manfred than he is to Matthew Arnold's tiresome worrier, and closest of all to Byron and Shelley themselves, and to their greatest fictive descendant, Browning's Childe Roland. Emerson, though, is an Empedocles-in-dialectical-reversal, a happy pilgrim whose daimonic drive irradiates every Dark Tower he astonishingly bypasses, almost indeed a Buster Keaton in his amazing survivals that thread through what ought to be the destructive labyrinths of the self. Yet, as quester, he is the Don rather than Sancho, most Faustian where he is most amiable. Is it then Emerson's outrageous accomplishment so to have purified Romanticism or internalized quest that it loses all its Empedoclean and Byronic hazard and sorrow? Can one surrender the darkness of the daimonic ground and yet retain its enchantment? We know that Hawthorne, Emerson's uneasy neighbor and walking companion, rather resentfully thought otherwise, and that *his* friend Melville satirized Emerson as only another Confidence Man, or as the Plotinus

Plinlimmon whose abstractions drained life of its vitality as much as of its suffering. Emerson—to them—for all his uncanny greatness remained the sophist of the visionary lie, the poet of ideas who blandly sought—in Dickinson's terms—to know the transport without the pain. Any American—for we are still, in our accursedness, Emerson's contemporaries and his involuntary disciples—needs to ask of this central American sage: "How can you hope to teach us to purify our selves and lives without teaching us some, any, mode of purgation? How can you urge us to daimonic expansion, from the Soul to the Oversoul, without our becoming what Stevens so bitterly calls "The Rabbit as King of the Ghosts," a grant of consciousness utterly devoid of any being whatsoever? What do you offer us which we do not already possess in quantities rather too large for our own exasperated good?"

I think that Emerson more than answers these questions, by making us see what it is in us that persists in asking them, and I will turn to the essay "Circles" again for demonstration, but first I ask the indulgence of a personal excursus. Whatever Romanticism *is*—and I am convinced it *is* now what it has been for at least the past two hundred years—I am certain it is not a Napoleonic obsession with titanic forms, and not a subtle, charming shrug that says, "This is not the place, this is not the time and you—there confronting me—you are not the person for me, nor am I the person for you." The Titanic form and the diffident ironist are not even the diseases of Romanticism, but symptoms of that greater malady Romanticism came hoping to heal. Romanticism, even in its most remorseless protagonists, is centrally a humanism, which seeks our renewal as makers, which hopes to give us the immodest hope that we—even we—coming so late in time's injustices can still sing a song of ourselves. Despite all its studying of the nostalgias, the high song that is Romanticism persists in saying: "Nothing need be lost—nothing is lost —if we will learn to listen again, and with the ear of the mind too, to see into the life of things and to see with the eye of the mind, to touch without self-appropriation." We live—of course—amid a parody of this high song. We are now afflicted

—more than we need be—by what masquerades as a new sensibility or consciousness but is only another exhausted sentimentality, a pseudo-shamanism, indeed what Blake prophesied accurately as a revival of what he sardonically called Druidism, a virulent natural religion exalting what Blake ironically termed "The selfish virtues of the natural heart." Our baffled younger questers who go apart peculiarly assert their discipleship to Blake, or to Emerson's one surly follower who was also a genius in his own stance and right, Thoreau, whose one consistent teaching was the Emersonian insistence upon continuous intellectual effort.

The last line of Emerson's verse-epigraph to "Circles" speaks of a new genesis that would be here, could we but know the full dimensions of our perceptions, our scanning of nature's sphere. Throughout, Emerson speaks for Blake's prolific half of the contraries, for outwardly pulsating energy which makes a new idea of reason with each fresh circumference. "Every action admits of being outdone," he insists, and again: "There is no outside, no inclosing wall, no circumference to us." This denial of Necessity, of the contrary that Blake calls the Devourer, reaches the moral extreme of insisting that "The only sin is limitation." And even natural context must yield to influx, as it does in a fine sentence that reverberates throughout Dickinson: "The natural world may be conceived of as a system of concentric circles, and we now and then detect in nature slight dislocations which apprise us that this surface on which we now stand is not fixed, but sliding." In Dickinson's terms, we have gone out upon Circumference, but Emerson betrays not the slightest sign of her wariness of our risk. Why is it that no plank in precarious fresh reason can give way for the Concord rhapsode; why does he not fear that we may fall through, as so many of us certainly will—indeed as we certainly must—in fact as we certainly do? An extraordinarily cunning brief paragraph answers us, and needs as much pondering as we can bring to it:

> Yet this incessant movement and progression which all things partake could never become sensible to us but

by contrast to some principle of fixture or stability in the
soul. Whilst the eternal generation of circles proceeds,
the eternal generator abides. That central life is somewhat superior to creation, superior to knowledge and
thought, and contains all its circles. Forever it labors to
create a life and thought as large and excellent as itself,
but in vain, for that which is made instructs how to
make a better.

We could—after reading this—burst out as did the elder
Henry James, who loved Emerson yet who understandably
protested: "O you man without a handle!" But even a moder-
ately close reading gives us handle enough, and tells us
plainly the central truth within ourselves that the earlier or
primary Emerson insists we learn and acknowledge. The soul
stands sure, if it stands at all; there is a substance in us that
prevails, because it always was. No more was it ever made
than God was made. How does it manifest itself to us? We
know the flux and outward move of our boundaries because
there is a place surely enough fixed within us that we can
take firm stance. At the center of us is a divinity that hopes
to look upon its makings and find them good, but that will be
frustrated only because the mind in creation is not—as Shelley skeptically conceived—like a fading coal, but more like
Isaiah's and Blake's expanding furnace, which teaches itself
to go beyond itself. Isaiah would have recoiled from Emerson's paradox, but Blake expresses the same celebratory fury
many times. The circles of creation emanate out from the
Merkabah's or Divine Chariot's fire-bursts, but the vehicular
form of divinity, as Blake oddly calls it, is not itself affected.
At the center of Emerson's central mind is a point where no
change can come, but this point is not in itself a final excellence or central truth. It will and must be bettered, not by
what it makes, but by what comes after, that is, by what its
own creation will teach to successors. This vision of Emerson's is not so much difficult as it is frustrating, for it leaves
us asking: "What are *we* to do when *we* must choose? Do we
abandon the fixed point, the soul's stability, and go with our
own creation, to see what fresh excellence it will instruct into

existence, or do we abide where our stance abides, secure and snug while our naked conceptions live and die in the world of what is becoming?" Just here, I am afraid, is where Emerson's answerings stop, and his Yankee caution inherits. He will not say, unlike Blake or Shelley, Nietzsche and Pater and Yeats, indeed unlike his disciples Thoreau and Whitman, all of whom in very different but parallel ways would send us out from our fixed souls and into a freedom they found terrible but necessary. Emerson is not a Trimmer, and he does not grow suddenly silent. Like Wordsworth, he has anchored upon a "possible sublimity," upon "something ever more about to be," upon a final step not quite taken. Why then are his answerings true answers? Nietzsche, who loved Emerson and scorned Carlyle, denied that Emerson gave answers at all. His best and funniest comment on Emerson can help us here. He wrote, in his "Twilight of The Idols":

> Emerson has that gracious and clever cheerfulness which discourages all seriousness; he simply does not know how old he is already, and how young he is still going to be; he could say of himself, quoting Lope de Vega: "I am my own heir." His spirit always finds reasons for being satisfied and even grateful; and at times he touches on the cheerful transcendency of the worthy gentleman who returned from an amorous rendezvous, as if he had accomplished his mission. "Though the power is lacking," he said gratefully, "the lust is nevertheless praiseworthy."

Potency is indeed the point at issue, for I take "Power" to be Emerson's key term. Either he opens us to more power in ourselves, or he is a cheerful and charming self-deceiver, and hardly the dangerous deceiver of others that Winters, sincere apostle of moral virtue, found him to be. The answer, and his answer, I judge to be in the formula: "opening towards power." The power is in him all right, as it is in you; he tells you it is there, tells you how to open yourself to it, and then abandons you either to abandon it yourself, or somehow, anyhow, decide what to do with it, while he quests off to his later, darker broodings about Fate and Necessity. He finds you simmering, brings you to a boil, but does not stay to make the coffee. Freud also passes beyond the Pleasure Principle to the confrontation with Ananke, Necessity, the Reality Principle, but Freud is a much firmer moralist, and achieves some useful balancings in his comments on the Pleasure Principle. Emerson, like all true questers, cares about the journeying and not the goal. Childe Roland, after a lifetime spent training for the sight, cannot see the Dark Tower until it is upon him. Emerson would not even see *then* that it *was* dark, and would bustle by cheerful and unharmed.

Yet his disciples, coming after him, have come to their griefs there one by one, from Whitman on to Hart Crane, Roethke, and our immediate contemporaries. Thoreau, whose Journals are not exactly heaped with praise of his fellow men, said there that his relation with Emerson was one long tragedy, but grudgingly added that: "There is no such general critic of men and things, no such trustworthy and faithful man. More of the divine realized in him than in any. A poetic critic, reserving the unqualified nouns for the gods."

What *is* this more of the realized divine that even the embittered Thoreau had to acknowledge? I return—for a last time—to "Circles." Emerson, stable at his own center, observes the farthest circumferences emanating out from him, rejoices that they will lead someone on out to a perfection greater than his own, and then hunkers down cheerfully in his center. This is an awfully canny godhood, but at least it *is* transparent to itself. And there I locate the final clue, in this transparency, this sense that all things have stopped revolving except in crystal, to adapt a highly Emersonian line of Stevens. I venture the generalization that Emersonian Transcendentalism is not a transcendence at all, but is the program of attaining this transparency, which is the peculiarly American mode of the Romantic epiphany or privileged moment. Immanence and transcendence are both spatial concepts; the Divine is either *in* the world or above and *over* the world, but the Emersonian transparency gives us the Divine as being found *through* the world, which is not a spatial category at all, but discontinuous in the extreme, and as much an ebbing out as a flowing in, as Whitman, Hart Crane, and their compeers discovered.

But I will not leave our father Emerson there, happily circulating—like his own Uriel—in his own bright and transparent cloud, while chuckling—in what became the mode of his disciple Frost—that "Evil will bless and ice will burn." His conscious glory was solipsistic and to some degree self-castrating; his greater glories came unconsciously and where they had to—even for him—in his sorrows, personal and intellectual. The later Emerson moves from the High Romanticism of *Nature*, "Self-Reliance," and "Circles" through the growing skepticism of "Experience" and *Representative Men* on to the extraordinary worship of the serpent Ananke in *The Conduct of Life,* particularly in its three great essays—"Illusions," "Power," and the devastating "Fate." This Emerson has abandoned the American Romanticism that he invented, and gives us instead a demonic parody of Romantic hopefulness. No new genesis is here, but only the most ancient of entropies, as Emerson—in spite of himself—at last becomes Browning's Childe Roland, who at the Dark Tower calls what comes to claim him by the dread name of Necessity. Only a decade after writing "Circles," he writes the essay "Fate," and we witness again what Shelley—brooding on Wordsworth and Coleridge while tracing the exemplary destiny of Rousseau—grimly called "The Triumph of Life." After the transparency, the spectral shadowing; after the celestial light, the colder light of common day. "Circles" had said: "Men cease to interest us when we find their limitations. The only sin is limitation." To which "Fate" replies as follows:

> Let us build altars to the Beautiful Necessity, which secures that all is made of one piece; that plaintiff and defendant, friend and enemy, animal and planet, food and eater are of one kind. . . . Why should we fear to be

crushed by savage elements, we who are made up of the same elements?

No—I want to reply, as Blake did to Wordsworth—you shall not bring me down to such fitting and being fitted, I will not join you in building altars to the Beautiful Necessity, which you of all men should not be doing in any case. If the daimon was your destiny, then you should have followed him out to the farthest rings of the circumferences he drew for you, since you knew better than I that the transparency is most absolute out there, where no Necessity can come. But I do not make this reply, because I am haunted by a Journal entry that Emerson had made a few years before, shortly after the death of his greatly loved five-year-old son, Waldo. The true Emersonian dialectic of imaginative autonomy as against Necessity, of transparency as against enforced opaqueness, is in this journal passage. I close this essay by quoting it, without final comment, as the epitome of the glory and sorrows of Emerson, and of our American Romanticism, wildest and freest at last, most a giant of the imagination where it most confronts its own dwarf of disintegration. Emerson writes:

> In short, there ought to be no such thing as Fate. As long as we use this word, it is a sign of our impotence and that we are not yet ourselves. There is now a sublime revelation in each of us which makes us so strangely aware and certain of our riches that although I have never since I was born for so much as one moment expressed the truth, and although I have never heard the expression of it from any other, I know that the whole is here,—the wealth of the Universe is for me, everything is explicable and practicable for me. And yet whilst I adore this ineffable life which is at my heart, it will not condescend to gossip with me, it will not announce to me any particulars of science, it will not enter into the details of my biography, and say to me why I have a son and daughters born to me, or why my son dies in his sixth year of joy. Herein, then, I have this

latent omniscience coexistent with omni-ignorance. Moreover, whilst this Deity glows at the heart, and by his unlimited presentiments gives me all Power, I know that tomorrow will be as this day, I am a dwarf, and I remain a dwarf. That is to say, I believe in Fate. As long as I am weak, I shall talk of Fate; whenever the God fills me with his fulness, I shall see the disappearance of Fate.

I am *Defeated* all the time; yet to Victory I am born.

:II:

4

The Native Strain

AMERICAN ORPHISM

> *I do not fear that the poetry of democratic na-*
> *tions will prove insipid or that it will fly too near*
> *the ground; I rather apprehend that it will range*
> *at last to purely imaginary regions. I fear that the*
> *productions of democratic poets may often be sur-*
> *charged with immense and incoherent imagery,*
> *with exaggerated descriptions and strange crea-*
> *tions; and that the fantastic beings of their brain*
> *may sometimes make us regret the world of real-*
> *ity.*
>
> TOCQUEVILLE, ca. 1835–40

* * *

In September 1866, Emerson, aged sixty-three, set down in
his journal an ultimately American insight: "There may be
two or three or four steps, according to the genius of each,
but for every seeing soul there are two absorbing facts,—*I
and the Abyss.*" "Seeing soul" means "poet," and Emerson
in his late phase is the poet of the goddess Ananke, the
American Necessity he calls "Fate":

> *Her planted eye today controls,*
> *Is in the morrow most at home,*
> *And sternly calls to being souls*
> *That curse her when they come.*

This grim Muse is hardly the presiding Deity of *Nature* and
most of the *Essays,* of *Walden,* of the first three *Leaves of*

Grass (1855, 1856, 1860), of Dickinson, or in our time of *Harmonium, The Bridge, Paterson,* and all the other grand monuments of our Optative Mood down to one of the most recent, Mark Strand's conclusion to his lyric "White":

> *And out of my waking*
> *the circle of light widens,*
> *and the day begins.*
> *Trees turn in the luminous*
> *reaches of sight,*
> *and birds, and the bright*
> *pockets of cloud.*
> *The rim of light*
> *is crowded with hills,*
> *stars, and the pale echoes of night.*
> *It reaches out.*
> *It rings the eye with white.*
> *All things are one.*
> *All things are joined even beyond*
> *the edge of sight.*
> *All things are white.*

All things are white, to Strand, when the axis of vision becomes coincident with the axis of things. When all things cease to be one, for him, their opacity appears as a darkness. But for Strand's precursor, Stevens, the whiteness was terrible, and marked an opaqueness rather than a transparency. In the culminating crisis of his vision, Stevens also echoed Emerson, confirming the dialectic of what must be the most central passage in our literature, the extraordinary and much maligned transformation of the Sage of Concord into a Transparent Eyeball. "The ruin or the blank that we see when we look at nature, is in our own eye," Emerson said later in his *Nature,* and the same blankness descends upon Stevens at his nadir of vision:

> *Here, being visible is being white,*
> *Is being of the solid of white, the accomplishment*

Of an extremist in an exercise . . .

*The season changes. A cold wind chills the
    beach.
The long lines of it grow longer, emptier,
A darkness gathers though it does not fall*

*And the whiteness grows less vivid on the wall.
The man who is walking turns blankly on the
    sand.*

Whether the whiteness is transparent or opaque, what matters is the diminishment of its vividness. When Wordsworth saw the glory fade away, he confronted a fearful life-crisis, which soon enough ended him effectually as a poet. But a British High Romantic, even of Wordsworth's preternatural strength, had the horror only of the loss of a poethood, when vision came to its crisis. Even the Orphic Shelley did not see himself as a liberating god; that was left for his later followers, who apprehended him as a divinity, from Beddoes on through Browning and then to the generation of Lionel Johnson and the young Yeats. The native strain of American poetry, at least from Emerson to my own contemporaries, is a curious variant or version of Orphism, and the crisis of vision in this tradition threatens always a loss of divinity far transcending even the splendor of poetic vocation.

The sources of Emerson's kind of Orphism have been traced in Plato, various Neoplatonists, Cambridge Platonists, and even in the curious New England mode of Swedenborgianism, as represented by Sampson Reed and other exotic contemporaries. But Emerson's Orphism is very much his own, and little is to be apprehended of Emerson by tracking him to any of his precursors, for no other Post-Enlightenment intellect, not even Nietzsche's, has set itself quite so strongly against the idea of influence, and done this so successfully, and without anxiety. Even Emily Dickinson owes more to Emerson than Emerson did to Coleridge, Wordsworth, or any other spiritual father. All that Emerson took from Orphic traditions can be gleaned by any reader with even a slight knowledge of ancient Greek religion. When Emerson, in his essay "The Poet," brings together the "highest minds of the world," those who never cease to explore the manifold meanings of every sensuous fact, he lists an extraordinary seven: "Orpheus, Empedocles, Heraclitus, Plato, Plutarch, Dante, Swedenborg." Presumably, all these excel as figurative interpreters of mere nature, and Orpheus heads the list as though he were an actual poet, with priority over all others. Whether, as Empedocles, Plato, Emerson, and so distinguished a recent scholar as Jane Harrison thought, Orpheus was an actual man, or whether he was only a myth, does not matter for anyone's understanding of Orphism, since what affects followers of so esoteric a faith at any time will be its unique aspects, and not its genetic elements. Orphism differs from every other Greek religion, including the worship of Dionysus to which it is so strangely both allied and opposed. Orpheus is a kind of shaman, as is Empedocles after him, a master of divination whose quest leads to godhood, if finally also to failure and to a terrible death. The hypothetical lost poems of the Orphics, which Emerson knew in their later, Neoplatonic elaborations, were evidently purgatorial and apocalyptic, offering pathways to release from metamorphic existence. Where Greek thought emphasized always the great reality of human mortality, Orphism was not only a doctrine of immortality, but of the actual if latent divinity of the soul. Such doctrine was Thracian and Bacchic; the Orphics combined it with Apollonian notions of ritual purification to produce a purgatorial faith. There are only two gods who matter deeply to the Orphics, and these are Eros or Phanes, and Dionysus or Bacchus, rather than Zeus and Apollo. I think, to leap ahead, that these are also the only gods who matter to Emerson and to all his descendants in American poetic tradition, though I would add one goddess who is also important in the Orphic pantheon, Ananke or dread Necessity. The divinities of American Romantic poetry are Eros, Bacchus, and Ananke, and the troublesome relations between these giant forms account for much of the peculiar individuality of post-Emersonian American poetry, when we compare it to the British poetry of the same period, continuing on into our own days.

In his essay "History," Emerson tells us that: "The power of music, the power of poetry, to unfix and as it were clap wings to solid nature, interprets the riddle of Orpheus." In a journal entry for November 28, 1836, Emerson illuminates the Orphic riddle:

> In what I call the cyclus of Orphic words, which I find in Bacon, in Cudworth, in Plutarch, in Plato, in that which the New Church would indicate when it speaks of the truths possessed by the primeval church broken up into fragments and floating hither and thither in the corrupt Church, I perceive [an adaptation] myself addressed thoroughly. They do touch the Intellect & cause a gush of emotion; [to] which we call the moral sublime; they pervade also the moral nature. Now the Universal Man when he comes, must so speak. He must not be one-toned. He must recognize by addressing the whole nature.

Emerson's Universal Man, he that shall come, is Orphic Man. But what is Orphic Man? Vico traced the lyre of Orpheus to the original possession of Hermes, and though Emerson never mentions Vico he seems to have arrived at just this Viconian connection (possibly by reading French Viconians like Cousin, Ballanche, and Michelet). Orphic Man is Hermetic in having priority, and so in being free of the anxiety of influence. Even as Orpheus dissolved the forms of barbarism so as to nurture Greek civilization (according to Vico), and again in the same way that Emerson's Orpheus brings forth a new flux out of solid nature, so Orphic Man performs rather than suffers a rending. But Orphic Man, who will tear nature apart, is still to come; the Orphic Poet is his prophet.

Emerson's Orphic Poet makes three major appearances, two in *Nature*, and the other in the essay "The Poet." All his appearances are dazzling, and consciously extravagant. In each, Emerson achieves an *ekstasis,* a stepping-out that is truly a wandering beyond limits. If there is a source for these passages, the frequently cited sentence from Proclus will do: "He who desires to signify divine concerns through symbols is orphic, and, in short, accords with those who write myths concerning the gods." In *Nature,* Emerson remarks that what the Orphic poet sings to him may be both history and prophecy. When the Orphic poet teaches Emerson in the essay "The Poet," his song is called "freer speech," and we need to remember that for Emerson "freedom" and "wild-ness" are synonymous. Yet these central utterances of Emerson's Orphic Poet, though not incompatible with one another, are very different in tone and in direction, the difference being only in part the consequence of the seven years that divided the more experienced Emerson, aged forty, from the apocalyptic and more Orphic Emerson who had reached his own first large utterance at the christological age of thirty-three. Where the first prose-chants of the Orphic poet are in the Optative Mood carried beyond all limits, the later one makes a careful (perhaps an overly care-ful) distinction between Orphic poet and Orphic poem, ad-mitting a kind of Shelleyan skepticism into the whole cate-gory of the Orphic.

Let me attempt to give the center of each crucial Orphic chant, without quoting either fully, as each is so ordered as to make such a center available. In *Nature,* the Orphic poet begins by comparing fallen man, "a god in ruins," to Nebu-chadnezzar, the hideous emblem whose degradation is also the climax of Blake's parallel manifesto, *The Marriage of Heaven and Hell.* Nebuchadnezzar—"dethroned, bereft of reason, and eating grass like an ox"—is every man who tries to live by the understanding alone. Yet spirit or "reason" can afflict even Nebuchadnezzar with a terrible cure, or as Emer-son more grandly and grimly phrases it, "But who can set limits to the remedial force of spirit?" This is a Jobean rhetor-ical question, and Emerson answers it with a majestic para-graph that begins, "Man is the dwarf of himself." Once unfallen spirit, Emerson tells us, man was a center from which nature emanated. But the creation is now too large for the self-ruined creator. The Orphic poet concludes, with simple but awesome power, by celebrating in fallen man the faculty of *instinct,* as superior to the will as reason is to the understanding:

> He sees that the structure still fits him, but fits him colossally. Say, rather, once it fitted him, now it corresponds to him from far and on high. He adores timidly his own work. . . . Yet sometimes he starts in his slumber, and wonders at himself and his house, and muses strangely at the resemblance betwixt him and it. He perceives that if his law is still paramount, if still he have elemental power, if his word is sterling yet in nature, it is not conscious power, it is not inferior but superior to his will. It is instinct.

By so exalting instinct as our only link to unfallen human potential, Emerson opened himself and his poetic descendants to daemonic influx, for whatever he meant by "instinct," he could not reconcile it with the Transcendentalist faith in Coleridgean "reason." Orphic instinct, in Emerson and in his descendants, manifests itself as Dionysiac possession, and also as a rival possession that begins as Eros and ends as Ananke, love yielding to necessity. Emerson's *Nature* knows only Dionysus and Eros as divinities, but Emerson was not yet at the turning. In the essay "The Poet," which is best viewed as a prelude to Emerson's greatest essay, "Experience," the shadows of instinctual necessity begin to darken instinctual love. Though Emerson calls the poet "the man without impediment" and nature nothing but "motion or change," his later Orphic poet sees Nature as dominant, indeed as Necessity ("Nature through all her kingdoms, insures herself"), while the poet is only a dying creature whose songs are detached from him, by Nature herself, that they may outlive him. Nothing could contrast more with the closing passage of *Nature,* where the Orphic poet returned to prophesy "the

kingdom of man over nature, which cometh not with observation," and so counseled every man: "Build therefore your
own world." Emerson's first Orphic poet could have written
Song of Myself or *The Bridge*'s more ecstatic passages; his
second Orphic poet could write only lyrics like "As I Ebb'd
With The Ocean of Life" or "The Broken Tower." Yet he was
right to call both poets Orphics, or at least American Orphics.

Orphism attracted Emerson for reasons akin to the cause
of its mingled attraction and repulsion for Plato, and yet
more closely akin to its wholly attractive power for Empedocles and much later for the Neoplatonists of all ages, down to
certain Late Romantics. For Orphism, uniquely among ancient faiths in the West, came near shamanism without actually quite being a thoroughgoing shamanism. Mircea Eliade
lists as shamanistic characteristics in Orpheus his descent to
the dead to bring back his wife's soul, his healing art, love for
music and animals, his "charms," and—most crucially for us
—his power of divination and the posthumous performance
of his skull as an oracle. But Eliade also shows that Bacchic
(and Orphic) enthusiasm does not equal shamanistic ecstasy,
which is rather more extreme. There are moments in Emerson when he almost suggests shamanistic ecstasy, in a few
earlier notebook verse fragments, even fewer later prose
passages in the Journal, and most memorably in the great
poem "Bacchus." Orphic enthusiasm is more generally the
expansive or Transcendental atmosphere in Emerson, who is
wary almost always as to finding a way back from the influx
of power to the stabler ways of prudence.

Yet the shamanistic ecstasy, like the Orphic enthusiasm, is
what Nietzsche called "the antithetical"; it is a movement
against the merely natural in man. Emerson's poet, like the
Orphic adept and like the quasi-Orphic Empedocles, wants
us to think of him as a liberating god, and not just as a man.
We come back again to the strangeness of Orphism among
the classical faiths. It holds that man is wicked, because descended from the Titans who devoured the child Dionysos-
Zagreus, and yet also divine, because descended also necessarily from the grotesquely cannibalized Bacchic babe. We

have in us what Plato calls "the Titan Nature," our original sin, and we have what was never nature's. Plato mocked the Orphic notion that redeemed life would be "an eternal intoxication," but Emerson welcomed and echoed it. By making his own version of Orphism the revealed religion of American poetry, Emerson did something both frightening and splendid to most of our good poets after him. He committed them to an enterprise that British High Romanticism was either too commonsensical or too repressed to attempt, an enterprise that can be summed up in the single word "divination." If we interpret divination in every possible sense, including the proleptic knowledge of actual experience, and the fearsome project of god-making, then we have a vision of the outrageous ambition of the native strain in our poetry, or what I have chosen to call American Orphism.

There are a myriad of figures to illustrate American Orphism, but I want to confine myself here first to our very best poets (or those who seem best to me)—Whitman, Dickinson, a certain aspect of Stevens, and Hart Crane—and then to my own contemporaries I admire most, A. R. Ammons and John Ashbery. Frost is a cunningly concealed Orphic, and Pound, in the *Cantos*, a very central one, but a discussion of all our Emersonian poets soon would become very nearly a discussion of all our poets. There are six or seven Emersons in Emerson's prose, and three or four more in his verse, and he would have been delighted at our total inability to reconcile all of them, for more than Whitman he was large; he did contain multitudes of his descendants. He was indeed the American Orpheus, though, as he said, he sang rather huskily in verse, yet so magnificently, I think, in prose. Orpheus turned orator, we could say, or turned sophist as I suppose the late Yvor Winters or Robert Penn Warren might say, in one of their kinder moods toward our greatest ancestor (sometimes they talk of him as though he were Orpheus turned Satan).

Emerson understood that poets, or seeing souls, could not as poets accept mortality. As a man he had to accept rather too much of it: his first wife, his little son, two beloved brothers. As an Orphic orator he began by accepting nothing but Dionysus and Eros, but ended by accepting Ananke, and with her something dread that transcended mortality, the Orphic doom of wandering in repetition, in a netherworld, carrying poetry rather than water in a sieve. Let us call the sieve our American pragmatic temperament, and the spilled poetry the religion of money, since Emerson's disciples included the dreamers who divined a business expansion that would make us liberating gods, the least ambiguous consequence of our Optative Mood. To call the Emersonian Henry Ford a master of divination, and so a major American Orphic, does not discredit the native strain, for Orphism, though esoteric, is a democratic religion.

After Emerson inevitably comes Whitman, since *Song of Myself* is the natural son of Emerson's *Nature* and of the crucial essays, particularly "Self-Reliance" and "The Poet." Whitman, in his three great editions of *Leaves of Grass,* is a religious poet, and his faith is American Orphism. But American Orphism is not a doctrine but a fury, and the rage is for priority. No American poet wants to be an Orphic; they all insist upon being Orpheus. Emerson denounced all influence as pernicious, and his involuntary disciples have fought so bitterly against influence that they have all become one version or another of their brilliantly scattered, ever metamorphic father, whose oracular Yankee skull goes on chanting in their repudiations of Transcendental influx.

Whitman prided himself on telling truths about death that Emerson had not told, as well as truths about the body, sex, and time that went beyond his precursor's knowledge. Perhaps he did, but they are all the same truth and approximate one American Orphic formula: Eros is at once life, love, sleep, and death, or as Jane Harrison said of the ancient Orphic Eros, "a life-impulse, a thing fateful to all that lives, a man because of his moralized complexity, terrible and sometimes intolerable." This Orphic Eros, Jane Harrison also observed, was inseparable from the mother, conceived not as Aphrodite but as the old figure of the Earth-goddess, or if

Aphrodite, then the ocean-goddess, or else the underworld mother, goddess of death. The mysteries of the Orphic Eros are the mysteries of the mother, and in turning from his spiritual father Emerson, as from his own phallic father, Whitman turned only toward an even more Orphic vision of death.

Whitman's invocations of the Orphic mother emphasize faith in a mystery, as here at the close of "The Sleepers" (1855 version):

> *I too pass from the night;*
> *I stay awhile away O night, but I return to you*
>   *again and love you;*
>
> *Why should I be afraid to trust myself to you?*
> *I am not afraid. . . . I have been well brought*
>   *forward by you;*
> *I love the rich running day, but I do not desert*
>   *her in whom I lay so long:*
> *I know not how I came of you, and I know not*
>   *where I go with you. . . . but I know I came*
>   *well and shall go well.*
> *I will stop only a time with the night. . . . and*
>   *rise betimes.*
>
> *I will duly pass the day O my mother and duly*
>   *return to you;*
> *Not you will yield forth the dawn again more*
>   *surely than you will yield forth me again,*
> *Not the womb yields the babe in its time more*
>   *surely than I shall be yielded from you in my*
>   *time.*

The riddle of the Sphinx, of human origins, and the greater riddle of death, are mysteries beyond Whitman's knowledge, but his moving faith is that the going will be as well for him as the coming, and that the going is only a return to a further gestation and to a proper rebirth "in my time," not the time prescribed for another. "Pure I come from the Pure, O

Queen," reads a fragment from one of the Orphic tablets, where the queen addressed is at once the Earth-mother and the goddess of Hades. "Thou art become God from Man. A kid thou art fallen into milk," reads a fragment from another tablet, which could find a number of contexts in Whitman that would fit. In the Dionysiac afflatus, Whitman knew his own divinity, as Emerson's writings had promised he would know. But this is the knowledge of enthusiasm, born from the Orphic flux and doomed to ebb away as all Orphic intensities ebb. Shamanism, with its archaic and highly effective techniques of ecstasy, has known always how to avoid this ebb and flow. Though certain current American Orphics have returned to some of these archaic techniques, they sacrifice their more authentic if more sorrowful heritage by doing so. Emerson definitely prophesied them in "The Poet," when he declared for the Orphic asceticism against the shamanistic immersion in what he called *"quasi*-mechanical substitutes for the true nectar, which is the ravishment of the intellect by coming nearer to the fact." We are to remember that Emerson existed to remind us that a fact was an epiphany of God, and that always we were to ask the fact for the form. Hence the great declaration in "The Poet," that Whitman, Dickinson, Stevens in their lives were to exemplify, and that Hart Crane broke himself by being so tragically unable to heed; this great wisdom, as to substitutes for the true nectar:

> These are auxiliaries to the centrifugal tendency of a man, to his passage out into free space, and they help him to escape the custody of that body in which he is pent up, and of that jailyard of individual relations in which he is enclosed. Hence a great number of such as were professionally expressers of Beauty, as painters, poets, musicians and actors, have been more than others wont to lead a life of pleasure and indulgence; all but the few who received the true nectar; and, as it was a spurious mode of attaining freedom, as it was an emancipation not into the heavens but into the freedom of baser places, they were punished for that advantage they won, by a dissipation and deterioration. But never can

any advantage be taken of nature by a trick. The spirit
of the world, the great calm presence of the Creator,
comes not forth to the sorceries of opium or of wine.
The sublime vision comes to the pure and simple soul
in a clean and chaste body. That is not an inspiration,
which we owe to narcotics, but some counterfeit excite-
ment and fury.

This may sound merely conventional, or even tiresomely
sensible, but like Whitman's almost pathological emphases
on purity and cleanliness and Dickinson's obsession with her
White Election, it is a sublime passage of Orphic enthusiasm
and about as ordinary as Whitman on death and the mother
or Dickinson on what and how she merely sees. For Orphic
asceticism, whether ancient or American, is a peculiar kind
of purgation, not at all resembling the various asceticisms
practiced in Christian traditions. The *askesis* of Empedocles,
who was at once a sort of Orphic, a sort of Pythagorean, and
something of a Thracian shaman, is much closer to what
Emerson urged and Whitman and Dickinson so differently
followed. The Purifications of Empedocles are meant to reconcile one goddess to us, and she is Ananke or Necessity. We
are daemons, exiled from our true home, and our sin is that
we trusted in the principle of strife. The four elements
scarcely can bear us, and toss us back and forth, so that we
have been all things, even plants and fish. Purifications must
redeem us and return us to godhood, and do this by persuad-
ing Necessity to remit her oracle that prescribes our wander-
ings.

Purification, in the shrewd and saintly Emerson, is mostly
the process of unlocking our gates, of opening ourselves to
vision. How strangely American it is that purification should
be release rather than repression, though this is release in the
sense best exemplified by Thoreau, a lesser Emerson we have
so overvalued in this century, and so oddly and wrongly at
Emerson's expense. Purification in Whitman is self-integra-
tion and consequent release of imagination, very much in the
Emersonian pattern. In Dickinson, purification becomes the

most intensely Orphic phenomenon in the history of the American poetic consciousness, and remains more difficult to understand than any parallel process in a major modern creator.

Dickinson's religion, despite the pieties of her biographers-to-date and most of her critics, was no more Christian than the faiths of Emerson, Thoreau, Whitman. Christian imagery she employed always to her own curious ends as she saw fit, free-style, picking it up or dropping it at will. But even as her mind is stronger and more individual, more profoundly original, than Emerson's, Thoreau's, Whitman's, so her American Orphism is more complete and more astringent than theirs. Jane Harrison observed that: "The religion of Orpheus *is* religious in the sense that it is the worship of the real mysteries of life, of potencies (daemons) rather than personal gods *(theoi);* it is the worship of life itself in its supreme mysteries of ecstasy and love." Bacchus and Eros are Dickinson's daemons also, but she addressed the third Orphic potency, Ananke, not as Emerson's Fate but as death. Death, which imaginatively failed to interest Emerson, was identified by Whitman with Eros but by Dickinson with Necessity, two startlingly irreconcilable Orphic choices. To understand this contrast, we can return again to the Orphism of Emerson.

What did Emerson ask of life? Ecstasy and love, but also alas a reconcilement with the way things are, not in society or even in our fallen nature, but in the daemonic world. Like Swedenborg, whom he both admired and distrusted, he believed in influx and consequently in contact. It is here that he locates Plato's one defect in power, and "power," for Emerson as for Nietzsche, is the true value-term. He says of Plato that "his writings have not . . . the vital authority which the screams of prophets and the sermons of unlettered Arabs and Jews possess. There is an interval; and to cohesion, contact is necessary." Contact is Dionysian, and returns us to the primal child in ourselves. An Orphic saying of Heraclitus tells us that "Time is a child who plays and moves the pieces, the lordship is to the child." But if our lord Time is a child, then he has all the aggressive and destructive fantasies of a child, and he acts them out. And, unlike a human child, Time can make no reparation.

Orphism, even in the antihistorical Emerson, worships origins, and ultimately therefore worships Time. Time's firstborn, in the Orphic vision, is Eros, who brings us our souls by literal inspiration, by prevailing winds. Our souls then are latent divinities, but if we are to reach this Eros in ourselves we need to get there by Dionysiac enthusiasm. When this influx fails us, when we are left with only the sinful Titanic elements in ourselves, then truly we fall into Time, and finally into Hades. Our souls cease to be airy and become of earth. In the intervals left to us, our religious sense grants us visions of only one deity: Ananke. She abides, and as failed Orphics we must abide with her.

Emerson, when he failed as an Orphic, failed only dialectically, for his temperament was too fortunate for absolute failure. The despair of Melville is both profound and profoundly appealing to us, but Emerson on principle as well as by temperament would not despair, not even if the despair were to be of Whitman's Orphic kind, as in the *Sea-Drift* poems. Here is Emerson in August 1859, lamenting his inability to write consecutively of the beatitudes of intellect:

> It is too great for feeble souls, and they are overexcited. The wineglass shakes, and the wine is spilled. What then? The joy which will not let me sit in my chair, which brings me bolt upright to my feet, and sends me striding around my room, like a tiger in his cage, and I cannot have composure and concentration enough even to set down in English words the thought which thrills me—is not that joy a certificate of the elevation? What if I never write a book or a line? for a moment, the eyes of my eyes were opened, the affirmative experience remains, and consoles through all suffering.

I think a passage like this explains why the later Emerson, of "Fate," "Illusions," "Power," and the other vastations that make up *The Conduct of Life*, is still among the eternally

undefeated. Though he yields to Fate and gives to Ananke
the worship he once gave to Eros, he can continue to insist
that: "We are as lawgivers; we speak for Nature; we prophesy
and divine." He had created an Orphism that survives its
own ruin; we are not saved, and yet the Dionysian enthusiasm goes on flickering in us. Those who came after him had
neither his extraordinary temperament nor his intensely
faithless faith. Whitman would not surrender except to Eros,
but the Dionysian died in him after his crisis of 1859–60, and
like Wordsworth he long outlived his own poethood. Whitman's Orphism is as incomplete as Emerson's is overcom-
plete.

Dickinson, always too difficult for brief summation, defies
all terms not her own. Her religion, though, if we try to call
it religion or a binding, is a heresy of which the orthodoxy is
Emersonian Orphism. Sometimes, but not often, she can be
as grim as the older Emerson is about Fate, as in this late
fragment:

> *We never know we go when we are going—*
> *We jest and shut the Door—*
> *Fate—following—behind us bolts it—*
> *And we accost no more—*

But generally she is far subtler in her relations to the goddess Ananke, treating Necessity as a sister not too much more
formidable than the poet herself. In the later poems there is
rather less transport than in those of the great years, 1859
through 1864, but the Dionysiac enthusiasm, the influx of
power, never leaves her, nor does Eros wane to make room
for Ananke. Almost from the start, all three deities are in her
poetry, and again nearly at her origins Ananke is made one
with death. Where Whitman found Eros and death one in the
Orphic mother, and Emerson hardly found death at all (in his
vision, not his life), Dickinson recognized death's place as
rightfully being in the Orphic pantheon. "Why Orphic?"
readers of Dickinson may well ask, seeing that she allows
Orpheus only one appearance in all of her poetry, though

then in a late poem where he is preferred to the Bible because he captivated and did not condemn. Because, like the Orphic poet in Emerson's *Nature*, she tells us powerfully but largely by her example, that reality is consciousness, and this is consciousness of three things: poetic ecstasy, love, and the necessity of dying. The rest, as her pride, power, and exclusiveness of vision imply, do not matter. Life is solipsistic transport, extended to the Bacchic commonal through her poems. Life again is the rapture and cruelty of Eros, in her case always without an object adequate to herself as extraordinary subject. And life, finally yet without paradox, is the confrontation with dying, not as a consequence of Orphic failure in divination, but as the final exercise in divination, the triumphant test that will achieve a decisive priority. For does any other poet whatsoever so persuade us that she will die her own death and not another poet's or person's? Rilke hoped to meet and marry his own death, as Shelley had hoped before him. Both these poets were conscious Orphics, both are persuasive, but both seem dubious or even a little confused about the high individuality of their own deaths when we compare them closely to the more formidable Dickinson. What are we to call her peculiarly self-reliant faith if not a version of Emerson's Orphism, the validly solipsistic, and so ultimately realist doctrine native to American poetry?

As a heretic from Emersonianism, Dickinson declined to entertain inconsistencies, as her precursor could with his outrageous charm. We can name Emerson accurately as a dozen things, and describe all of them with ease and an exuberance he happily supplies us. Unfortunately, we then cannot reconcile that dozen to produce a coherent Emerson. We can name Dickinson accurately as only one thing, but we have failed so far to describe that massive unity, despite all her exuberance, which is not so contagious a quality. The critics of Emerson do not agree, and they are all of them somewhat correct. The critics of Dickinson are all honorable failures.

Yet they have shown us, however tentatively, everything she was not, at times even everything she would not condescend to be. Her hands, as she says, are narrow, yet she says also she can spread them wide: "To gather Paradise—." Elsewhere she tells us Paradise is "an uncertain certainty," and we know she means the Paradise of Poets, which is Orphic. Emerson, who fought against the past as inhibition, was chosen by Orphism because he was susceptible to what he called the Newness, and so asserted his own priority. Dickinson knew every Orphic priority except one, freedom from death's necessity, and so she labored to win a freedom Emerson more happily assumed, the wildness of an absolute priority, an Orphic death that she could die as if no one else had died so inventively before her. More than Emerson or Whitman, she seems now a perfect sphere of a consciousness, a divinity not wholly latent.

Of the Orphic inheritors in modern American poetry, Wallace Stevens is the largest. His most mysterious and difficult poem is the great elegy, "The Owl in the Sarcophagus," where the Orphic trinity appears as sleep, peace, and death: a Dionysiac sleep, erotic peace, and transformed Ananke of a death, all of these oxymorons blending into a Whitmanian consolation, for, as an American Orphic, Stevens is closer to Whitman than to Emerson or Dickinson. In *Notes Toward a Supreme Fiction*, Stevens reservedly mentions that: "A dead shepherd brought tremendous chords from hell/And bade the sheep carouse. Or so they said." But this already modified Orphism is darker in the "Owl" elegy, where sleep is "the accomplished, the fulfilling air" that redeems the Orphic soul, yet is also "a diamond jubilance beyond the fire," a reduction of Dionysian enthusiasm to "the unique composure" Stevens will accept as compromise. Eros, always elusive in Stevens, is in his vision of the last things the inhuman figure of peace, of passion spent, "a thousand begettings of the broken bold." Whitman's Orphic mother, divested of her erotic intensities, stands separately in Stevens as a last knowledge that death has, "there on the edges of oblivion." Time as the Orphic child of Heraclitus returns in the poem's moving final image:

> *It is a child that sings itself to sleep,*
> *The mind, among the creatures that it makes,*
> *The people, those by which it lives and dies.*

If this is still Orphic faith, admittedly it is faint, but we may remember the wisdom of Stevens in the even later poem, "The Sail of Ulysses":

>   *Need makes*
> *The right to use. Need names on its breath*
> *Categories of bleak necessity,*
> *Which, just to name, is to create*
> *A help, a right to help, a right*
> *To know what helps and to attain,*
> *By right of knowing, another plane.*

Here Stevens comes full circle around to late Emerson again, for this is the doctrine of *The Conduct of Life,* and Stevens too, for all his ironic wariness, concludes by building altars to the Beautiful Necessity. Emerson and Stevens are allied finally as failed Orphics who refuse to accept defeat.

I conclude though with the most magnificent of failed Orphics, Hart Crane, who was too pure to deny his defeat, and also with a closing glance at the best of our contemporary American Orphics, who understand their tradition perhaps too well. Crane's acts of worship directed to Bacchus and to Eros are clearer than his as intense worship of Ananke, which is simply his love of everything that is irreconcilable, his Shelleyan sense that even love and the means of love are not to be charmed into reconcilement. Crane is profoundly moving when he asks for "That patience that is armour and that shields/Love from despair—when love foresees the end—." The most Orphic poem Crane wrote is "Atlantis," the first section of *The Bridge* to be composed, and the prophecy of this Orphic poet's high spiritual failure (but aesthetic triumph, since it makes no sense to go on calling *The Bridge* a failure, even as the poem becomes more vital with each passing year). "Atlantis" is Orphic rather as its Platonic source is Orphic, that is, on the whole unwillingly. Plato resorts to Orphic mythology, as in his fable of Er, because he needs a purifying vision of judgment, and because he shares the Orphic conviction that our Titan nature requires to be cleansed; but Plato seems uneasy about Orphism, with its necessary emphasis on the irrational soul attaining an airy redemption. Crane too would have liked to have been more rational and less enthusiastic in his glimpses of salvation, but here his poetic tradition may have served him badly. His religious sensibility was too pure and acute to accept the failure of his Dionysiac and erotic quests to attain some reconcilement with the way things were, and it is at least a partial truth to say that Crane's Transcendentalism helped destroy him, which was the violent but insightful judgment of Yvor Winters.

The most convinced American Orphics since Crane were probably the late Theodore Roethke and the formidably active James Dickey, but I choose two poems by my own contemporaries as epilogue for this discussion. One is "Evening in the Country" from the book *The Double Dream of Spring* by John Ashbery; the other is "Prodigal" from the vòlume *Corsons Inlet* by A. R. Ammons. Both poems are beautifully chastened meditations that combine a kind of convalescence from Dionysiac enthusiasm, a continued erotic hope, and a recognition that necessity is stronger than either poetic influx or love's potential. Though both poets are battered Orphics, they are Orphics nevertheless, Ashbery as Stevens' continuator and Ammons as Emerson's. Ashbery's "Evening in the Country" begins with a declaration of happiness that is also a disavowal of ambition:

> *My resolve to win further I have*
> *Thrown out, and am charged by the thrill*
> *Of the sun coming up.*

From this acceptance of diminishment there rises a poignant declaration of faith in what is essentially an American Orphic act of purification:

Light falls on your shoulders, as is its way,
And the process of purification continues happily,
Unimpeded, but has the motion started
That is to quiver your head, send anxious beams
Into the dusty corners of the rooms
Eventually shoot out over the landscape
In stars and bursts? For other than this we know
*   nothing*
And space is a coffin, and the sky will put out
*   the light.*
I see you eager in your wishing it the way
We may join it, if it passes close enough:
This sets the seal of distinction on the success or
*   failure of your attempt.*

The light here is the Stevensian one of the imagination that falls upon reality, adding nothing but itself. One purification is rewarded only by the impulse that may lead to another, and so "the seal of distinction" here will be set without regard to success or failure of a Transcendental attempt. For these are the humane exhaustions of an American Orphism that has burned nearly to the socket.

Ammons' "Prodigal" also addresses itself to a moment of visionary convalescence:

after the mental
blaze and gleam,
the mind in both motions building and tearing
*   down.*

But Ammons, though as spent a Dionysiac seer as Ashbery and as much a yielder to the goddess Ananke, moves again toward an Orphic Eros with something of the old Emersonian acceptance and of the great Whitmanian force:

the mind whirls, short of the unifying
reach, short of the heat
to carry that forging:

    after the visions of these losses, the spent
seer, delivered to wastage, risen
   into ribs, consigns knowledge to
   approximation, order to the vehicle
of change, and fumbles blind in blunt innocence
   toward divine, terrible love.

5

Death and the Native Strain in American Poetry

Shall we be found hanging in the trees next spring?
Of what disaster is this the imminence:
Bare limbs, bare trees and a wind as sharp as salt?

The stars are putting on their glittering belts,
They throw around their shoulders cloaks that flash
Like a great shadow's last embellishment.

It may come tomorrow in the simplest word,
Almost as part of innocence, almost,
Almost as the tenderest and the truest part.

This is Wallace Stevens in expectation of an imminent death. The context is the American Sublime; the poem is his masterpiece, "The Auroras of Autumn." When the poem attains its resolution, the auroras cease to be a spell of light or false sign of heavenly malice, and are seen as an innocence of the earth. Death, which may come tomorrow, is not called part of that innocence, but *almost* part of it—even almost what it is in Whitman, the tenderest and truest part of innocence. Whitman and Stevens, both central to American poetic tradition, are wholly at the American imaginative center in their visions of death. Mortality, when confronted by the native strain in our poetry, is neither religiously denied nor transformed into something strangely rich. Death is part of the family, and its enigma is assimilated to the mystery of origins, where it is granted the true priority.

I want to contrast the visions of death in British and American poetry, and though I will take my instances of both free-style, I will keep coming back to a central poet of each tradition and a central text of death in each poet. Yeats and Stevens are inevitable contraries, being the largest heirs, respectively, of British and American Romanticism. I want two mysterious, hieratic poems, pre-elegies for the poet's own death, and out of a number of possibilities I choose Yeats' "Cuchulain Comforted" and Stevens' "The Owl in the Sarcophagus." Yet to apprehend these poems we need to know other poems by Yeats and Stevens, and the inescapable poems of their precursors: Blake, Shelley, Keats and Browning for Yeats; these same poets, but also the American line of Emerson, Whitman, and Dickinson for Stevens. This discussion, then, attempts to illuminate Yeats by his ancestors and by his contrary, Stevens, and also to see through Stevens and his American ancestry a peculiarly national vision of death. Yeats, though esoteric, moves towards a broader European account (and acceptance) of death, but the American poetic story of death is less universal, and probably more of an evasion of death, an evasion that is the ultimate triumph of imaginative solipsism.

Blake and Emerson, two very different Romantic founding fathers, had a common disinterest in death, unlike their major disciples. Blake said he could not think that death was more than a going-out from one room into another, which is a dismissal we might expect from a consciousness strong enough to believe that "The ruins of Time build mansions in Eternity." Emerson, in his best essay, "Experience," has resort to death as a final antidote to the illusoriness of all phenomena: "Nothing is left us now but death. We look to that with a grim satisfaction, saying, There at least is reality that will not dodge us." Yet this is Emerson in a fine exasperation with his (and our) own skepticism. More often, he is subtly dialectical in his devaluation of death. Aged thirty-nine, he writes in his journal, "The only poetic fact in the life of thousands and thousands is their death. No wonder they specify all the circumstances of the death of another person."

At forty, he protests, "Now, if a man dies, it is like a grave dug in the snow, it is a ghastly fact abhorrent to Nature, and we never mention it. Death is as natural as life, and should be sweet and graceful." At the age of fifty-one, he sums up the strength of his wisdom, but with the resignation of the seer who doubts the communicability of his vision:

> A man of thought is willing to die, willing to live; I suppose because he has seen the thread on which the beads are strung, and perceived that it reaches up and down, existing quite independently of the present illusions. A man of affairs is afraid to die, is pestered with terrors, because he has not this vision. Yet the first cannot explain it to the second.

Emerson and Blake, who disagree on most things, including the relative goodness of the natural man, are nearly at one in their realization that death is not *materia poetica.* Wordsworth, the other prime founder of Romanticism in the poetry of our language, is much closer to all later Romantics in his poetic anxieties about death. Yeats, though consciously repelled by Wordsworth, followed after Wordsworth's imaginative patterns quite as much as Stevens did, and Stevens is an overt Wordsworthian. In this, Yeats and Stevens repeat the contrast between Shelley and Keats, both of whom developed Wordsworth's central arguments—but Shelley by opposing their naturalism and Keats by making such naturalism even more heroic.

Wordsworth fought the *consciousness* of death because he had begun by identifying the poetic spirit with the intimation of immortality. His means for fighting a self-consciousness so destructive was to beget again the glory of his youth by the pursuit and recapture of after-images, defined by Geoffrey Hartman as re-cognitions leading to recognitions. By entering again into the gleam of immortality, through recollected images, Wordsworth almost persuaded himself that he could renovate his consciousness so as to attain again the child's freedom from any sense of mortality.

Shelley, a skeptic yet a visionary, apprehended the Words-worthian gleam as a constant inconstant, a flickering sense of what he called the Intellectual Beauty. Primarily an erotic poet, Shelley centered his concern on the shadow of ruin that haunted every manifestation of the Intellectual Beauty, par-ticularly in heterosexual love, in all its glory and in its cyclic decay. Death, for Shelley, is essentially the absence or ruin of Eros. For Keats, with his faith in the senses, death is part of the body, and part therefore of Eros. Even as Keats is incapable of unperplexing joy from pain, so he discovers we cannot unperplex bodily love from death. It is—Keats sings —in the very temple of delight that veiled Melancholy has her solitary shrine. After the quester, Keats adds, proves capable of viewing this, he is capable only of a distinguished death: "to be among her cloudy trophies hung." As Hart Crane says of his idioms in one of his elegies, so we might say of Keats' questers: "They are no trophies of the sun." Like Stevens after him, Keats yields graciously to what Freud would call the Reality Principle. Yeats outrageously and splendidly would not so yield, and in this he had both English Romantic and Victorian precursors (Browning most power-fully), even as Stevens was schooled in yielding by the two best American poets, Whitman and Dickinson.

Browning's triumph over the Reality Principle does not come through his vehement temperament, much impressed as we may be when he growls at us that he would no more fear death than he would any other battle. We are more moved when Childe Roland dauntless touches the slug-horn to his lips even as a horrible and nameless death closes upon him. But a kind of vehemence is involved in Childe Roland too, and I will return to Browning's magnificent invention when "Cuchulain Comforted" becomes the main text, for "Cuchulain Comforted" is Yeats' version of "Childe Roland to the Dark Tower Came." Though Santayana attacked Browning and Whitman together as "poets of Barbarism," there is nothing in common between the two, including their clashing visions of death. This rapid induction to a contrast between British and American poetries of death can move to

Yeats and Stevens by way of Whitman's contrast to Browning, with a side glance at Dickinson's severe originalities in this, her great subject.

Whitman, in the concluding sections of *Song of Myself*, meets death as being indistinguishable from an Orphic Eros, a release that is fulfillment:

> *And as to you Death, and you bitter hug of*
> *   mortality,*
> *it is idle to try to alarm me.*
>
> *To his work without flinching the accoucheur*
> *   comes,*
> *I see the elder-hand pressing receiving*
> *   supporting,*
> *I recline by the sills of the exquisite flexible*
> *   doors,*
> *And mark the outlet, and mark the relief and*
> *   escape.*

Here, as at the end of "The Sleepers," neither we nor Whitman know precisely whether we are talking about a womb or a tomb, birth or death. Yet Whitman, unlike Browning or Yeats, is not concerned about personal immortality in the sense of an individual survival. "I shall clasp thee again," Browning insists, and in his last *Epilogue* reminds us he always "Held we fall to rise, are baffled to fight better,/Sleep to wake." Browning's is a highly individual, truly a private Protestantism, yet it is still Protestant, but Whitman's religion is American Orphism, which is a very different faith. Dickinson, who had in common with Whitman only Emerson as prime precursor, shares in this Orphism but with a very different emphasis, and an accent entirely her own creation.

Emerson was Orphic about everything except death, which may suggest he was more an Orphic speculator than an Orphic believer. He had fostered a faith that Whitman, Thoreau, and Dickinson all possessed, yet he entertained it more speculatively than they did. American Orphism, which seems to me still the religion of the ongoing native strain in our poetry, emphasizes not the potential divinity of man but the actual divinity already present in the creative spirit. Divination, in every sense of that term, is the enterprise of the native strain in American poetry. What Wordsworth hesitantly affirmed becomes literal doctrine in American Romanticism. The American Orphic not only worships the gods Bacchus, Eros, and Ananke or Necessity, as the ancient followers of Orpheus did, but he seeks to become those gods. Zeus, Apollo, Jehovah and Christ count for less in American poetry than Bacchus, Eros and Ananke do, for the American Orpheus begins in the Evening-land, and so starts out in the belief that he is already a quasi-god, who perhaps can evade true death through divination, by joining gods like Dionysus, Eros, and Ananke, all of whom include death, and so surmount it.

Dickinson is too strong and too subtle to divinate without every kind of shading reservation. What matters in her is consciousness, and this is rarely so much consciousness of death as it is the consciousness of consciousness, even when it is death that is being apprehended:

> *This Consciousness that is aware*
> *Of Neighbors and the Sun*
> *Will be the one aware of Death*
> *And that itself alone*
>
> *Is traversing the interval*
> *Experience between*
> *And most profound experiment*
> *Appointed unto Men—*
>
> *How adequate unto itself*
> *Its properties shall be*
> *Itself unto itself and none*
> *Shall make discovery.*
>
> *Adventure most unto itself*
> *The Soul condemned to be—*

Attended by a single Hound
Its own identity.

A consciousness that she tells us is not solipsistic, since it is aware of other selves and of the external world, will some day be aware of dying, and will be altogether solitary, autonomous, and unable to communicate its final knowing to others. This final adventure will be a quest indistinguishable from the quester, and yet the quester will know herself as a shaman might, surviving so long as her totemic hound survives. This division between soul or character, and self or personality or identity is a distinction made in different ways in Browning, Whitman and Yeats, yet never as starkly as Dickinson conveys it. What matters in her is a heroism that says only consciousness matters. Death interests her as a challenge to consciousness, but not as a challenge to any other capacity for heroism.

Heroism meant nearly everything to Yeats; he overvalued violence because he was so desperate in his search for the heroic character. His central hero is the legendary Cuchulain, who inspired his finest verse-dramas, *At the Hawk's Well* and *The Only Jealousy of Emer.* Yeats's last play, left unrevised, is *The Death of Cuchulain;* his last poem-but-one is the majestic "Cuchulain Comforted," as good a poem as ever he wrote. Yeats dated it 13 January 1939; on January 28 he died. Dorothy Wellesley, who heard Yeats read aloud a prose version of the poem, gives this as part of her memory of it: One of the shades speaks to Cuchulain, the just-slain hero:

> . . . you will like to know who we are. We are the people who run away from the battles. Some of us have been put to death as cowards, but others have hidden, and some even died without people knowing they were cowards . . .

In the poem, "Cuchulain Comforted," the Shrouds tell Cuchulain their character: "Convicted cowards all, by kindred slain / Or driven from home and left to die in fear." They omit those who die, their cowardice still unknown by others. Cuchulain, "violent and famous," is the antithesis of a coward, and so is Browning's obsessive quester, Childe Roland, who nevertheless enters the after-life ringed by cowards and traitors, failed fellow-questers, just as Cuchulain does. Is Yeats, like Browning, struggling with an obscure sense of self-betrayal, of a moral cowardice he believes himself not to have expiated?

As Helen Vendler has noted, the beautiful close of "Cuchulain Comforted," "They had changed their throats and had the throats of birds," echoes Dante's great vision of Brunetto Latini, who is in Hell, yet seems one of the victorious and not among the defeated. This is the accent of celebration and not of bitterness, and we can say therefore that Yeats, though equivocal, is not turning against the theme of heroism in this death-poem. The cowards are transfigured, even as Roland's failed companions are transfigured when they stand ranged about him as a living flame, as he sounds his last trumpet of a prophecy. The hero has joined the failures, blent into one final state where the antithesis between heroism and cowardice, success and failure, has broken down far more thoroughly, somehow, than the unbreakable antithesis between life and death.

Yeats compels us, in "Cuchulain Comforted" as in a surprising number of other poems, to a close knowledge of his system in *A Vision.* The weight of Yeats-criticism is against me here, but the critics are wrong. "Cuchulain Comforted" does not make full sense unless we understand the precise difference between the supernatural states inhabited in the poem respectively by the Shrouds and by Cuchulain. In terms of Yeats' system, the Shrouds are moving through the last moments of the state called the Shiftings, until in the poem's last line they pass into the state Yeats calls the Beatitude. Cuchulain, less advanced than the Shrouds, moves in the poem from the Phantasmagoria or third phase of the state of Meditation into the Shiftings. To translate this, we need to turn to *A Vision.*

After you die, Yeats tells us there, you find yourself in a state he calls The Vision of the Blood Kindred, a kind of farewell to the sensuous world, to things as they were, to images and impulses. The following state is the Meditation, which is in three phases, called in sequence the Dreaming Back, the Return, and the Phantasmagoria. In the whole of the Meditation your labor is to see your past life as a coherent whole, an achieved form, like a work of art. Yet the Meditation is not a creative state; it is confused, imperfect, unhappy, and begins with the painful Dreaming Back, in which all the events of your past life recur. In the Return phase, which is a kind of antithesis of artistic creation, you deconstruct all the events of your life until they are turned into pure knowledge, divested of all accident, all passion. You are ready then for the Phantasmagoria, which is where we meet Cuchulain in the poem, leaning upon a tree, suffering again the wounds and blood of his destruction, and so at work exhausting, as Yeats says, "not nature, not pain and pleasure, but emotion." When emotion is exhausted, in this nightmare parody of po-etic vision, Cuchulain will be ready to join the Shrouds in the Shiftings, where moral good and moral evil, and particularly courage and cowardice, are cast off by the Spirit. In this shifting of your whole morality as a man, you are emptied out, and are made ready for the Shrouds' transfiguration into complete equilibrium or wholeness, at once a condition of unconsciousness and an epiphany or privileged moment of consciousness: "They had changed their throats and had the throats of birds."

Though "Cuchulain Comforted" takes you only so far (for dramatic reasons), Yeats's system in *A Vision* takes you all the way back to rebirth again. The Shrouds, and Cuchulain when he is ready, will pass next to the Purification, which means mostly that you become very simple, free of all complexity, in an occult state. You may linger in the Purification for centuries, while your thin Spirit seeks out a living person to somehow help you into the Foreknowledge, a kind of launch-ing pad towards Rebirth.

If we return to "Cuchulain Comforted" with these arbitrary but peculiarly fascinating Yeatsian distinctions firmly in mind, we can begin to understand the poem's design upon us. The cowards, until the last line of the poem, remain cowards, "Mainly because of what we only know/The rattle of those arms makes us afraid." What is it that they know? In the terms of Yeats' system, they know what Cuchulain has not yet realized, that all of us must live again, and since they are not yet in the Beatitude, they retain enough of their nature to fear the hero's weapons. But in deeper terms, belonging to European literary tradition at least since Homer, they know something that humanly impresses us more. They are comforted by their momentary communal experience ("And all we do/All must together do") but they know what Yeats the poet so greatly knows, which is what Homer knew, that in dying as in living any sense of community is rapidly evanescent. Cuchulain may be degraded (if indeed that is Yeats' entire intention, which I doubt), yet he remains the hero. In encountering Cuchulain, who can bear the solitude of dying as he can bear the solitude of being reborn, they encounter their own foreboding that in rebirth they must experience again the condition of being alone, which as cowards they cannot tolerate.

What then is Yeats most crucially saying about death, or rather about dying, in this fascinating but veiled Dantesque poem, with its muted *terza rima?* Very much, I think, what his master Shelley said about death in "Adonais" and "The Triumph of Life" and what his fellow-student of Shelley, Browning, was saying in "Childe Roland to the Dark Tower Came." The consciousness of death's necessity calls into question the purposiveness of all human action that is not somehow communal, and yet the dignity of dying, for a poet, demands a questing mode of action that is either wholly solitary or that admits the possibility of the community only of a band of brothers, the precursors of poet and hero, or as we now should say, the poet-as-hero. Yeats, as perhaps the last of the High Romantics of European tradition, confirms his tradition's view of death even as he seems to qualify or even degrade it. Death matters because it can be *materia poetica,* but only when it becomes an opportunity for the poet to pass a Last Judgment upon himself. Was he enough of a hero? Did he surmount his precursors, or if he joined them in failure, was he at least worthy of such a joining? Death is, therefore, even for a poet or hero, a social phenomenon essentially, and the standards it must meet (or evade) involve some sort of vision of the communal, however specialized that vision may be.

How un-American this is, and how far even from Emerson, let alone Whitman and Dickinson and their descendants all through American poetry, including Hart Crane and Wallace Stevens. Because our poets are such gorgeous solipsists, from Emerson on, their vision of dying has no relation to this European dialectic of the communal and the solitary. Browning, a passionate egomaniac, is all but selfless compared to Whitman and Dickinson, whose spirits make contact only with divisions in their own selves. Yeats, compared with Wallace Stevens, is drowned in the dramas of other selves; there are *people* in his poems, but Stevens magnificently knows only himself, attaining his greatest peace when he can intone most persuasively:

> *And if there is an hour there is a day,*
>
> *There is a month, a year, there is a time*
> *In which majesty is a mirror of the self:*
> *I have not but I am and as I am, I am.*

What can so great an "I am" meditate when it comes into the region where we all must die? Browning is not a better poet than Dickinson, or Yeats than Stevens; the problem here is not one of aesthetic loss and gain, but of an imaginative difference that I am rather dismayed to find may be at its root a social difference. Our native strain goes down deeper still, and must be related to the differences between British and American Puritanism, since both poetries for the last two hundred years are, in a clear sense, displaced Protestantisms. But rather than lose myself in a labyrinth I am not competent to explore, I want to return us to a text, with a brief overview of Stevens' "The Owl in the Sarcophagus," after which I will conclude with a contrast between Yeats and Stevens as representative British and American poets of death.

"The Owl in the Sarcophagus" is an elegy for Stevens' friend, Henry Church, to whom *Notes Toward a Supreme Fiction* had been dedicated. Written in 1947, when Stevens was sixty-eight, it is also a kind of pre-elegy for Stevens' own death, some eight years later. In Stevens' work, it stands chronologically and thematically between "Credences of Summer," essentially a celebratory, naturalistic, Keatsian poem, and "The Auroras of Autumn," a Wordsworthian poem of natural loss, and of the compensatory imagination rising up, not to redress loss, but to intimate what Stevens beautifully calls "an innocence of the earth." "The Owl in the Sarcophagus" yields up the world celebrated, however qualifiedly, in "Credences of Summer" and reaches towards the divination of "The Auroras of Autumn," where the only consolation offered is the wisdom of acceptance, of completion, a wisdom testifying to the mind's power over our consciousness of death. "The Owl in the Sarcophagus" does not go so far; it does not leave us with Stevens' "The vital, the never-failing genius,/Fulfilling his meditations, great and small." But it does give us a lasting sense of "the beings of the mind/In the light-bound space of the mind, the floreate flare . . ." or more starkly of what Stevens also calls "the mythology of modern death."

"The Owl in the Sarcophagus" is a vision of two forms that move among the dead, "high sleep" and "high peace," two brothers, and a third form, "the mother of us all,/The earthly mother and the mother of/The dead." This is an American Orphic Trinity, ultimately derived from Emerson, though Stevens was evidently not wholly aware of his full relation to this particular precursor. Stevens' "high sleep" is a version of Dionysus, however strange or even oxymoronic the image of a Dionysiac sleep must seem. But then, Stevens' "high peace" is a transformed Eros, and an erotic peace is rather far from the experience of most of us. The Orphic Great Mother, probably derived by Stevens from Whitman's "The Sleepers," is a transfigured Ananke, Necessity divested of her dread and made into a figure of ultimate consolation (as she is also in certain passages of Emerson's *The Conduct of Life*). In Stevens' elegy, the consolation is attained by a magical metamorphosis of the mind's consciousness of death into the opposite of such consciousness, a child asleep in its own life:

> *These are death's own supremest images,*
> *The pure perfections of parental space,*
>
> *The children of a desire that is the will,*
> *Even of death, the beings of the mind*
> *In the light-bound space of the mind, the*
>   *floreate flare*
>
> *It is a child that sings itself to sleep,*
> *The mind, among the creatures that it makes,*
> *The people, those by which it lives and dies.*

When we contrast Stevens and Yeats on death, we might begin by remembering Stevens' insistence that poetry must satisfy the human desire for resemblances. Against *A Vision*'s multi-phased life-after-death or rather death-between-lives, we can set a sardonic prose statement by Stevens:

> What a ghastly situation it would be if the world of the dead was actually different from the world of the living and, if as life ends, instead of passing to a former Victorian sphere, we passed into a land in which none of our problems had been solved, after all, and nothing resembled anything else in shape, in color, in sound, in look or otherwise.

The world of the dead in "The Owl in the Sarcophagus" is only what, "Generations of the imagination piled/In the manner of its stitchings," and Stevens speaks of his mother of the dead as "losing in self/The sense of self," very much in Dickinson's manner. His elegy is profoundly American in making dying an ultimate solipsistic adventure, at once Bacchic, erotic and necessitarian, and as much an act of solitary fulfillment as the writing of a poem is. Dying has priority in divination, even as becoming a poet establishes priority in divination. Major American poets see dying as only another assertion in the self's expansiveness, another huge effort to subsume the universe. Dying, whatever else it is for our native strain, for the genius of America, is not a social act. Even Yeats knows what European poets always knew, that dying makes a gesture towards community, but the American imagination has another goal always.

The greatness of *Cuchulain Comforted* is that, like *The Man and the Echo* and certain other late poems of Yeats, it shows its poet both powerfully employing and yet standing clear of his own mythologies. This is his advantage over Stevens, and the general advantage of the less solipsistic British over our own poets. Still, the whole movement of modern poetry is towards a progressive internalization of every sort of quest, and Yeats is most Romantic and most like American poets when he defies everything that is external and societal. Against *Cuchulain Comforted,* with all its magnificence of Yeats-against-Yeats, its seeming degradation of heroism, we can set Yeats himself, in a late prose manifesto, celebrating the unique power of the poets: "The world knows nothing because it has made nothing, we know everything because we have made everything."

6

Wallace Stevens

THE POEMS OF OUR CLIMATE

Poets influence us because we fall in love with their poems. All love unfortunately changes, if indeed it does not end, and since nothing is got for nothing, we also get hurt when we abandon, or are abandoned by, poems. Criticism is as much a series of metaphors for the acts of loving what we have read as for the acts of reading themselves. Walter Pater liked to use the word "appreciations" for his critical essays, and I present this particular series of metaphors as an appreciation of Wallace Stevens. Precisely, I mean to appreciate his success in writing the poems of our climate more definitively than any American since Whitman and Dickinson. What justifies an estimate that sets him higher than Frost, Pound, Eliot and Williams? If he is, as so many readers now believe, a great poet, at least the equal of such contemporaries as Hardy, Yeats, Rilke and Valéry, what are the qualities that make for greatness in him? How and why does he move us, enlighten us, enlarge our existences, and help us to live our lives?

Though the admirers of Stevens are a mighty band these days, they have not convinced all skeptics or detractors. We have had some difficulty in exporting him to the British, who with a few noble exceptions continue to regard him as a rather luxurious and Frenchified exquisite, a kind of upper-middle-class mock-Platonist who represents at best an American Aestheticism, replete with tropical fruits and aroma-laden invitations to the voyage. Their Stevens is the celebrator of Florida and of pre-Castro Havana, a vulgarian-in-spite-of-himself. Some American apostles of the Pound-

Eliot-Williams-Olson axis are holdouts also; thus we find Hugh Kenner growling, in his recent *The Pound Era,* that all Stevens comes to is the ultimate realization of the poetics of Edward Lear. We can find also, apart from different adherents of the Gorgeous Nonsense school, those critics who complain that Stevens increasingly became desiccated and mock-philosophical; here one can remember Jarrell's crack about G. E. Moore at the spinet. Finally, sometimes we can hear the complaint of those who insist they are weary of poems about poetry, and so are rendered weariest by the recorder of *Notes Toward a Supreme Fiction.* Probably new fault-findings, more soundly based upon Stevens' actual limitations, will arrive as the decades pass. Someone will rise to ask the hard question: How many qualifications can you get into a single poem and still have a poem? Do we not get more than enough of these interjections that Stevens himself describes as "a few words, an and yet, and yet, and yet—"?

But an appreciation does not address itself to answering negative critics, or to proposing fresh negations. The reader who loves Stevens learns a passion for Yes, and learns also that such a passion, like the imagination, needs to be indulged. "It must give pleasure," Stevens says, following a supreme tradition, and his poems do give pleasure. This pleasure, though naturalistic, essentially helps to satisfy the never-satisfied mind, and to the pursuit of the meaning of that satisfaction I now turn. Courageously waving before me the gaudy banners of the Affective Fallacy, I ask myself what it is that reading Stevens does for me, and what is it that I then attempt to do for other readers of Stevens? Is it an effectual though reduced Romantic Humanism that is rekindled for us? Is it a last splendid if willfully grotesque triumph of the American Sublime? Is it, O glorious if this be so, an achieved survival of the Genteel Tradition, another final hedge against the barbarians who are, as we all know, not only within the gates but also indistinguishable, alas, except upon certain moonlit nights, from our very selves? Is the prudential Seer of Hartford only the most eloquent elaborator of our way of life, the Grand Defender of our sanctified evasions, our privileged status as the secular clergy of a society we cannot serve, let alone save? Have we committed the further and grievous sin of making a Stevens in our own image, a poet of professors as Auden and Eliot and Arnold used to be? Having employed Stevens as a weapon in the mimic wars of criticism against the anti-Romantic legions of the Eliotics and Arnoldians, are we now confronted by his poems as so many statues in the formal parks of our university culture? Are his poems still Spirit to us, or are they only what Emerson, most prudential of New England seers, shrewdly called Commodity? Have we made him too into Literature? Do we need now to defend him against ourselves?

Several critics have regarded Stevens as essentially a comic poet. I think this characterization is not adequate to even his more sardonic aspect, but at least it reminds us of how humorous he could be. One of my favorite poems in *Harmonium*, which I rarely persuade anyone else to like, is called "Two Figures in Dense Violet Light." I take it as being a superbly American kind of defeated eroticism, the complaint of a would-be lover who is ruefully content to be discontent, because he rather doubts that high romance can be domesticated anyway in a world still so ruggedly New. One might think of this poem's speaker as being a decadent Huckleberry Finn dressed up to play the part of Romeo:

> *I had as lief be embraced by the porter at the*
> *hotel*
> *As to get no more from the moonlight*
> *Than your moist hand.*
>
> *Be the voice of night and Florida in my ear.*
> *Use dusky words and dusky images.*
> *Darken your speech.*
>
> *Speak, even, as if I did not hear you speaking,*
> *But spoke for you perfectly in my thoughts,*
> *Conceiving words,*

As the night conceives the sea-sounds in silence,
And out of their droning sibilants makes
A serenade.

Say, puerile, that the buzzards crouch on the
    ridge-pole
And sleep with one eye watching the stars fall
Below Key West.

Say that the palms are clear in a total blue,
Are clear and are obscure; that it is night;
That the moon shines.

Though more than usually mocking and self-mocking, this is surely another of Stevens' hymns to the Interior Paramour, another invocation of his Muse, his version of Whitman's Fancy. But Whitman's Fancy, though she rarely emanated very far out from him, did have a touch or two of an exterior existence. Stevens' Paramour, poor girl, is the most firmly Interior being in Romantic tradition. Compared to her, the epipsyches of Nerval, Poe, Shelley and the young Yeats are buxom, open-air, Renoir-like ladies. Stevens knows this, and the violet light of his poem is so dense that the two figures might as well be one. "What a love affair!" we cannot help exclaiming, as the Grand Solipsist murmurs to his Paramour: "Speak, even, as if I did not hear you speaking,/But spoke for you perfectly in my thoughts." This is a delicious Dialogue of One, all right, and we find its true father in some of Emerson's slyly bland observations on the Self-Reliance of Spheral Man. Recalling one Boscovich, an Italian Newtonian who had formulated a more-than-usually crazy version of the molecular theory of matter, Emerson mused: "Was it Boscovich who found that our bodies never come in contact? Well, souls never touch their objects. An innavigable sea washes with silent waves between us and the things we aim at and converse with."

In Stevens, this "innavigable sea" is called "the dumb-foundering abyss/Between us and the object," and no poet has been more honestly ruthless about the actual dualism of our everyday perceptions and imperceptions. Except for a peculiar roster of fabulistic caricatures, there aren't any *people* in Stevens' poems, and this exclusion is comprehensive enough to include Stevens himself as whole man or as person. But the "whole man" or "person" in a poem is generally only another formalizing device or dramatizing convention anyway, a means of self-presentation that Stevens did not care to employ. In the difficult poem, "The Creations of Sound," written against Eliot, who appears in it as X, Stevens declares himself as:

> *. . . a separate author, a different poet,*
> *An accretion from ourselves, intelligent*
> *Beyond intelligence, an artificial man*
>
> *At a distance, a secondary expositor,*
> *A being of sound, whom one does not approach*
> *Through any exaggeration.*

For all his antimythological bias, the old Stevens turned to Ulysses, "symbol of the seeker," to present his own final quest for a transcendental self. Unlike the Ulysses of Tennyson, at once somewhat Homeric, Dantesque, Shakespearean and Miltonic, the Ulysses of Stevens is not seeking to meet anything even partly external to himself. What other Ulysses would start out by saying: "As I know, I am and have/The right to be"? For Stevens, "the right to know/And the right to be are one," but his Ulysses must go on questing because:

> *Yet always there is another life,*
> *A life beyond this present knowing,*
> *A life lighter than this present splendor,*
> *Brighter, perfected and distant away,*
> *Not to be reached but to be known,*
> *Not an attainment of the will*
> *But something illogically received,*

A divination, a letting down
Resolved in dazzling discovery.

There is, despite so many of his critics, no doubt concerning the precursor of this ultimate Stevens. For that "something illogically received," we can recall the divinations of the inescapable father of the American Sublime, who uttered the grand formula: "All I know is reception; I am and I have: but I do not get, and when I have fancied I had gotten anything, I found I did not." In the same essay, the superb "Experience," Emerson mused: "I am very content with knowing, if only I could know." Both Emerson and Stevens hold hard to what both call "poverty," imaginative need, and they believe that holding hard long enough will compel the self to attain its due sphericity. Between the skeptically transcendental grandfather and the transcendentally skeptical grandson came the heroic father, spheral man himself, unqualified in his divinations, who tells us what we miss in Emerson and Stevens alike, and what we cannot resist in him:

> *Encompass worlds, but never try to encompass*
> *me,*
> *I crowd your sleekest and best by simply looking*
> *toward you.*
>
> *Writing and talk do not prove me,*
> *I carry the plenum of proof and every thing else*
> *in my face,*
> *With the hush of my lips I wholly confound the*
> *skeptic.*

For the absolutely transcendental self, the man-god, we read Whitman only, but I am astonished always how much of it abides in Stevens, despite nearly all his critics, and despite the Idiot Questioner in Stevens himself. His evasive glory is hardly distinguishable from his imperfect solipsism, or from ours. And there I verge upon what I take as the clue to his greatness; in the curiously esoteric but centrally American tradition of Emerson, Whitman, Thoreau and Dickinson, Stevens is uniquely the twentieth century poet of that solitary and inward glory we can none of us share with others. His value is that he describes and even celebrates (occasionally) our selfhood-communings as no one else can or does. He knows that "the sublime comes down/To the spirit and space," and though he keeps acknowledging the spirit's emptiness and space's vacancy, he keeps demonstrating a violent abundance of spirit and a florabundance of the consolations of space. He is the poet we always needed, who would speak for the solitude at our center, who would do for us what his own "Large Red Man Reading" did for those ghosts that returned to earth to hear his phrases, "and spoke the feeling for them, which was what they had lacked." Or, to state this function positively, Stevens, more even than Wordsworth, is the essential poet who can recognize that:

> *There is a human loneliness,*
> *A part of space and solitude,*
> *In which knowledge cannot be denied,*
> *In which nothing of knowledge fails,*
> *The luminous companion, the hand,*
> *The fortifying arm, the profound*
> *Response, the completely answering voice,*
> *The which is more than anything else*
> *The right within us and about us,*
> *Joined, the triumphant vigor, felt,*
> *The inner direction on which we depend,*
> *That which keeps us the little that we are,*
> *The aid of greatness to be and the force.*

There is nothing communal here. Stevens celebrates an apprehension that has no social aspect whatsoever and that indeed appears resistant to any psychological reductions we might apply. As no one is going to be tempted to call Stevens a mystical poet, or in any way religious, we rightly confront a considerable problem in description whenever Stevens is most himself. His True Subject appears to be his own sense of glory, and his true value for his readers appears to be that he reminds us of our own moments of solipsistic bliss, or at least of our aspirations for such moments.

The Stevens I begin to sketch has little in common with the poet of "decreation" most of his better critics have described for us. There is indeed a Stevens as seen by Hillis Miller, a poet of the almost-Paterian flux of sensations, of a cyclic near-nihilism returning always upon itself. There is also truly a Stevens as seen by Helen Vendler: Stevens the venerable ironist, apostle of "the total leaflessness." I do not assert that these are merely peripheral aspects of the poet, but they seem to me aspects only, darker saliences that surround the central man, shadows flickering beyond that crucial light cast by the single candle of Stevens' self-joying imagination, his version of "A Quiet Normal Life":

> *His place, as he sat and as he thought, was not*
> *In anything that he constructed, so frail,*
> *So barely lit, so shadowed over and naught,*
>
> *As, for example, a world in which, like snow,*
> *He became an inhabitant, obedient*
> *To gallant notions on the part of cold.*
>
> *It was here. This was the setting and the time*
> *Of year. Here in his house and in his room,*
> *In his chair, the most tranquil thought grew*
>   *peaked*
>
> *And the oldest and the warmest heart was cut*
> *By gallant notions on the part of night—*
> *Both late and alone, above the crickets' chords,*
>
> *Babbling, each tone, the uniqueness of its sound.*
> *There was no fury in transcendent forms.*
> *But his actual candle blazed with artifice.*

Stevens' customary anxiety about transcendent forms is evident, yet it is also evident that his actual candle is pre-

cisely a transcendent form. Wordsworth was sanely English
in refusing to go too far into his True Subject, which was his
own sense of actual sublimity. Emerson, deliberately and
wildly American, made possible for all his descendants the
outrageous True Subject of the American Sublime. Mocking
as always where he is most vulnerable and most involved,
here is Stevens' "The American Sublime":

> *How does one stand*
> *To behold the sublime,*
> *To confront the mockers,*
> *The mickey mockers*
> *And plated pairs?*
>
> *When General Jackson*
> *Posed for his statue*
> *He knew how one feels.*
> *Shall a man go barefoot*
> *Blinking and blank?*
>
> *But how does one feel?*
> *One grows used to the weather,*
> *The landscape and that;*
> *And the sublime comes down*
> *To the spirit itself,*
>
> *The spirit and space,*
> *The empty spirit*
> *In vacant space.*
> *What wine does one drink?*
> *What bread does one eat?*

Juxtapose this to one of the pure versions of the American
Sublime:

> In the highest moments, we are a vision. There is
> nothing that can be called gratitude nor properly joy.
> The soul is raised over passion. It seeth nothing so much
> as Identity. It is a Perceiving that Truth and Right ARE.

Hence it becomes a perfect Peace out of the knowing
that all things will go well. Vast spaces of nature, the
Atlantic Ocean, the South Sea; vast intervals of time
years, centuries, are annihilated to it; this which I think
and feel underlay that former state of life and circumstances, as it does underlie my present, and will always
all circumstance, and what is called life and what is
called death.

This excerpt from Emerson's 1838 Journal was modified
into one of the most famous passages in the essay, "Self-
Reliance." Nervous as Stevens is at confronting possible
mockers, his American Sublime is no appreciable distance
from Emerson's. One doesn't see Stevens posing for his
statue, but he still admits that the Sublime comes down to
what one feels and what one sees, and his emptiness of spirit
and vacancy of space were part of the weather, inner and
outer, and not permanent metaphysical reductions. That
which he was, that only could he see, and he never wearied
of affirming his version of Self-Reliance:

>   *. . . What*
> *One believes is what matters. Ecstatic identities*
> *Between one's self and the weather and the*
>   *things*
> *Of the weather are the belief in one's element,*
> *The casual reunions, the long-pondered*
> *Surrenders, the repeated sayings that*
> *There is nothing more and that it is enough*
> *To believe in the weather and in the things and*
>   *men*
> *Of the weather and in one's self, as part of that*
> *And nothing more.*

How can a solipsism present itself in the accents of glory,
we may be uneasy enough to ask, and again, can a solipsism
be a possible humanism? I begin an answer with the dark
Wittgensteinian aphorism: What the solipsist *means* is right.

For, though solipsism is refutable by its status as tautology, this is what Wittgenstein means when he speaks of a *deep* tautology, which leads to a true realism. Stevens too knows, as Emerson knew, that what he *says* is wrong, but that his meaning is right. The European Sublime had a communal aspect, however solitary its stimulus, but we are of an even more displaced Protestant national sensibility, and, accordingly, we come to reality only through knowing first the scandalous reality of our own selves. Or, as Stevens said:

> *The lean cats of the arches of the churches,*
> *That's the old world. In the new, all men are*
> > *priests.*

Stevens is a priest, not of the invisible, but of that visible he labors to make a little hard to see. He serves that visible, not for its own sake, but because he wants to make his own sublimity more visible to himself. Endlessly qualifying his sense of his own greatness, he still endlessly returns to rest upon such a sense. Yet he knows that he needs us, his possible readers, to do for him "what he cannot do for himself, that is to say, receive his poetry." As he proudly tells us, he addresses us as an elite, being in this one respect, at least, more honest than a far more esoteric and difficult poet, Whitman. In *The Noble Rider and the Sound of Words*, Stevens says:

> . . . all poets address themselves to someone and it is of the essence of that instinct, and it seems to amount to an instinct, that it should be to an elite, not to a drab but to a woman with the hair of a pythoness, not to a chamber of commerce but to a gallery of one's own, if there are enough of one's own to fill a gallery. And that elite, if it responds, not out of complaisance, but because the poet has quickened it, because he has educed from it that for which it was searching in itself and in the life around it and which it had not yet quite found, will thereafter do for the poet what he cannot do for himself, that is to say, receive his poetry.

There are two questions to be asked of this passage: What is it in this poet that gives him the instinct to address himself not to a drab but to a woman with the hair of a pythoness, and what is it that we keep searching for in ourselves that Stevens would quicken in us, that he would educe from us? The answer to both questions must be the same answer: a quality that Stevens calls "nobility." As he knew, it is hardly a word that now moves us, and I suspect he chose the word defiantly and therefore wrongly. Stevens says, in the same essay, that "It is one of the peculiarities of the imagination that it is always at the end of an era." Certainly Stevens now seems peculiarly to have been at the end of an era, where he himself could still be visualized as a *noble* rider moving to the sound of words. I myself have come to think that the principal peculiarity of the imagination is that it does not exist, or to state my thought another way, that people talking about the arts do better when they begin to talk as though the imagination did not exist. Let us reduce to the rocky level, and say, as Hobbes did, that "decaying sense" most certainly does exist. Stevens had then a decaying sense of nobility, which he called an imagination of nobility. "Noble," in its root, means to be knowing or seeing, and Stevens had therefore a decaying sense of a certain seeing that was also a knowing. I turn again to Stevens' central precursor for the inevitable vision of this nobility in its American variety:

> . . . This insight, which expresses itself by what is called Imagination, is a very high sort of seeing, which does not come by study, but by the intellect being where and what it sees; by sharing the path or circuit of things through forms, and so making them translucid to others.
> . . .

"Leave the many and hold the few," Emerson also advises in his late poem, "Terminus," thus sanctioning the democratic poet, like Whitman, in the pragmatic address to an actual elite. Stevens needed little sanctioning as to audience, but he was rather anxious about his own constant emphasis upon the self as solitary "scholar," and his recourse was to plead "poverty." He cannot have been unaware that both "scholar" and "poverty" in his rather precise senses were Emersonian usages. A great coverer of traces, Stevens may be judged nevertheless to have turned more to a tradition than to a man. American Romanticism found its last giant in Stevens, who defines the tradition quite as strongly as it informs him.

"The prologues are over. . . . It is time to choose," and the Stevens I think we must choose writes the poems not of an empty spirit in vacant space, but of a spirit so full of itself that there is room for nothing else. This description hardly appears to flatter Stevens, yet I render it in his praise. Another of his still neglected poems, for which my own love is intense, is entitled simply, "Poem With Rhythms":

> *The hand between the candle and the wall*
> *Grows large on the wall.*

> *The mind between this light or that and space,*
> *(This man in a room with an image of the*
>   *world,*
> *That woman waiting for the man she loves.)*
> *Grows large against space:*

> *There the man sees the image clearly at last.*
> *There the woman receives her lover into her*
>   *heart*
> *And weeps on his breast, though he never comes.*

> It must be that the hand
> Has a will to grow larger on the wall,
> To grow larger and heavier and stronger than
> The wall; and that the mind
> Turns to its own figurations and declares,
> *"This image, this love, I compose myself*
> *Of these. In these, I come forth outwardly.*
> *In these, I wear a vital cleanliness,*
> *Not as in air, bright-blue-resembling air,*
> *But as in the powerful mirror of my wish and*
>   *will."*

The principal difference between Stevens and Whitman appears to be that Stevens admits his mind is alone with its own figurations, while Whitman keeps inaccurately but movingly insisting he wants "contact" with other selves. His "contact" is an Emersonian term, and we know, as Whitman's readers, that he actually cannot bear "contact," any more than Emerson, Dickinson, Frost or Stevens can tolerate it. "Poem With Rhythms," like so much of Stevens, has a hidden origin in Whitman's "The Sleepers," particularly in a great passage apparently describing a woman's disappointment in love:

> *I am she who adorn'd herself and folded her*
> *   hair expectantly,*
> *My truant lover has come, and it is dark.*
>
> *Double yourself and receive me darkness,*
> *Receive me and my lover too . . . he will not let*
> *   me go*
> *without him.*
>
> *I roll myself upon you as upon a bed . . . I*
> *   resign myself*
> *to the dusk.*
>
> *He whom I call answers me and takes the place*
> *   of my lover,*
> *He rises with me silently from the bed.*
>
> *Darkness, you are gentler than my lover . . . his*
> *   flesh was*
> *   sweaty and panting,*
> *I feel the hot moisture yet that he left me.*
>
> *My hands are spread forth . . . I pass them in all*
> *   directions.*
> *I would sound up the shadowy shore to which*
> *   you are*
> *   journeying.*
>
> *Be careful, darkness! . . . already, what was it*
> *   touch'd me?*

I thought my lover had gone . . . else darkness
  and he are one,
I hear the heart-beat . . . I follow . . . I fade
  away.

This juxtaposition of major Whitman to relatively minor
Stevens is not altogether fair, but then I don't think I hurt
Stevens by granting that Whitman, upon his heights, is likely
to make his descendant seem only a dwarf of disintegration.
Whitman-as-Woman invokes the darkness of birth, and
blends himself into the mingled Sublimity of death and the
Native Strain. Stevens-as-Interior-Paramour invokes only his
mind's own figurations, but he sees himself cleansed in the
vitalizing mirror of will as he could never hope to see himself
in the mere outwardness of air. Whitman oddly but beautifully persuades us of a dramatic poignance that his actual
solipsism does not earn, while Stevens rather less beautifully
knows only the nondramatic truth of his own fine desperation.

What then is Stevens giving us? What do we celebrate with
and in him when he leads us to celebrate? His vigorous affirmation, "The Well Dressed Man With a Beard," centers on
"a speech/Of the self that must sustain itself on speech." Is
eloquence enough? I turn again to the fountain of our will,
Emerson, who had the courage to insist that eloquence was
enough, because he identified eloquence with "something
unlimited and boundless," in the manner of Cicero. Here is
Stevens mounting through eloquence to his individual sense
of "something unlimited and boundless," a "something" not
beyond our apprehension:

Last night at the end of night his starry head,
Like the head of fate, looked out in darkness,
  part
Thereof and part desire and part the sense
Of what men are. The collective being knew
There were others like him safely under roof:

The captain squalid on his pillow, the great
Cardinal, saying the prayers of earliest day;
The stone, the categorical effigy;
And the mother, the music, the name; the
    scholar,
Whose green mind bulges with complicated
    hues:

True transfigurers fetched out of the human
    mountain,
True genii for the diminished, spheres,
Gigantic embryos of populations,
Blue friends in shadows, rich conspirators,
Confiders and comforters and lofty kin.

To say more than human things with human
    voice,
That cannot be; to say human things with more
Than human voice, that, also, cannot be;
To speak humanly from the height or from the
    depth
Of human things, that is acutest speech.

A critic who has learned, ruefully, to accept the reductive view that the imagination is only decaying sense, must ask himself: Why is he so moved by this transfiguration of language into acutest speech? He may remember, in this connection, the prose statement by Stevens that moves him most:

> Why should a poem not change in sense when there is a fluctuation of the whole of appearance? Or why should it not change when we realize that the indifferent experience of life is the unique experience, the item of ecstasy which we have been isolating and reserving for another time and place, loftier and more secluded. . . .

The doctrinal voice of Walter Pater, another unacknowledged ancestor, is heard in this passage, as perhaps it must be heard in any modern Epicureanism. Stevens, I suggest, is the Lucretius of our modern poetry, and like Lucretius seeks his truth in mere appearances, seeks his spirit in things of the weather. Both poets are beyond illusions, yet both invest their knowing of the way things are with a certain grim ecstasy. But an American Lucretius, coming after the double alienation of European Romanticism and domestic Transcendentalism, will have lost all sense of the communal in his ecstasy. Stevens fulfilled the unique enterprise of a specifically American poetry by exposing the essential solipsism of our Native Strain. No American feels free when he is not alone, and every American's passion for Yes affirms a hidden belief that his soul's substance is no part of the creation. We are mortal gods, the central strain in our poetry keeps saying, and our aboriginal selves are forbidden to find companionship in one another. Our ecstasy comes only from self-recognition, yet cannot be complete if we reduce wholly to "the evilly compounded, vital I . . . made . . . fresh in a world of white." We need "The Poems of Our Climate" because we are, happily, imperfect solipsists, unhappy in a happily imperfect and still external world—which is to say, we need Stevens:

> *There would still remain the never-resting mind,*
> *So that one would want to escape, come back*
> *To what had been so long composed.*
> *The imperfect is our paradise.*
> *Note that, in this bitterness, delight,*
> *Since the imperfect is so hot in us,*
> *Lies in flawed words and stubborn sounds.*

:III:

7

The New Transcendentalism

THE VISIONARY STRAIN IN

MERWIN, ASHBERY, AND AMMONS

> *I mean we have yet no man who has leaned en-*
> *tirely on his character, and eaten angels' food;*
> *who, trusting to his sentiments, found life made of*
> *miracles; who, working for universal aims, found*
> *himself fed, he knew not how; clothed, sheltered,*
> *and weaponed, he knew not how, and yet it was*
> *done by his own hands.*
>
> EMERSON, *The Transcendentalist* (1842)

* * *

My subject is a still little-noted phenomenon, the revival of
the Native Strain or Emersonian vision, in the poetry of my
own generation of American poets, born in the decade 1925–
1935. I cannot survey all these poets here, and will discuss
aspects of the work of only three: W. S. Merwin, A. R. Ammons, and John Ashbery. My choice is affected by the limitations of personal taste, and I know it could be argued that the
true continuators of the Emersonian strain are to be located
elsewhere, not so much in the School of Stevens and Frost as
in that of Williams and Pound. But I am troubled by the
equivocal nature (as it seems to me) of the achievement of
Olson, Duncan and their fellows, down to Ginsberg, Snyder
and younger figures. Emersonian poetry is a diffuse though
recognizable tradition: it includes Jeffers as well as Hart
Crane, the Pound of *The Pisan Cantos* together with the
Stevens of "The Auroras of Autumn," middle Roethke just as
much as the later Aiken. The problem of American poetry
after Emerson might be defined as: "Is it possible to be un-

Emersonian, rather than, at best, anti-Emersonian?" Poe is not an Emersonian poet, but then he is also not a good poet. Perhaps only our Southern poets, down to Tate and Warren, could be as un-Emersonian as they were anti-Emersonian; the best of them now (Dickey and Ammons) are wholly Emersonian. Even in Emerson's own time, irreconcilable poets emerged from his maelstrom: Dickinson, Thoreau, Whitman, Very, even Tuckerman, whom Winters judged to be as firm a reaction against Emerson as Hawthorne and Melville were. American Romanticism is larger than Emersonianism, but in our time it may no longer be possible to distinguish between the two phenomena. The prophet of a national poetic sensibility in America was the Concord rhapsode, who contains in the dialectical mysteries of his doctrines and temperament very nearly everything that has come after.

Let me begin with a representative text, by the indubitably representative poet of my generation, the Protean Merwin. The poem is the wonderful "The Way to the River" from the volume, *The Moving Target*, of 1963. As the poem is about fifty lines, I will summarize rather than quote it entire. Addressed to the poet's wife, the poem is a kind of middle-of-the-journey declaration, a creedal hymn reaffirming a covenant of love and a sense of poetic vocation. Historically (and prophetically) the poem sums up the dilemma of "the Silent Generation" of young Americans, on the eve of the astonishing change (or collapse) of sensibility that was to begin at Berkeley in 1964. After nearly a decade, one sees how brief an episode (or epicycle) this Time of Troubles was. Merwin, with his curious proleptic urgency, memorably caught the prelude to that time:

> *The way to the river leads past the names of*
> *Ash the sleeves the wreaths of hinges*
> *Through the song of the bandage vendor*
>
> *I lay your name by my voice*
> *As I go*

The way to the river leads past the late
Doors and the games of the children born
  looking backwards
They play that they are broken glass
The numbers wait in the halls and the clouds
Call
From windows
They play that they are old they are putting the
  horizon

Into baskets they are escaping they are
Hiding

I step over the sleepers the fires the calendars
My voice turns to you

This is the "poverty" of Emerson and Stevens: imaginative need. Merwin joins a tradition that includes the E. A. Robinson of "The Man Against the Sky," the Frost of "Directive," the Stevens of "The Auroras of Autumn" as he too follows Emerson in building an altar to the Beautiful Necessity:

To the city of wires I have brought home a
  handful
Of water I walk slowly
In front of me they are building the empty
Ages I see them reflected not for long
Be here I am no longer ashamed of time it is too
  brief its hands
Have no names
I have passed it I know

Oh Necessity you with the face you with
All the faces

This is written on the back of everything

But we
Will read it together

The Merwin of this—still his present phase—began with the central poem, "Lemuel's Blessing," which follows the Smart of "Jubilate Agno" for its form (as do so many recent American poets, including Ginsberg, Strand, Donald Finkel) but which is also an Emersonian manifesto. Addressing a Spirit ("You that know the way") Merwin prayed: "Let the memory of tongues not unnerve me so that I stumble or quake." This hymn to Self-Reliance expanded into the most ambitious poem of *The Moving Target,* a majestic celebration of what Emerson called the Newness, "For Now:" "Goodbye what you learned for me I have to learn anyway/You that forgot your rivers they are gone/Myself I would not know you." In *The Lice,* his next volume (and his best), Merwin defined the gods as "what has failed to become of us," a dark postscript to the Emersonian insistence that the poets are as liberating gods. The poems of *The Lice* are afflicted by light, as in this wholly characteristic brief lyric, the poignant "How We Are Spared":

> *At midsummer before dawn an orange light*
> *returns to the mountains*
> *Like a great weight and the small birds cry out*
> *And bear it up*

With his largest volume, *The Carrier of Ladders,* Merwin appears to have completed his metamorphosis into an American visionary poet. The book's most astonishing yet most problematic poems are four ode-like "Psalms," subtitled: "Our Fathers," "The Signals," "The September Vision" and "The Cerements." No recent American poet, not even the Roethke of *The Far Field* or Dickey in his latest work, has attempted so exalted a style:

> *I am the son of hazard but does my prayer*
> *reach you O star of the uncertain*
> *I am the son of blindness but nothing that we*
> *have made watches us*
> *I am the son of untruth but I have seen the*

> *children in Paradise walking in pairs each*
> *hand in hand with himself*
> *I am the son of the warder but he was buried*
> *with his keys*
> *I am the son of the light but does it call me*
> *Samuel or Jonah*
> *I am the son of a wish older than water but I*
> *needed till now*
> *I am the son of ghosts clutching the world like*
> *roads but tomorrow I will go a new way*

The form is again that of the "Jubilate Agno," but the most important line in this first "Psalm," and in all of Merwin, is very far from Smart's pious spirit:

> *I am the son of the future but my own father*

As a poet, this latest Merwin hardly approaches that impossible self-begetting; the accent of the Pound-Eliot tradition hovers everywhere in even the most self-consciously bare of these verses. Merwin is more impressive for his terrible need, his lust for discontinuity, than for any actual inventiveness. The poignance of his current phase is the constant attempt at self-reliance, in the conviction that only thus will the poet *see.* Merwin's true precursors are three honorable, civilized representative poets: Longfellow and MacLeish and Wilbur, none of whom attempted to speak a Word that was his own Word only. In another time, Merwin would have gone on with the cultivation of a more continuous idiom, as he did in his early volumes, and as Longfellow did even in the Age of Emerson. The pressures of the quasi-apocalyptic nineteen-sixties have made of Merwin an American Orphic bard despite the sorrow that his poetic temperament is not at home in suffering the Native Strain. No poet legitimately speaks a Word whose burden is that his generation will be the very last. Merwin's litanies of denudation will read very oddly when a fresh generation proclaims nearly the same dilemma, and then yet another generation trumpets finality.

Merwin's predicament (and I hope I read it fairly, as I am not unsympathetic to his work) is that he has no Transcendental vision, and yet feels impelled to prophesy. What is fascinating is that after one hundred and thirty years, the situation of American poetry is precisely as it was when Emerson wrote his loving but ironic essay on his younger contemporaries and followers, *The Transcendentalist*, where they are seen as exposing our poverty but also their own. With that genial desperation (or desperate geniality) that is so endearing (and enraging) a quality in his work, Emerson nevertheless urged his followers out into the wilderness:

> But all these of whom I speak are not proficients; they are novices; they only show the road in which man should travel, when the soul has greater health and prowess. Yet let them feel the dignity of their charge, and deserve a larger power. Their heart is the ark in which the fire is concealed which shall burn in a broader and universal flame. Let them obey the Genius then most when his impulse is wildest; then most when he seems to lead to uninhabitable deserts of thought and life; for the path which the hero travels alone is the highway of health and benefit to mankind. What is the privilege and nobility of our nature but its persistency, through its power to attach itself to what is permanent?

Merwin prays to be sustained during his time in the desert, but his poems hardly persuade us that his Genius or Spirit has led him into "uninhabitable deserts of thought and life." Readers distrustful of *The Carrier of Ladders* either emphasize what they feel is a dominance of style over substance or they complain of spiritual pretentiousness. What I find more problematic is something that Emerson foresaw when he said of his Transcendentalist that "He believes in miracle, in the perpetual openness of the human mind to new influx of light and power; he believes in inspiration, and in ecstasy," and yet went on to observe that such a youth was part of an American literature and spiritual history still "in the optative mood." Merwin's optative mood seems only to concern his impersonal identity as poet-prophet; instead of a belief in an influx of light and power, he offers us what we might contrive to know anyway, even if we had not been chilled with him by his artful mutations:

> *To which I make my way eating the silence of*
> *   animals*
> *Offering snow to the darkness*
>
> *Today belongs to few and tomorrow to no one*

Emerson's favorite oracular guise was as an Orphic poet. Of the Orphic deities—Eros, Dionysus, and Ananke—Merwin gives us some backward glances at the first, and a constant view of the last, but the Dionysiac has gone out of his poetry. Without the Bacchic turbulence, and haunted by a light that he presents as wholly meaningless, Merwin seems condemned to write a poetry that is as bare of true content as it is so elegantly bare in diction and design. Only the *situation* of the Emersonian Transcendentalist or Orphic Poet survives in Merwin; it is as though for him the native strain were pure strain, to be endured because endurance is value enough, or even because the eloquence of endurance is enough.

Of the poets of Merwin's generation, Ashbery and Ammons seem to me the strongest, and the likeliest to achieve the kind of splendor that Stevens, Frost, Hart Crane and only a few other American poets of this century were able both to touch and then to maintain. Except for their excellence, Ashbery and Ammons have no common qualities. Ashbery has been misunderstood because of his association with the "New York School" of Kenneth Koch, Frank O'Hara and other comedians of the spirit, but also because of the dissociative phase of his work as represented by much of a peculiar volume, *The Tennis Court Oath.* But the poet of *The Double Dream of Spring* and the prose *Three Poems* is again the Stevensian meditator of the early *Some Trees.* No other American poet has labored quite so intensely to exorcise all the demons of discursiveness, and no contemporary American poet is so impressively at one with himself in expounding a discursive wisdom. Like his master, Stevens, Ashbery is essentially a ruminative poet, turning a few subjects over and over, knowing always that what counts is the mythology of self, blotched out beyond unblotching.

Ashbery's various styles have suggested affinities to composer-theorists like Cage and Cowell, to painters of the school of Kline and Pollock, and to an assortment of French bards like Roussel, Reverdy and even Michaux. But the best of Ashbery, from the early *Some Trees* on through "A Last World" and "The Skaters" to the wonderful culminations of his great book, *The Double Dream of Spring* and the recent *Three Poems*, shows a clear descent from the major American tradition that began in Emerson. Even as his poetic father is Stevens, Ashbery's largest ancestor is Whitman, and it is the Whitmanian strain in Stevens that found Ashbery. I would guess that Ashbery, like Stevens, turned to French poetry as a deliberate evasion of continuities, a desperate quest for freedom from the burden of poetic influence. The beautiful group called "French Poems" in *The Double Dream of Spring* were written in French and then translated into English, Ashbery notes, "with the idea of avoiding customary word-patterns and associations." This looks at first like the characteristic quarrel with discursiveness that is endemic in modern verse, but a deeper familiarity with the "French Poems" will evoke powerful associations with Stevens at his most central, the seer of "Credences of Summer":

> *And it does seem that all the force of*
> *The cosmic temperature lives in the form of*
> * contacts*
> *That no intervention could resolve,*
> *Even that of a creator returned to the desolate*
> *Scene of this first experiment: this microcosm.*
>
>   .   .   .   .   .
>   .   .   .   .   .
> * . . . and then it's so natural*

That we experience almost no feeling
Except a certain lightness which matches
The recent closed ambiance which is, besides
Full of attentions for us. Thus, lightness and
    wealth.

But the existence of all these things and
    especially
The amazing fullness of their number must be
For us a source of unforgettable questions:
Such as: whence does all this come? and again:
Shall I some day be a part of all this fullness?

The poet of these stanzas is necessarily a man who must have absorbed "Credences of Summer" when he was young, perhaps even as a Harvard undergraduate. Every strong poet's development is a typology of evasions, a complex misprision of his precursor. Ashbery's true precursor is the composite father, Whitman-Stevens, and the whole body to date of Ashbery's work manifests nearly every possible revisionary ratio in regard to so formidable an American ancestry. Though the disjunctiveness of so much of Ashbery suggests his usual critical placement with the boisterousness of Koch or the random poignances of O'Hara, he seems most himself when most ruefully and intensely Transcendental, the almost involuntary celebrator "of that *invisible light* which spatters the silence/Of our everyday festivities." Ashbery is a kind of invalid of American Orphism, perpetually convalescing from the strenuous worship of that dread Orphic trinity of draining gods: Eros, Dionysus, Ananke, who preside over the Native Strain of our poetry.

I propose to track Ashbery back to his origins in another essay, but here I have space only to investigate some poems of his major phase, as it seems developing in his two most recent books. To enter at this point a judgment of current American poets now entering their imaginative maturity, Ashbery and A. R. Ammons are to me the indispensable figures, two already fully achieved artists who are likely to develop into worthy rivals of Frost, Stevens, Pound, Williams, Eliot, Crane, and Warren. Merwin, James Wright, Merrill, perhaps Snyder in the school of Williams and Pound, perhaps James Dickey of a somewhat older generation (if he yet returns to the strength of earlier work) are candidates also. Yet all prophecy is dangerous here; there are recent poems by Howard, Hollander, Kinnell, Pack, Feinman, Hecht, Strand, Rich, Snodgrass, among others, which are as powerful as all but the very best of Ammons, Ashbery, Wright. Other critics and readers would nominate quite different groupings, as we evidently enter a time of singular wealth in contemporary verse.

Ashbery's poetry is haunted by the image of transparence, but this comes to him, from the start, as "a puzzling light," or carried by beings who are "as dirty handmaidens/To some transparent witch." Against Transcendental influx, Ashbery knows the wisdom of what he calls "learning to accept/The charity of the hard moments as they are doled out," and knows also that: "One can never change the core of things, and light burns you the harder for it." Burned by a visionary flame beyond accommodation (one can contrast Kinnell's too-easy invocations of such fire), Ashbery gently plays with Orphic influx ("Light bounced off the ends/Of the small gray waves to tell/Them in the observatory/About the great drama that was being won."). Between Emerson and Whitman, the seers of this tradition, and Ashbery, Ammons and other legatees, there comes the mediating figure of Stevens:

> *My house has changed a little in the sun.*
> *The fragrance of the magnolias comes close,*
> *False flick, false form, but falseness close to kin.*
>
> *It must be visible or invisible,*
> *Invisible or visible or both;*
> *A seeing and unseeing in the eye.*

These are hardly the accents of transport, yet Stevens does stand precariously, in the renewed light. But even the skepticism is Emerson's own; his greatest single visionary oration is *Experience,* a text upon which Dickinson, Stevens and Ashbery always seem to be writing commentaries:

> Thus inevitably does the universe wear our color, and every object fall successively into the subject itself. The subject exists, the subject enlarges; all things sooner or later fall into place. As I am, so I see; use what language we will, we can never say anything but what we are. . . . And we cannot say too little of our constitutional necessity of seeing things under private aspects, or saturated with our humors. And yet is the God the native of these bleak rocks. . . . We must hold hard to this poverty, however scandalous, and by more vigorous self-recoveries, after the sallies of action, possess our axis more firmly. . . .

The Old Transcendentalism in America, like the New, hardly distinguishes itself from a visionary skepticism, and makes no assertions without compensatory qualifications. Still, we tend to remember Emerson for his transparencies, and not the opaquenesses that more frequently haunted him and his immediate disciples. I suspect that this is because of Emerson's *confidence,* no matter where he places his emphases. When Stevens attains to a rare transparence, he generally *sees* very little more than is customary, but he *feels* a greater peace, and this peace reduces to a confidence in the momentary capability of his own imagination. Transcendentalism, in its American formulation, centers upon Emerson's stance of Self-Reliance, which is primarily a denial of the anxiety of influence. Like Nietzsche, who admired him for it, Emerson refuses to allow us to believe we must be latecomers. In a gnomic quatrain introducing his major essay on self-reliance, Emerson manifested a shamanistic intensity still evident in his descendents:

> *Cast the bantling on the rocks,*
> *Suckle him with the she-wolf's teat,*
> *Wintered with the hawk and fox,*
> *Power and speed be hands and feet.*

This is splendid, but Emerson had no more been such a bantling than any of my contemporaries are, unless one wants the delightful absurdity of seeing Wordsworth or Coleridge as a she-wolf. "Do not seek yourself outside yourself" is yet another motto to *Self-Reliance,* and there is one more, from Beaumont and Fletcher, assuring us that the soul of an honest man:

> *Commands all light, all influence, all fate*
> *Nothing to him falls early or too late.*

These are all wonderful idealisms. Whitman, who had been simmering, read *Self-Reliance* and was brought to the boil of the 1855 "Song of Myself." Ashbery, by temperament and choice, always seems to keep simmering, but whether he took impetus from Whitman, Stevens or even the French partisans of poetic Newness, he has worked largely and overtly in this Emersonian spirit. Unfortunately, like Merwin and Merwin's precursor, Pound, Ashbery truly absorbed from the Emerson-Whitman tradition the poet's over-idealizing tendency to lie to himself, against his origins and against experience. American poets since Emerson are all antithetical completions of one another, which means mostly that they develop into grotesque truncations of what they might have been. Where British poets swerve away from their spiritual fathers, ours attempt to rescue their supposedly benighted sires. American bards, like Democritus, deny the swerve, so as to save divination, holding on to the Fate that might make them liberating gods. Epicurus affirmed the swerve, ruining divination, and all poetry since is caught between the two. Emerson, though close to Democritus, wants even divination to be a mode of Self-Reliance. That is, he genuinely shares the Orphic belief that the poet is already divine, and realizes more of this divinity in writing his poems. Lucretian poets like Shelley who find freedom by swerving away from fathers (Wordsworth and Milton, for Shelley) do not believe in divination, and do not worship an Orphic Necessity as the final form of divinity. Orphic poets,

particularly American or Emersonian Orphics, worship four
gods only: Ananke, Eros, Dionysus and—most of all surely—
themselves. They are therefore peculiarly resistant to the
idea of poetic influence, for divination—to them—means
primarily an apprehension of their own possible sublimity,
the gods they are in process of becoming. The gentle Ashbery, despite all his quite genuine and hard-won wisdom, is
as much in this tradition as those spheral men, Emerson,
Whitman, Thoreau, and that sublime egoist, Stevens, or the
American Wordsworth.

The Double Dream of Spring has a limpidly beautiful
poem called "Clouds," which begins:

> *All this time he had only been waiting,*
> *Not even thinking, as many had supposed.*
> *Now sleep wound down to him its promise of*
>   *dazzling peace*
> *And he stood up to assume that imagination.*
>
> *There were others in the forest as close as he*
> *To caring about the silent outcome, but they had*
>   *gotten lost*
> *In the shadows of dreams so that the external*
>   *look*
> *Of the nearby world had become confused with*
>   *the cobwebs inside.*

Sleep here has a Whitmanian-Stevensian cast ("The Sleepers," "The Owl in the Sarcophagus") and the gorgeous solipsism so directly celebrated here has its sources in the same
ultimately Emersonian tradition. Though "he," the poet or
quest-hero, is distinguished from his fellows as not having
yielded to such solipsism, the poem ends in a negative apoth-
eosis:

> *He shoots forward like a malignant star.*
> *The edges of the journey are ragged.*
> *Only the face of night begins to grow distinct*

As the fainter stars call to each other and are
    lost.

Day re-creates his image like a snapshot:
The family and the guests are there,
The talking over there, only now it will never
    end.
And so cities are arranged, and oceans traversed,

And farms tilled with especial care.
This year again the corn has grown ripe and
    tall.
It is a perfect rebuttal of the argument. And
    Semele
Moves away, puzzled at the brown light above
    the fields.

The harvest of natural process, too ripe for enigmas, re-
futes quest, and confirms the natural realism of all solipsists.
This poem, urging us away from the Emersonian or Central
Self, concludes by yielding to that Self, and to the re-birth of
Dionysus, Semele's son. Like his precursor, Stevens, Ashbery
fears and evades the Native Strain of American Orphism and
again like Stevens he belongs as much to that strain as Hart
Crane or John Wheelwright does. In the recent prose *Three
Poems,* he ruefully accepts his tradition and his inescapable
place in it:

> . . . Why, after all, were we not destroyed in the
> conflagration of the moment our real and imaginary
> lives coincided, unless it was because we never had a
> separate existence beyond that of those two static and
> highly artificial concepts whose fusion was nevertheless
> the cause of death and destruction not only for ourselves
> but in the world around us. But perhaps the explanation
> lies precisely here: what we were witnessing was merely
> the reverse side of an event of cosmic beatitude for all
> except us, who were blind to it because it took place
> inside us. Meanwhile the shape of life has changed defi-
> nitively for the better for everyone on the outside. They
> are bathed in the light of this tremendous surprise as in

the light of a new sun from which only healing and not
corrosive rays emanate; they comment on the miracu-
lous change as people comment on the dazzling beauty
of a day in early autumn, forgetting that for the blind
man in their midst it is a day like any other, so that its
beauty cannot be said to have universal validity but
must remain fundamentally in doubt.

—The Recital, p. 114

The closest (though dialectically opposed) analogue to this
passage is the great concluding rhapsody of Emerson's early
apocalypse, *Nature*, when the Orphic Poet returns to
prophesy:

> . . . As when the summer comes from the south the
> snow-banks melt and the face of the earth becomes
> green before it, so shall the advancing spirit create its
> ornaments along its path, and carry with it the beauty
> it visits and the song which enchants it; it shall draw
> beautiful faces, warm hearts, wise discourse, and heroic
> acts, around its way, until evil is no more seen. The
> kingdom of man over nature, which cometh not with
> observation,—a dominion such as now is beyond his
> dream of God,—he shall enter without more wonder
> than the blind man feels who is gradually restored to
> perfect sight.

Ashbery's apocalyptic transformation of the Self, its elevation to the Over-Soul, is manifest to everyone and everything
outside the Self, but not to the blind man of the Self. The
Emersonian Self will know the metamorphic redemption of
others and things only by knowing first its gradual freedom
from blindness as to its own glory. Ashbery's forerunners, the
makers of *Song of Myself* and *Notes toward a Supreme Fiction*, were primary Emersonians, involuntary as Stevens was
in this identity. Ashbery is that American anomaly, an antithetical Transcendentalist, bearer of an influx of the Newness
that he cannot know himself.

In turning to A. R. Ammons, the wisest and I prophesy
most enduring poet of his generation, we confront the most

direct Emersonian in American poetry since Frost. For an account of Ammons' work from its origins to the lyrics of *Uplands* (1970) and *Briefings* (1971), I refer to my book, *The Ringers in the Tower* (Chicago, 1971). Here I wish to describe the great achievement of the latest Ammons, as gathered in the large *Collected Poems 1951–1971* (1972), particularly three long poems: *Essay on Poetics, Extremes and Moderations, Hibernaculum,* but also two crucial recent lyrics.

The *Essay on Poetics* begins by giving us Ammons' central signature, the process by which he has made a cosmos:

> *Take in a lyric information*
> *totally processed, interpenetrated into*
> *wholeness where*
>
> *a bit is a bit, a string a string, a*
> *cluster a cluster, everything beefing up*
> *and verging out*
>
> *for that point in the periphery where*
> *salience bends into curve*
> *and all saliences bend to the same angle of*
>
> *curve and curve becomes curve, one curve, the*
> *   whole curve:*
> *that is information actual*
> *at every point*
>
> *but taking on itself at every point*
> *the emanation of curvature, of meaning, all*
> *the way into the high*
>
> *recognition of wholeness, that synthesis,*
> *feeling, aroused, controlled, and released . . .*

Ammons' "periphery" is at once the "circumference" of Emerson and Dickinson, and also the nerve-ending of the quester who goes out upon circumference. Ammons' "salience" is the further projecting or out-leaping from the longest periphery that the seer has attained. That makes Ammons' "salience" his equivalent of the Pound-Williams "image" or the Stevensian "solar single,/Man-sun, man-moon, man-earth, man-ocean." Far back, but indubitably the starting-place, Ammons' *Essay on Poetics* touches Whitman's 1855 "Preface" and Whitman's fecund ground, Emerson's "The Poet," a prose rhapsody mostly of 1842. Ammons expounds a "science" that now seems curious, but Emerson called it "true science." More than Whitman, or even Thoreau or Dickinson or Frost, Ammons is the Poet that Emerson prophesied as necessary for America:

> . . . For through that better perception he stands one step nearer to things, and sees the flowing or metamorphosis; perceives that thought is multiform; that within the form of every creature is a force impelling it to ascend into a higher form; and following with his eyes the life, uses the forms which express that life, and so his speech flows with the flowing of nature. All the facts of the animal economy, sex, nutriment, gestation, birth, growth, are symbols of the passage of the world into the soul of man, to suffer there a change and reappear a new and higher fact. He uses forms according to the life, and not according to the form. This is true science. The poet alone knows astronomy, chemistry, vegetation and animation, for he does not stop at these facts, but employs them as signs. He knows why the plain or meadow of space was strown with these flowers we call suns and moons and stars; why the great deep is adorned with animals, with men, and gods; for in every word he speaks he rides on them as the horses of thought.

As in "Tintern Abbey," standing closer to things is to see into their life, to see process and not particulars. But it is not Wordsworthian nor even neo-Platonic to possess a speech that is magic, to speak words that are themselves the metamorphosis. This violent Idealism is Emerson's Transcendental science, a knowing too impatient for the disciplines of mysticism, let alone rational dialectic. To read Emerson's "The Poet" side-by-side with any British Romantic on poetry, except Blake, is to see how peculiar the Emersonian wildness is. Only a step away and Emerson will identify a true poet's words with Necessity, as though nature's absolute confounding of our faculties simultaneously could make us skeptics and scientists affirming an inevitable insight. Emerson, here as so often, seems to break down the humanly needful distinctions between incoherence and coherence, relying upon his tone to persuade us of an intelligibility not wholly present. Ammons, like any strong poet, handles influence by misprision. His Emersonianism is so striking and plausible a twisting askew of that heritage as to raise again the labyrinthine issue of what poetic influence is, and how it works.

To talk about a poem by Ammons in terms of Emerson or Whitman is to invoke what one might term the Human Analogue, as opposed to Coleridge's Organic Analogue. No poem rejoices in its own solitary inscape, any more than we can do so. We have to be talked about in terms of other people, for no more than a poem is, can we be "about" ourselves. To say that a poem is about itself is killing, but to say it is about another poem is to go out into the world where we live. We idealize about ourselves when we isolate ourselves, just as poets deceive themselves by idealizing what they assert to be their poems' true subjects. The actual subjects move towards the anxiety of influence, and now frequently *are* that anxiety. But a deeper apparent digression begins to loom here, even as I attempt to relate the peripheries and saliences of Ammons to the great circumference of his ancestors.

Reductively, the anxiety of influence *is* the fear of death, and a poet's vision of immortality includes seeing himself free of all influence. Perhaps sexual jealousy, a closely related anxiety, also reduces to the fear of death, or of the ultimate tyranny of space and time, since influence-anxiety is related to our horror of space and time as a dungeon, as the danger of domination by the Not-Me. Anxiety of influence is due then partly to fear of the natural body, yet poetry is written by the natural man who is one with the body. Blake insisted that there was also the Real Man—the Imagination. Perhaps there is, but he cannot write poems, at least not yet.

The poem attempts to relieve the poet-as-poet from fears that *there is not enough for him,* whether of space (imaginative) or time (priority). A subject, a mode, a voice; all these lead to the question: "What, besides my death, is my own?" Poets of the Pound-Williams school, more than most contemporary poets, scoff at the notion of an anxiety of influence, believing as they think they do that a poem is a machine made out of words. Perhaps, but mostly in the sense that we, alas, appear to be machines made out of words, for poems actually are closer to—as Stevens said—men made up out of words. Men make poems as Dr. Frankenstein made his *daemon,* and poems too acquire the disorders of the human. The people in poems do not have fathers, but the poems do.

Ammons, like Merwin and Ashbery, is aware of all this, for strong poets become strong by meeting the anxiety of influence, not be evading it. Poets adept at forgetting their ancestry write very forgettable poems. Ammons' *Essay on Poetics* swerves away from Emerson by the exercise of a variety of revisionary ratios, cunningly set against mere repetition:

> *the very first actions of contact with an ocean*
> *   say ocean over and*
> *over: read a few lines along the periphery of*
> *   any of the truly*
> *great and the knowledge delineates an open*
> *   shore:*
>
> *what is to be gained from the immortal person*
> *   except the experience*
> *of ocean: take any line as skiff, break the*
> *   breakers, and go out*
> *into the landless, orientationless, but perfectly*
> *   contained, try*
>
> *the suasions, brief dips and rises, and the*
> *   general circulations,*
> *the wind, the abundant reductions, stars, and*
> *   the experience is*

obtained: but rivers, brooks, and trickles have
their uses and

special joys and achieve, in their identities,
difficult absoluteness
but will you say, what of the content—why
they are all made of water
but will you, because of the confusion, bring
me front center as

a mere mist or vapor . . .

This is the faith of Emersonian Self-Reliance, yet severely
mitigated by the consciousness of latecoming. At the close of
the poem, Ammons attains a majestic bleakness not wholly
compatible with this apparent humility:

. . . along the periphery of integrations, then, is
an exposure
to demons, thralls, witcheries, the maelstrom
black of
possibility, costly, chancy, lethal, open: so I am
not so much

arguing with the organic school as shifting true
organisms from
the already organized to the bleak periphery of
possibility,
an area transcendental only by its bottomless
entropy . . .

The later Ammons writes out of a vision "transcendental
only by its bottomless entropy," yet still Emersonian, though
this is the later Emerson of *The Conduct of Life*, precursor
of Stevens in *The Rock* and Frost throughout *In The Clearing. Extremes and Moderations* is Ammons' major achievement in the long poem, written in "the flow-breaking four-
liner," starting out in an audacious transcendentalism and
modulating into the prophetic voice Ammons rarely seeks,
yet always attains at the seeking:

. . . O city, I cry at
the gate, the glacier is your
mother, the currents of the deep father you, you
   sleep

in the ministry of trees, the boulders are your
   brother sustaining
you: come out, I cry, into the lofty
   assimilations: women, let
down your hair under the dark leaves of the
   night grove, enter
the currents with a sage whining, rising into
   the circular

dance: men, come out and be with the wind,
   speedy and lean, fall
into the moon-cheered waters, plunge into the
   ecstasy of rapids:
children, come out and play in the toys of
   divinity: glass, brick,
stone, curb, rail are freezing you out of your
   motions, the

uncluttered circulations: I cry that, but perhaps
   I am too secular
or pagan: everything, they say, is artificial:
   nature's the
artwork of the Lord: but your work, city is
   aimed unnaturally
against time: your artifice confronts the Artifice:
   beyond

the scheduled consummation, nothing's to be
   recalled: there is
memory enough in the rock, unscriptured
   history in
the wind, sufficient identity in the curve
of the valley . . .

This is the extreme of which Ammons' earlier and masterly lyric, "The City Limits," was the moderation. By "extremes"

Ammons signifies what Emerson's circle called the Newness, onsets of transcendental influx. "Moderations" are the rescues of these evaded furies that Ammons attempts for the poetry of life, while carefully distinguishing even the extremes from mere phantasmagorias:

> *. . . that there should have been possibilities*
> *enough to*
> *include all that has occurred is beyond belief,*
> *an extreme the*
> *strictures and disciplines of which prevent*
> *loose-flowing*
> *phantasmagoria . . .*

Though the poem concludes in a moving ecological outrage, an outrage the poet appears to believe is his theme, its concerns hover where Ammons' obsessions always congregate, his resistance to his own transcendental experience. This resistance is made, as all constant readers of Ammons learn, in the name of a precarious naturalism, but the concealed undercurrent is always the sense of an earlier bafflement of vision, a failure to have attained a longed-for unity with an Absolute. The latest Ammons rarely makes reference to this spent seership, but the old longing beautifully haunts all of the difficult recent radiances. Here is a typical late lyric, "Day," manifesting again the extraordinary and wholly deceptive ease that Ammons has won for himself, an ease of mode and not of spirit, which continues to carry an exemplary burden of torment:

> *On a cold late*
> *September morning,*
> *wider than sky-wide*
> *discs of lit-shale clouds*
>
> *skim the hills,*
> *crescents, chords*

of sunlight
now and then fracturing

the long peripheries:
the crow flies
silent,
on course but destinationless,

floating:
hurry, hurry,
the running light says,
while anything remains.

The mode goes back through Dickinson to Emerson, and is anything but the Pound-Williams "machine made out of words" that Hugh Kenner describes and praises in his crucially polemical *The Pound Era.* "The long peripheries," for Ammons, are identical with poems, or rather with what he would like his poems to be, outermost perceptions within precise boundaries, or literally "carryings-over" from the eye's tyranny to the relative freedom of a personally achieved idiom. What now distinguishes a lyric like "Day" from the characteristic earlier work in the Ammons canon is the urgency of what another late long poem, *Hibernaculum,* calls "a staying change," this seer's response to our current time-of-transition from our recent confusions to whatever is coming upon us: "I think we are here to give back our possessions before/they are taken away." This is the motto preceding an immense intimation of another Newness:

. . . I

accost the emptiness saying let all men turn
   their
eyes to the emptiness that allows adoration's life:
that is my whole saying, though I have no
   intention to

stop talking: our immediate staying's the rock
  but
the staying of the rock's motion: motion, that
  spirit!
we could veer into, dimpling, the sun or into the
  cold

orbital lofts, but our motion, our weight, our
  speed
are organized here like a rock, our spiritual stay:
the blue spruce's become ponderous with snow:
  brief

melt re-froze and knitted ice to needles and ice
to snow so the ridges eight inches high hold: the
branches move back and forth, stiff wailers:

the cloud-misty moonlight fills small fields,
  plots,
woodnooks with high light, snow transluminant
  as
fire . . .

Contrast to this an equally superb Emersonian epiphany:

Last night the moon rose behind four distinct pine-tree tops in the distant woods and the night at ten was so bright that I walked abroad. But the sublime light of night is unsatisfying, provoking; it astonishes but explains not. Its charm floats, dances, disappears, comes and goes, but palls in five minutes after you have left the house. Come out of your warm, angular house, resounding with few voices, into the chill, grand, instantaneous night, with such a Presence as a full moon in the clouds, and you are struck with poetic wonder. In the instant you leave far behind all human relations, wife, mother and child, and live only with the savages—water, air, light, carbon, lime, and granite. . . . I become a moist, cold element. 'Nature grows over me.' Frogs pipe; waters far off tinkle; dry leaves hiss; grass bends and rustles,

and I have died out of the human world and come to
feel a strange, cold, aqueous, terraqueous, aerial,
ethereal sympathy and existence. I sow the sun and
moon for seeds.

Emerson and Ammons share a nature that on the level of
experience or confrontation cannot be humanized. Yet they
share also a Transcendental belief that one can come to
unity, at least in the pure good of theory. Their common tone
is a curious chill, a tang of other-than-human relationship to
an Oversoul or Overall that is not nature, yet breaks through
into nature. Like Emerson, its founder, Ammons is a poet of
the American Sublime, and a residue of this primordial
strength abides in all of his work.

Collected Poems 1951–1971 closes with a magnificent poem
that is Ammons' overt *apologia,* and I will close this essay by
giving the poem entire, and then attempting a defining observation upon its place in the tradition of American poetry.
Here is "The Arc Inside and Out":

If, whittler and dumper, gross carver
into the shadiest curvings, I took branch
and meat from the stalk of life, threw

away the monies of the treasured,
treasurable mind, cleaved memory free
of the instant, if I got right down

shucking off periphery after periphery
to the glassy vague gray parabolas
and swoops of unnailable perception,

would I begin to improve the purity,
would I essentialize out the distilled
form, the glitter-stone that whether

the world comes or goes clicks gleams
and chinks of truth self-making, never
to be shuttered, the face-brilliant core

stone: or if I, amasser, heap shoveler,
depth pumper, took in all springs and
oceans, paramoecia and moons, massive

buttes and summit slants, rooted trunks
and leafages, anthologies of wise words,
schemata, all grasses (including the

tidal Spartinas, *marginal, salty*
broadsweeps) would I finally come on a
suasion, large, fully-informed, restful

scape, turning back in on itself, its
periphery enclosing our system with
its bright dot and allowing in nonparlant

quantities at the edge void, void, and
void, would I then feel plenitude
brought to center and extent, a sweet

easing away of all edge, evil, and surprise:
these two ways to dream! dreaming them's
the bumfuzzlement—the impoverished

diamond, the heterogeneous abundance
starved into oneness: ultimately, either
way, which is our peace, the little

arc-line appears, inside which is nothing,
outside which is nothing—however big,
nothing beyond: however small, nothing

within: neither way to go's to stay, stay
here, the apple an apple with its own hue
or streak, the drink of water, the drink,

the falling into sleep, restfully ever the
falling into sleep, dream, dream, and
every morning the sun comes, the sun.

The "arc" here, like Dickinson's "Circumference," ultimately derives from Emerson's subtle essay, "Circles":

Our life is an apprenticeship to the truth that around every circle another can be drawn; that there is no end in nature, but every end is a beginning . . .

The natural world may be conceived of as a system of concentric circles, and we now and then detect in nature slight dislocations which apprise us that this surface on which we now stand is not fixed, but sliding. . . . The one thing which we seek with insatiable desire is to forget ourselves, to be surprised out of our propriety, to lose our sempiternal memory and to do something without knowing how or why; in short to draw a new circle. . . .

Ammons' "little arc-line" is both his Blakean Minute Particular or vision that cannot be further reduced, and his Emersonian "new circle" or vision that cannot be further expanded. He begins his poem by a vehement reduction to "the face-brilliant core stone" and proceeds by an equally vehement expansion to a "suasion, large, fully-informed." Both reduction and expansion are lovingly dismissed as rival dreamings. This poet's reality, still transcendent, is the arc-line, at once peripheral and salient, a particular apple or a particular gulp of water, that itself is dream-inducing, but this is a dream of Whitman's or Stevens' colossal sun, of a reality so immediate as to carry its own transcendence. Ammons remains, somewhat despite himself, the least spent of our seers.

8

Dark and Radiant Peripheries

MARK STRAND AND A. R. AMMONS

> *A man's fortunes are the fruit of his character.*
> *A man's friends are his magnetisms. We go to*
> *Herodotus and Plutarch for examples of Fate; but*
> *we are examples. . . .*
>
> EMERSON, Fate

*   *   *

The four books of new American poetry that have moved me most in the last two years are *Uplands* and *Briefings* by A. R. Ammons and *Reasons for Moving* and *Darker* by Mark Strand. Ammons was born in North Carolina in 1926; Strand, in Prince Edward Island, Canada, in 1934. Born equidistant between them in time and space, I discover that reading their recent books has defined the limits of my own generation of poets for me. The generation includes formidable accomplishments: the works of Ashbery, Merrill, Merwin, Kinnell, Snyder, Ginsberg, and James Wright, and Richard Howard's recent series of dramatic monologues; Hollander's ambitious long poem, *Visions from the Ramble;* Alvin Feinman's one distinguished and difficult volume, *Preambles;* and powerful individual lyrics by perhaps half a dozen more. If Derek Walcott of the West Indies be added, the whole body of work by poets now in their first prime in America is immensely heartening, particularly at so dark a moment. Granted some good fortune (and if we can save them from a killing neglect even as we allow the academies to be overrun by the rabblement of the New Sensibility), they should surpass the rich generation that included Roethke, Jarrell,

Warren, Bishop, Lowell, Berryman, Duncan, Olson, Schwartz, Wilbur, Hecht, and James Dickey. Ammons in his new phase and Strand in his first full finding of himself are both miraculously strong poets, artists so complete and individualized that we are absurd to neglect them in our poverty, in our profound and desperate imaginative need of them. I juxtapose them here for their mutual excellence, but also for their revelatory contrast to one another. Ammons is the direct and rightful heir, since Robinson and Frost, of Emerson's central line that commenced with Thoreau and Whitman; there are no strong twentieth-century influences upon him, despite the affinities of his metric with the early work of Pound and Williams. Strand is a dark child of Stevens, despite early debts to several poets of the generation just before his own. Ammons is a seer; Strand, a quester engulfed by phantasmagoria. Both have the magnificence of having been found by inevitable and obsessive themes, which they have conquered and made their own, but neither has found sanctuary by such conquest. The scourge of Ammons is the ceaseless conflict in him of violently personal ideas of permanence and change; he is a poet for whom the outward world exists, but only as a combatant in the war between the sky and the mind. Strand's affliction is the family romance, and his main resource the transformations of the self as it dodges a proleptic consciousness of its own death in an outward world that somehow seems not to exist. He is as overtly Freudian in his visions as Ammons is knowingly Emersonian. The greater poems of *Darker* are monuments to the already passing time of what Rieff termed Psychological Man, even as the truly astonishing poems in *Uplands* and *Briefings* may well be our last cairns to the memory of Transcendental Man. Ammons holds radical light; Strand keeps moving from "It is dark" to "It is darker." They represent two permanent (until now, anyway) strains of American Romanticism that cannot be reconciled with one another, though both exist strongly in our five major poets: Emerson, Whitman, Dickinson, Frost, and Stevens.

I

Reasons for Moving (1968) was preceded by Strand's first book, *Sleeping with One Eye Open* (1964), privately printed and largely apprentice work. The epigraph to *Reasons for Moving*, from Borges (and ultimately from the Chinese), establishes the irreality that never ceases to haunt Strand: "—while we sleep here, we are awake elsewhere and that in this way every man is two men." The title poem, which appeared in the first book under the title "A Reason for Moving," is now called "Keeping Things Whole":

> *In a field*
> *I am the absence*
> *of field.*
> *This is*
> *always the case.*
> *Wherever I am*
> *I am what is missing.*
>
> *When I walk*
> *I part the air*
> *and always*
> *the air moves in*
> *to fill the spaces*
> *where my body's been.*
>
> *We all have reasons*
> *for moving.*
> *I move*
> *to keep things whole.*

Beneath the grace, this is desperate enough to be outrageous. This "I" might wish he were asleep elsewhere as well as here, and so be no man rather than two. His absence seems a void that his presence could not fill, or a wound that his presence could not heal. The poet of *Reasons for Moving* writes Borges-like parables in a limpid mode that sometimes has overtones of Elizabeth Bishop or Roethke or even Wilbur, but the pervasive reductiveness resembles the winter vision of the prime precursor, Stevens. This is the Stevens of "The Snow Man," "The Man Whose Pharynx Was Bad," "The Death of a Soldier," and the other small ecstasies of reduction to a basic slate or universal hue that mark *Harmonium*'s other music, the contrary to its Floridean excesses and gaudiness. The true epigraph to all of Strand is: "The poem refreshes life so that we share,/For a moment, the first idea. . . ." But the first idea in Stevens is quite deliberately unbearable, since to behold constantly nothing that is not there and the nothing that is would make us inhuman, or at least hopeless company for one another. Contemplating this aspect of Stevens, and its effect upon a younger poet of genius like Strand, I am reminded of Goethe's grim warning that anyone who destroys all illusion in himself and in others will be punished tyrannically by nature.

Some of the parables in *Reasons for Moving* read like scenarios by Beckett or Pinter, but the book's best poem, its last and longest, is harrowingly unlike its overt analogues and likely sources. "The Man in the Mirror" is at once phantasmagoria and simple narcist self-confrontation, an inescapable, daily, waking nightmare. First staring at his reflection, seeing an alien sleeper, the poet gasps: "How long will all this take?"—reminding me of Shelley's encounter with his double, before drowning, and the double's terrible "How long do you mean to be content?" Remembering the earlier Narcissus-delight ("how we used to stand/wishing the glass/would dissolve between us"), Strand is compelled to see the now-terrible reflection depart from him:

> *Your suit floating, your hair*
> *moving like eel grass*
> *in a shallow bay, you drifted*
> *out of the mirror's room, through the hall*
>
> *and into the open air.*
> *You seemed to rise and fall*
> *with the wind, the sway*
> *taking you always farther away, farther away.*

Alone ("The mirror was nothing without you") the poet waits, avidly, until the prodigal's return, as "a bruise coated with light." But the returned double is only a perpetual vision of loss, central emblem of the self unable to bear the self, ambivalence without resolution:

> *It will always be this way.*
> *I stand here scared*
> *that you will disappear,*
> *scared that you will stay.*

This is the last vision of *Reasons for Moving*, and is (consciously) no distance at all from the book's opening fantasy, the poet "eating poetry" in a library, romping like a dog "with joy in the bookish dark." The dark covers the honest terror of Narcissus, always at work composing more letters to himself, and always in the same vein: "You shall live/by inflicting pain./You shall forgive." The world outside this occluded self is almost formless, almost indeed without weather:

> *There is no rain.*
> *It is impossible to say what form*
> *The weather will take.*
> *We blow on our hands,*
> *Trying to keep them warm,*
> *Hoping it will not snow.*

"What the solipsist *means* is right," a gnomic Wittgensteinian truth, is in traditional American terms the Emersonian admonition "Build therefore your own world," which in turn is founded on the central Emersonian motto: "What we are, that only can we see." For Emerson knew he could only show (and not say) the truths, all eloquence (his own included) necessarily obscured. Pears, expounding early Wittgenstein, reads to me like an exegete of Emerson:

> But what is this unique self, of whose existence he
> feels assured? It is neither his body nor his soul nor

anything else in his world. It is only the metaphysical
subject, which is a kind of focal vanishing point behind
the mirror of his language. There is really nothing except the mirror and what the mirror reflects. So the only
thing that he can legitimately say is that what is reflected in the mirror is reflected in the mirror. But this
is neither a factual thesis nor a substantial necessary
truth about what is reflected in the mirror, but a
tautology. It means only that whatever objects exist exist. So when solipsism is worked out, it becomes clear
that there is no difference between it and realism.
Moreover, since the unique self is nothing, it would be
equally possible to take an impersonal view of the vanishing point behind the mirror of language. Language
would then be any language, the metaphysical subject
would be the world spirit, and idealism would lie on the
route from solipsism to realism.

That route was Emerson's, from the solipsism of the early
Notebooks through the idealism of *Nature* on to the realism
of *The Conduct of Life*. Ammons is an Emersonian who has
passed to idealism; Strand follows no route, and never de-
parts from solipsism. The splendor of his poetry, only in-
timated by *Reasons for Moving*, emerges in *Darker* (1970),
where nearly every poem *shows* what can be shown of the
solipsist's predicament, while wisely eschewing the saying of
what cannot be said. Pears, following Wittgenstein, speaks of
"deep tautologies," and Strand, without metaphysical design, gives them to us. "There is what there is" might be the
motto of *Darker*. Here is its characteristic kind of poem:

> *I empty myself of the names of others. I empty*
>   *my pockets.*
> *I empty my shoes and leave them beside the*
>   *road.*
> *At night I turn back the clocks;*
> *I open the family album and look at myself as a*
>   *boy.*
>
> *What good does it do? The hours have done*
>   *their job.*

I say my own name. I say goodbye.
The words follow each other downwind.
I love my wife but send her away.

My parents rise out of their thrones
into the milky rooms of clouds. How can I sing?
Time tells me what I am. I change and I am the
    same.
I empty myself of my life and my life remains.

This poem's title, "The Remains," means everything about
the self that ought to have only posthumous existence, when
the poet will survive only in the regard of other selves. But
his dread (which is one with the reality of him) is that already
he survives only insofar as he has become an otherness capable of extending such regard. Dread born of spectral duality,
dread identical with what Blake called the Spectre of Ur-
thona, is peculiarly an anxiety that shadows poets, and is
almost a distinguishing mark of Romantic tradition. "The
Remains" is a poem written by Strand's *alastor* or Spirit of
Solitude, his true voice of feeling. Its despairing wish—to be
delivered from the self's prison without abandoning a self
that can be embraced only when it in prison lies—is repeated
throughout *Darker* in many superb modulations:

that the lies I tell them are different
from the lies I tell myself,
that by being both here and beyond
I am becoming a horizon . . .

And there is the sleep that demands I lie down
and be fitted to the dark that comes upon me
like another skin in which I shall never be
    found,
out of which I shall never appear. . . .

Why do you never come? Must I have you by
    being

somebody else? Must I write My Life *by*
  somebody else?
My Death *by somebody else? Are you listening?*
Somebody else has arrived. Somebody else is
  writing.

The mode is phantasmagoria, of which the American master will always be Whitman, the one supreme Emersonian
bard. No poem by Strand (so far) is as dark and powerful as
Whitman's "A Hand-Mirror" ("Looking-Glass" in its manuscript title) where the self has the strength of Satan to bear
its outward and inward loss. Closer to Strand (and more ap-
proachable) is the Stevens who charted the "mythology of
self,/Blotched out beyond unblotching." Strand's peculiar
courage is to take up the quirky quest when "amours shrink-
/Into the compass and curriculum/Of introspective exiles,
lecturing," concerning which Stevens warned: "It is a theme
for Hyacinth alone." Throughout *Darker,* Strand's risk is
enormous. He spares us the opaque vulgarity of "confessional" verse by daring to expose how immediate in him a
more universal anguish rages:

> *The huge doll of my body*
> *refuses to rise.*
> *I am the toy of women.*
> *My mother*
>
> *would prop me up for her friends.*
> *"Talk, talk," she would beg.*
> *I moved my mouth*
> *but words did not come.*
>
> *My wife took me down from the shelf.*
> *I lay in her arms. "We suffer*
> *the sickness of self," she would whisper.*
> *And I lay there dumb.*
>
> *Now my daughter*
> *gives me a plastic nurser*

filled with water.
"You are my real baby," she says.

Strand's unique achievement is to raise this mode to an aesthetic dignity that astonishes me, for I would not have believed, before reading him, that it could be made to touch upon a sublimity. *Darker* moves upon the heights in its final poems, "Not Dying" and the longer "The Way It Is," the first work in which Strand ventures out from his eye's first circle, toward a larger art. "Not Dying" opens in narcist desperation, and reaches no resolution, but its passion for survival is prodigiously convincing. "I am driven by innocence," the poet protests, even as like a Beckett creature he crawls from bed to chair and back again, until he finds the obduracy to proclaim a grotesque version of natural supernaturalism:

> *I shall not die.*
> *The grave result*
> *and token of birth, my body*
> *remembers and holds fast.*

"The Way It Is" takes its tone from Stevens at his darkest ("The world is ugly/And the people are sad") and quietly edges out a private phantasmagoria until this merges with the public phantasmagoria we all of us now inhabit. The consequence is a poem more surprising and profound than Lowell's justly celebrated "For the Union Dead," a juxtaposition made unavoidable by Strand's audacity in appropriating the same visionary area:

> *I see myself in the park*
> *on horseback, surrounded by dark,*
> *leading the armies of peace.*
> *The iron legs of the horse do not bend.*
>
> *I drop the reins. Where will the turmoil end?*
> *Fleets of taxis stall in the fog, passengers fall*
> *asleep. Gas pours*

from a tri-colored stack.
Locking their doors,
people from offices huddle together,
telling the same story over and over.

Everyone who has sold himself wants to buy
    himself back.
Nothing is done. The night
eats into their limbs
like a blight.

Everything dims.
The future is not what it used to be.
The graves are ready. The dead
shall inherit the dead.

Self-trained to a private universe of irreality, where he has learned the gnomic wisdom of the deep tautology, Strand peers out into the anxieties of the public world, to show again what can be shown, the shallow tautologies of a universal hysteria, as much a hysteria of protest as of societal repression. Wherever his poetry will go after *Darker,* we can be confident it goes as a perfected instrument, able to render an image not of any created thing whatsoever, but of every nightmare we live these days, separately or together.

II

Ammons, though only recently much discussed, published his first volume, *Ommateum,* in 1955. His greatly productive phase comprised five volumes from 1964 to 1968, the last of these the very fine *Selected Poems* (1968). *Uplands* (1970) and *Briefings* (1971) mark a new and major period in his work. For an account of his earlier achievement, I refer the reader to Richard Howard's *Alone with America* and to my *The Ringers in the Tower.*

Of the poets in my own generation, Ammons seems to me the likeliest to attain a central position in our imaginative history. He is less representative than Merwin, less dramatic than James Wright, and—while ultimately difficult—less immediately challenging in his difficulties than Ashbery. His centrality stems from his comprehensiveness, for he offers a heterocosm, an alternate world to the nature he uneasily meets, and also from his certain place in the Emerson-Whitman-Dickinson-Frost-Stevens-Crane succession that Roethke narrowly missed joining. Ammons makes a strong seventh in a line of major poets of the "native strain" or "native element" that various critics have identified for us. I am aware of how immensely our major poets differ from one another, but in a larger perspective than we ordinarily employ they can be seen to verge upon a common vision. Even Dickinson and Stevens belong to Emerson's universe of mind, as Whitman, Frost, and Crane more clearly do. Ammons, though a Southerner and a man obsessed with Minute Particulars, is the most Emersonian poet we have had since Whitman's petering out after 1860.

Uplands consists of about thirty lyrics and two longer poems; *Briefings* (the richer book) has more than eighty lyrics. Taking the two books together (as I will here) we have almost fifty short poems of nearly unsurpassed excellence, to match which I would have to go back past Roethke and Lowell to the final phases of Wallace Stevens. This is an enormous assertion, which I shall try to justify by concentrating on only a double handful of poems: "Upland," "Periphery," "Conserving the Magnitude of Uselessness," "Laser," (all from *Uplands*); and "He Held Radical Light," "Countering," "Cut the Grass," "Levitation," "Pluralist," and the wholly astonishing "The City Limits" (all from *Briefings*).

Strand's phantasmagoria persuasively insists that the external world is not our home. Ammons as persuasively knows no other, and proposes a very grim radiance to us as our true dwelling place. Strand's dread emblem is Narcissus; Ammons has no mythological emblem, yet from the mirror of the fallen world, Blake's Vegetable Glass of Nature, the dark double he disdains to regard keeps peering out at him. The darker temptation for the Ammons of *Selected Poems* was to merge himself with the natural mirror, but this temptation was set aside in a series of harrowing poems in which the poet, as "spent seer," yielded up all his ideas of order to the wind as "vehicle of change." Earlier Ammons is too complex for rapid summary, but a juxtaposition of two passages, the first from "Hymn," the second from "Guide," can help to evidence the characteristic inner conflict that precedes the tentative resolutions of the new poems:

I know if I find you I will have to leave the
  earth
and go on out
    over the sea marshes and the brant in bays
and over the hills of tall hickory
and over the crater lakes and canyons
and on up through the spheres of diminishing
  air
past the blackest noctilucent clouds
    where one wants to stop and look
way past all the light diffusions and
  bombardments
up farther than the loss of sight
    into the unseasonal undifferentiated empty
  stark.

*   *   *

      You cannot come to unity and remain
  material:
in that perception is no perceiver:
    when you arrive
you have gone too far:
      at the Source you are in the mouth of
  Death:

You cannot
    turn around in
the Absolute: there are no entrances or exits
        no precipitations of forms
to use like tongs against the formless:

>   *no freedom to choose:*
> *to be*
>
>   *you have to stop not-being and break*
> *off from* is *to flowing and*
>   *this is the sin you weep and praise:*
> *origin is your original sin:*

The dialectic of earlier Ammons shuttles back and forth, incessantly, from the desire for "the unseasonal undifferentiated empty stark" to the consciousness that "origin is your original sin," a consciousness of separateness as necessity. The two masterpieces of *Selected Poems* are "Corsons Inlet" and "Saliences," where this dialectic is most strikingly set forth. In the lyrics of *Uplands* and *Briefings* the dialectic has been allowed to recede into the background, and the spent seer, trapped in a universal predicament, broods on every sharp instance where the ideas of permanence and change come together in a single body. The body's (or area's) outer edges, the long peripheries or nerve endings of perception, now obsess this Emersonian seeker who has learned, to an ultimate sorrow, that indeed there is an outside or circumference to us. "The only sin is limitation," Emerson insisted in "Circles," but Ammons has translated limitation into origin. What remained for Emerson, once he had translated limitation by Fate, was the one part of Power in us that at given moments could overwhelm the ninety-nine parts of Fate. The later Ammons holds to his bargain with the wind. To claim even one part of Power is to claim order, and all of order now belongs to the vehicle of change. Permanence abides in the still-explicable sphere of origins, in the particulars of being that yield with marvelous slowness to the necessity of entropy, if they yield at all:

>   *take the Alleghenies for example,*
>   *some quality in the air*
>   *of summit stones lying free and loose*
>   *out among the shrub trees: every*

> *exigency seems prepared for that might*
> *roll, bound, or give flight*
> *to stone: that is, the stones are*
> *prepared: they are round and ready.*

This outward-opening conclusion of *Uplands* is Ammons'
new mode, fearfully strong in its apparent tentativeness. The
seer now praises a kind of sacred hesitation, as at the close of
the central lyric, "Periphery":

> *so I complained and said maybe I'd brush*
>
> *deeper and see what was pushing all this*
> *periphery, so difficult to make any sense*
>   *out of, out:*
> *with me, decision brings its own*
>
> *hesitation: a symptom, no doubt, but open*
> *and meaningless enough without paradigm:*
>   *but hesitation*
> *can be all right, too: I came on a spruce*
>
> *thicket full of elk, gushy snow-weed,*
> *nine species of lichen, four pure white*
>   *rocks and*
> *several swatches of verbena near bloom.*

The gift of hesitation is the beauty of the particular. Hesitation is a symptom as the desire for unseasonal unity was a
symptom, for hesitation like desire is a metonymy. The part
taken for a whole allows wisdom, the wisdom that stops short
of satisfaction. Seeking the Other in the Emersonian Not-Me
of nature, the seer had learned indirection and finally resignation. Now, not seeking, not even watching or waiting, he
is found—not by the Other—but by momentary visitations of
radiance almost wherever the nerve endings give out. Emersonianism, the most impatient and American of perceptual
traditions, has learned patience in the latest Ammons.

"Conserving the Magnitude of Uselessness," the wisest

lyric in *Uplands,* is a large, clear celebration of this new patience, a hymn "to all things not worth the work/of having." Like the late Frost of *In the Clearing,* Ammons now sees "the salvation of waste" and writes his version of that great poem, "Pod of the Milk-Weed." "Over-all is beyond me," the earlier Ammons had lamented, but now he joins himself to those poets, band of brothers at the Dark Tower, "rank as weeds themselves and just as abandoned" who know that "nothing useful is of lasting value."

Supplementing this new relaxation is the persistence in Ammons of the native strain at its highest pitch, as in "Laser":

> *but any found image falls*
> *back to darkness or*
> *the lesser beams splinter and*
> *go out:*
> *the mind tries to*
> *dream of diversity, of mountain*
> *rapids shattered with sound and light,*
>
> *of wind fracturing brush or*
> *bursting out of order against a mountain*
> *range: but the focused beam*
> *folds all energy in:*
> *the image glares filling all space:*
> *the head falls and*
> *hangs and cannot wake itself.*

Emerson's one part of Power, when it now comes, arrives only as destruction. Yet transcendental vision will not let Ammons be, despite his hard-won wisdom of metonymy. The greater lyrics of *Briefings* record the instances of a radiance that refuses not to be considered, that will not release its seer. "He Held Radical Light" defines this poet's burden: "reality had little weight in his transcendence." Wisdom, hard-won, yields to the Emersonian kind of Bacchic possession: "when the/light churned and changed/his head to music, nothing could keep him/off the mountains, his/head back, mouth working,/wrestling to say, to cut loose/from the high, unimaginable hook." Like Emerson, Ammons learns the necessity of guarding himself against the remedial force of the higher reason or imagination in him. The splendid "Countering" records the cunning of the unwilling seer who evades the crystal transparency that would engulf him:

> *to keep the*
> *life and*
> *shape, to keep*
> *the sphere, I hide*
> *contours,*
> *progressions between*
> *turning lines . . .*

Yet I will misrepresent *Briefings* if I consign all its visions to an unwilling medium. Its finest poems *do* celebrate a radiance, a light seen and held, though only on the peripheries, the same nerve endings where Strand counts his litanies of what is always darker. Ammons in his backyard, in "Cut the Grass," gives me a sense of "the wonderful workings of the world," and then of the best sense of Transcendentalism, which means just what a lady once defined it to Emerson as meaning: "a little beyond." The grasscutter thinks of the ocean, "multiple to a blinding oneness," and realizes the pleasure of his burden:

> *I'll have to say everything*
> *to take on the roundness and withdrawal of the*
> *deep dark:*
> *less than total is a bucketful of radiant toys.*

What begins to break through in the final poems of *Briefings* is a unique pride and saving comedy, yet still Transcendental in its emphasis. In "Levitation," the ground, "that disastrous to seers/and saints/is always around/evening scores, calling down . . . ," is shaken by its sudden realization that "something might be up there/able to get away." But the "something," the seer ascending like Stevens' Canon Aspirin, does not know it can and will get away, and turns:

> *cramped in abstraction's gilded loft*
> *and*
> *tried to think of something beautiful to say:*

Next to the humor there rides always the terror of the unsought particulars as they too transcend, as they rise free of the sin of their separate origins. In "Pluralist," indeed a "comforting/(though scary) exemplum," the maple tree expresses contrary notions:

> *one side going west and the*
> *other east or northeast or one*
> *up and the other*
> *down: multiple angling:*
> *the nodding, twisting, the*
> *stepping out and back*
> *is like being of two minds*
> *at least. . . .*

But the exemplum is "that maple trees/go nowhere at all." That this both scares and comforts is finally no comfort, for Ammons is so much of a seer, however spent, that his comforts sometimes cannot be ours, any more than Frost's savage consolations console us, though they impress and go on moving us.

Briefings ends with a poem so extraordinarily a high song of triumph and so beyond my capacity for praise that I want to end the Ammons half of this essay by quoting it in entirety, before allowing myself some brief statements about the poetry of my generation and the place of Strand and Ammons in it. To find a lyric rival for "The City Limits" I have to go back to very late Stevens, to "The Course of a Particular" (which Winters has the credit of first acclaiming) and "A

Discovery of Thought." The eye of the Southern countryman Ammons completes its first circle in this more-than-Emersonian evocation of "a high testimony," as even the spent seer, by implication, feels accepted into as much light as he can take:

When you consider the radiance, that it does
    not withhold
itself but pours its abundance without selection
    into every
nook and cranny not overhung or hidden; when
    you consider

that birds' bones make no awful noise against
    the light but
lie low in the light as in a high testimony;
    when you consider
the radiance, that it will look into the guiltiest

swervings of the weaving heart and bear itself
    upon them,
not flinching into disguise or darkening; when
    you consider
the abundance of such resource as illuminates
    the glow-blue

bodies and gold-skeined wings of flies
    swarming the dumped
guts of a natural slaughter or the coil of shit
    and in no
way winces from its storms of generosity; when
    you consider

that air or vacuum, snow or shale, squid or
    wolf, rose or lichen
each is accepted into as much light as it will
    take, then
the heart moves roomier, the man stands and
    looks about, the

leaf does not increase itself above the grass, and
   the dark
work of the deepest cells is of a tune with May
   bushes
and fear lit by the breadth of such calmly
   turns to praise.

III

Considering the radiance that has been given us by American poets born between 1926 and 1934, poets now in their first prime, we can begin to anticipate a superb decade ahead, if fortune and the rapid decline of our institutions and culture will permit it. Anyone attempting to compile an anthology of contemporary American verse right now (as I have been trying to do) finds himself under absurd extra-literary pressures, which do not arise from the cowardice or short-sightedness of editors and publishers, but from the failures of nerve and judgment in our academies. Shamanistic puritans, white and black, middle-aged and young, infest us, and this rabblement cries out daily to be fed what it thinks it wants —which is not even what it needs, let alone what the rest of us need. We need poetry, and so do they, for without poetry we shall perish together. The right use of this generation's poets, of Ammons, Strand, Ashbery, Merwin, Wright, and a dozen more, is available to us, even as the best of our past literature is, but it seems to me daily less likely that we will come to that humanizing use. Strand's darkened but deep tautologies and Ammons' strained but authentic radiances are alike noble in their economy and inevitability, in their creative swerves away from the great poetic fathers' splendors, which are also for us true anxieties. Both Strand and Ammons, and the other superb poets of their generation, need our exuberance and regard as readers. They, and we, will lose if we allow current squalors to distract us from what is most enduring in our poetic traditions.

9

John Ashbery

THE CHARITY OF THE HARD

MOMENTS

Of the American poets now in mid-career, those born in the decade 1925–1935, John Ashbery and A.R. Ammons seem to me the strongest. This essay, an overview of Ashbery's published work to date, is meant as a companion-piece to the essay on Ammons printed in my book of studies in Romantic tradition, *The Ringers in the Tower* (University of Chicago Press, 1971). Ashbery goes back through Stevens to Whitman, even as Ammons is a more direct descendant of American Romanticism in its major formulation, which remains Emerson's. Otherwise, these two superb poets have nothing in common except their authentic difficulty. Ammons belongs to no school, while Ashbery can be regarded either as the best poet by far of the "New York School" or—as I would argue—so unique a figure that only confusion is engendered by associating him with Koch, O'Hara, Schuyler and their friends and disciples.

I remember purchasing *Some Trees*, Ashbery's first commercially published volume (Yale Press, 1956, Introduction by Auden) in December, 1956, after reading the first poem ("Two Scenes") in a bookstore. The poem begins: "We see us as we truly behave" and concludes with "In the evening/Everything has a schedule, if you can find out what it is." A skeptical honesty, self-reflexive, and an odd faith in a near-inscrutable order remain characteristic of Ashbery's work. Also still characteristic is the abiding influence of Stevens. I remember being fascinated by the swerve away from Stevens' "Credences of Summer" in "Two Scenes":

This is perhaps a day of general honesty
Without example in the world's history
Though the fumes are not of a singular
  authority
And indeed are dry as poverty.

Where Stevens, in a moment of precarious satisfaction, entertained the possibility of overcoming "poverty," imaginative need, the young Ashbery identified self-knowledge with such need. Auden, hardly an admirer of Stevens, introduced Ashbery as an ephebe of Rimbaud, seer "of sacred images and ritual acts." But, actual disciple of Stevens (in his most Whitmanian aspect) and of Whitman ultimately, Ashbery necessarily began in a poetic world emptied of magical images and acts. The highly Stevensian "The Mythological Poet" opposed "a new/Music, innocent and monstrous/As the ocean's bright display of teeth" to "the toothless murmuring/Of ancient willows," sacred images for outworn seers. In the title-poem, clearly the book's best, Ashbery had found already his largest aesthetic principle, the notion that every day the world consented to be shaped into a poem. "Not every day," Stevens warns in his "Adagia," which Ashbery couldn't have read then, but Stevens' point was that on some days it could happen. The point is Emersonian or Whitmanian, and though Ashbery antithetically completes Stevens in this principle, he is ultimately, like Whitman and Stevens, a descendant of Emerson's *Nature,* though at the start a wry one:

> *. . . you and I*
> *are suddenly what the trees try*
>
> *To tell us we are:*
> *That their merely being there*
> *Means something; that soon*
> *We may touch, love, explain.*
>
> *And glad not to have invented*
> *Such comeliness, we are surrounded . . .*

The Not-Me, as Emerson said, is nature and my body together, as well as art and all other men. Such a conviction leads Ashbery, even as it impelled Whitman and Stevens, to a desperate quest that masks as an ease with things. The poem is to be discovered in the Not-Me, out in the world that includes the poet's body. Rhetorically, this tends to mean that every proverbial cliché must be recovered, which becomes almost a rage in Ashbery's *Three Poems*. Where the middle Ashbery, the poet of the outrageously disjunctive volume, *The Tennis Court Oath*, attempted too massive a swerve away from the ruminative continuities of Stevens and Whitman, recent Ashbery goes to the dialectical extreme of what seems at first like a barrage of bland commonplaces. Emerson, in *Nature*, anticipated Ashbery with his characteristic sense that parts of a world and parts of speech are alike emblematic, so that either, however worn out, could yet be an epiphany, though the world *seemed* so post-magical:

> . . . the memorable words of history and the proverbs of nations consist usually of a natural fact, selected as a picture or parable of a moral truth. Thus: a rolling stone gathers no moss; a bird in the hand is worth two in the bush; a cripple in the right way will beat a racer in the wrong; make hay while the sun shines; 'tis hard to carry a full cup even; vinegar is the son of wine; the last ounce broke the camel's back; long-lived trees make roots first . . .

Emerson insisted each worn proverb could become *transparent*. In his rare startlements into happiness, Ashbery knows this transparency, but generally his hopes are more modest. He is, in temperament, more like Whitman than like Emerson or Stevens. Even the French poet he truly resembles is the curiously Whitmanian Apollinaire, rather than Reverdy:

> *Et ce serait sans doute bien plus beau*
> *Si je pouvaise supposer que toutes ces choses*

dans lesquelles
  je suis partout
Pouvaient m'occuper aussi
Mais dans ce sens il n'y a rien de fait
Car si je suis partout a cette heure il n'y a
  cependant que
    moi qui suis en moi

Let us, swerving away from Apollinaire, call these Ashbery's two contradictory spiritual temptations, to believe that one's own self, like the poem, can be found in "all the things everywhere," or to believe that "there is still only I who can be in me." The first temptation will be productive of a rhetoric that puts it all in, and so must try to re-vitalize every relevant cliché. The second temptation rhetorically is gratified by ellipsis, thus leaving it all out. I suppose that Ashbery's masterpiece in this mode is the long spiel called "Europe" in *The Tennis Court Oath,* which seems to me a fearful disaster. In Stevens, this first way is the path of Whitmanian expansiveness, which partly failed the not always exuberant burgher of Hartford, while the second is the way of reductiveness, too great a temptation for him, as Stevens came to realize. The road through to poetry for Stevens was a middle path of invention that he called "discovery," the finding rather than the imposition of an order. Though there are at least three rhetorics in Stevens, matching these three modes of self-apprehension, none of the three risks Ashbery's disasters, whether of apparently joining together bland truisms or of almost total disjunctiveness. But I think that is close to the sorrow of influence in Ashbery, which is the necessary anxiety induced in him by the siren song of Stevens' rhetorics. Ashbery (who is not likely to be pleased by this observation) is at his best when he is neither re-vitalizing proverbial wisdom nor barely evading an ellipsis, but when he dares to write most directly in the idiom of Stevens. This point, and Ashbery's dazzling deflection of it, will be my concern when I arrive at *The Double Dream of Spring.*

My own melancholy, confronting Ashbery, is provoked by

his second public volume, *The Tennis Court Oath* (Wesleyan University Press, 1962). Coming to this eagerly as an admirer of *Some Trees,* I remember my outrage and disbelief at what I found:

> *for that we turn around*
> *experiencing it is not to go into*
> *the epileptic prank forcing bar*
> *to borrow out onto tide-exposed fells*
> *over her morsel, she chasing you*
> *and the revenge he'd get*
> *establishing the vultural over*
> *rural area cough protection*
> *murdering quintet. . . .*

This is from the piece called "Leaving The Atocha Station," which (I am told) has a certain reputation among the rabblement of poetasters who proclaim themselves anti-academic while preaching in the academies, and who lack consciousness sufficient to feel the genuine (because necessary) heaviness of the poetic past's burden of richness. *The Tennis Court Oath* has only one good poem, "A Last World." Otherwise, its interest is now entirely retrospective; how could Ashbery collapse into such a bog by just six years after *Some Trees,* and how did he climb out of it again to write *Rivers and Mountains,* and then touch a true greatness in *The Double Dream of Spring* and *Three Poems?*

Poets, who congenitally lie about so many matters, *never* tell the truth about poetic influence. To address an audience sprinkled with poets, on the subject of poetic influence, is to risk a *sparagmos* in which the unhappy critic may be mistaken for Orpheus. Poets want to believe, with Nietzsche, that "forgetfulness is a property of all action," and action for them is writing a poem. Alas, no one can write a poem without remembering another poem, even as no one loves without remembering, though dimly or subconsciously, a former beloved, however much that came under a taboo. Every poet is forced to say, as Hart Crane did in an early poem: "I can remember much forgetfulness." To live as a poet, a poet needs the illusive mist about him that shields him from the light that first kindled him. This mist is the nimbus (however false) of what the prophets would have called his own *kabod*, the supposed radiance of his own glory.

In *Some Trees*, Ashbery was a relatively joyous ephebe of Stevens, who evidently proved to be too good a father. Nietzsche suggested that: "If one has not had a good father, it is necessary to invent one." Yes, and for a poet, if one's father was too good, it becomes necessary to re-invent one's father's sorrows, so as to balance his glory. This necessity, which Ashbery met in all his subsequent work, is merely evaded throughout *The Tennis Court Oath*, where a great mass of egregious disjunctiveness is accumulated to very little effect. Apollinaire had counselled *surprise* for the modern poet's art, but what is surprising about a group of poems that will never yield to any reading or sustained re-reading? Poems may be like pictures, or like music, or like what you will, but if they *are* paintings or musical works, they will not be poems. The Ashbery of *The Tennis Court Oath* may have been moved by De Kooning and Kline, Webern and Cage, but he was not moved to the writing of poems. Nor can I accept the notion that this was a necessary phase in the poet's development, for who can hope to find any necessity in this calculated incoherence? Yet the volume matters, and still upsets me because it is Ashbery's, the work of a man who has written poems like "Evening In The Country," "Parergon," the astonishingly poignant and wise "Soonest Mended," and "Fragment," probably the best longer poem by an American poet of my own generation, and unmatched I believe by anything in the generation of Lowell.

Isolated amid the curiosities of *The Tennis Court Oath* is the beautiful "A Last World," which in its limpidity and splendor would fit well into one of Ashbery's later volumes. The poem prophesies the restorative aesthetic turn that Ashbery was to take, and reveals also what has become his cen-

tral subject and resource, the imagination of a later self questing for accommodation not so much with an earlier glory (as
in Wordsworth) but with a possible sublimity that can never
be borne, if it should yet arrive. Stevens more than Whitman
is again the precursor, and the greatness of Ashbery begins
to emerge when the anxiety of influence is wrestled with,
and at least held to a stand-off.

"A Last World," like any true poem, has the necessity of
reminding us that the meaning of one poem can only be
another poem, a poem not itself, and probably not even one
by its own author. Ashbery emerges into a total coherence
when he compels himself to know that every imagining is a
misprision, a taking amiss or twisting askew of the poetic
given. Mature creation, for a poet, rises directly from an
error about poetry rather than an error, however profound,
about life. Only a wilful *misinterpretation* of a poetry already
known too well, loved too well, understood too well, frees a
maturing maker's mind from the compulsion to repeat, and
more vitally from the fear of that compulsion. This is not
what "A Last World" *thinks* it is about, but the poem so
presents itself as to compel us to read it as an allegory of this
poet's struggle to win free of his own evasions, and not the
aesthetic evasions alone, but of everything that is elliptical in
the self.

The Stevensian "he" of "A Last World" becomes a constant presence in the next two volumes, modulating from
Ashbery as a self-deceiver to a perpetually late learner who
is educated with the reader, so as to become a convincing
"we":

> *Everything is being blown away;*
> *A little horse trots up with a letter in its*
> *mouth,*
> *which is read with eagerness*
> *As we gallop into the flame.*

This, the poem's conclusion, is the ostensible focus of "A
Last World"; the present is the flame, things vanish perpetu-

ally as we come up to them, and we are—at best—romance questers made pathetic as we read the message so charmingly delivered to us, which is hardly going to save us from joining a general state of absence. The poem seems to end dispassionately in loss, yet its tone is serene, and its atmosphere suffused with a curious radiance. This radiance is a revisionary completion of the difficult serenity of late Stevens, a completion that is also antithetical to Stevens' rockier composure, or as his "Lebensweisheitspielerei" calls it, his sense of "stellar pallor":

> *Little by little, the poverty*
> *Of autumnal space becomes*
> *A look, a few words spoken.*
>
> *Each person completely touches us*
> *With what he is and as he is,*
> *In the stale grandeur of annihilation.*

Stevens, contemplating the departure of the proud and the strong, bleakly celebrated those left as "the unaccomplished,/The finally human,/Natives of a dwindled sphere." Ashbery, counterpointing his vision against that of Stevens' *The Rock*, celebrates loss as an accomplishment, a treasure, a mint flavoring in Stevens' land of hay, which was too ripe for such enigmas:

> *Once a happy old man*
> *One can never change the core of things, and*
> *   light burns you the harder for it,*
> *Glad of the changes already and if there are*
> *   more it will never be you that minds*
> *Since it will not be you to be changed, but in*
> *   the evening in the severe lamplight doubts*
> *   come*
> *From many scattered distances, and do not come*
> *   too near.*
> *As it falls along the house, your treasure*

> *Cries to the other men; the darkness will have*
> *none of you,*
> *and you are folded into it like mint into*
> *the sound of haying.*

Loss is not gain here, and yet Ashbery takes Stevens' vision back from the last world of *The Rock* to "A Postcard from the Volcano" of 1936, where at least we leave behind us "what still is/The look of things." Absence or denudation is the common perception of the two poets, but Ashbery, though always anxious, is too gentle for bitterness, and rhetorically most himself where least ironic. Stevens' "qualified assertions" (Helen Vendler's apt phrase) become in Ashbery a series of progressively more beautiful examples of what we might call "qualified epiphanies," the qualifications coming partly from Ashbery's zeal in tacitly rejecting a poetry of privileged moments or privileged phrases. But this zeal is misplaced, and almost impossible to sustain, as will be seen in his later development.

Rivers and Mountains (1966) is a partial recovery from *The Tennis Court Oath,* though only one poem in it, "The Skaters," seems to me major Ashbery when compared to what comes after. But then, "The Skaters" is nearly half the volume, and its most luminous passages are of the same poetic ambience as the work beyond. With *Rivers And Mountains,* Ashbery began to win back the dismayed admirers of his earliest work, myself included. The curious poem called "The Recent Past," whatever its intentions, seems to be precisely addressed to just such readers, in very high good humor:

> *You were my quintuplets when I decided to*
> *leave you*
> *Opening a picture book the pictures were all of*
> *grass*
> *Slowly the book was on fire, you the reader*
> *Sitting with specs full of smoke exclaimed*

How it was a rhyme for "brick" or "redder".
The next chapter told all about a brook.

You were beginning to see the relation when a
*   tidal wave*
Arrived with sinking ships that spelled out
*   "Aladdin".*
I thought about the Arab boy in his cave
But the thoughts came faster than advice.
If you knew that snow was still toboggan in
*   space*
The print could rhyme with "fallen star".

As far as intention matters, the "you" here is another Ashbery, to whom almost the entire book is directed, as will be
the recent *Three Poems.* "These Lacustrine Cities" sets the
book's project:

Much of your time has been occupied by creative
*   games*
Until now, but we have all-inclusive plans for
*   you . . .*

"Clepsydra," the longer poem just preceding "The Skaters," is printed as the first attempt at the project's realization,
and is a beautiful failure, outweighing most contemporary
poetic successes. The water-clock of the title is ultimately
Ashbery himself, akin to the sun-flower of Blake's frighten-
ingly wistful lyric. A history-in-little of Ashbery's poethood,
"Clepsydra" is Ashbery's gentle equivalent of Stevens' sur-
passingly bitter "The Comedian as the Letter C," and is as
dazzling an apparent dead end. I judge it a failure not because its exuberance is so negative, in contrast to the Whitmanian "The Skaters," but because its solipsism, like that of
the "Comedian," is too perfect. Though splendidly coherent,
"Clepsydra" gives the uncanny effect of being a poem that
neither wants nor needs readers. It sits on the page as a
forbiddingly solid wall of print, about as far from the *look* of

Apollinaire as any verse could be. From its superbly opaque opening ("Hasn't the sky?") to its ominous closing ("while morning is still and before the body / Is changed by the faces of evening") the poem works at turning a Shelleyan-Stevensian self-referential quality into an absolute impasse. Perhaps here, more than in "The Skaters" even, or in his masterpiece, "Fragment," Ashbery tries to write the last poem about itself and about poetry, last by rendering the mode redundant:

> . . . *Each moment*
> *Of utterance is the true one; likewise none are*
>   *true,*
> *Only is the bounding from air to air, a*
>   *serpentine*
> *Gesture which hides the truth behind a*
>   *congruent*
> *Message, the way air hides the sky, is, in fact,*
> *Tearing it limb from limb this very moment: but*
> *The sky has pleaded already and this is about*
> *As graceful a kind of non-absence as either*
> *Has a right to expect: whether it's the form of*
> *Some creator who has momentarily turned away,*
> *Marrying detachment with respect* . . .

"Detachment with respect" is Ashbery's attitude towards transcendental experience, for which he tends to use the image of transparence, as Whitman and Stevens, following Emerson, did also. Stevens, as Helen Vendler notes, tends to *sound* religious when his poems discourse upon themselves, and "Clepsydra" like much of the *Three Poems* similarly has an oddly religious tone. All of Ashbery (I am puzzled as to why Richard Howard thinks Ashbery an "anti-psychological" poet), including "Clepsydra," is profound self-revelation. Ashbery—like Wordsworth, Whitman, Stevens, Hart Crane —writes out of so profound a subjectivity as to make "confessional" verse seem as self-defeating as that mode truly has been, from Coleridge (its inventor) down to Lowell and his disciples. "Clepsydra," so wholly self-enclosed, is an oblique lament rising "amid despair and isolation/of the chance to know you, to sing of me/Which are you." The poem's subject overtly is Ashbery's entrapped subjectivity, objectified in the pathetic emblem of the water-clock, and represented in large by the outrageously even tone that forbids any gathering of climaxes. This refusal to vary his intensities is one of Ashbery's defense mechanisms against his anxiety of poetic influences. I can think of no poet in English, earlier or now at work, who insists upon so subtly unemphatic a pervasive tone. As a revisionary ratio, this tone intends to distance Ashbery from Whitman and from Stevens, and is a kind of *kenosis*, a self-emptying that yields up any evident afflatus:

> *. . . Perhaps you are being kept here*
> *Only so that somewhere else the peculiar light*
> *of someone's*
> *Purpose can blaze unexpectedly in the acute*
> *Angles of the rooms. It is not a question, then,*
> *Of having not lived in vain . . .*

The *kenosis* is too complete in "Clepsydra"; the tone, however miraculously sustained, too wearying for even so intelligent a poet rightly to earn. With relief, I move on to "The Skaters," Ashbery's most energetic poem, the largest instance in him of the revisionary movement of *daemonization*, or the onset of his personalized Counter-Sublime, as against the American Sublime of Whitman and Stevens. Yet, "The Skaters" is almost outrageously Whitmanian, far more legitimately in his mode than Ginsberg manages to be:

> *Old heavens, you used to tweak above us,*
> *Standing like rain whenever a salvo . . . Old*
> *heavens,*
> *You lying there above the old, but not ruined,*
> *fort,*
> *Can you hear, there, what I am saying?*

"The Skaters" is not a parody, however involuntary, of *Song of Myself,* though sometimes it gives that impression. *Song of Myself* begins where the British Romantic quest-poem is sensible enough to end: with an internal romance, of self and soul, attaining its consummation. Whitman, having married himself, goes forth as an Emersonian liberating god, to preside over the nuptials of the universe. The daemonic parodies of this going forth stand between Whitman and Ashbery: *Paterson, the Cantos, The Bridge, Notes toward A Supreme Fiction, Preludes To Attitude, The Far Field.* What remains for Ashbery, in "The Skaters," is a kind of Counter-Sublime that accepts a reduction of Whitmanian ecstasy, while re-affirming it nevertheless, as in the vision early in the poem, when the poet's whole soul is stirred into activity, flagellated by the decibels of the "excited call" of the skaters:

> *The answer is that it is novelty*
> *That guides these swift blades o'er the ice*
> *Projects into a finer expression (but at the*
>   *expense*
> *Of energy) the profile I cannot remember.*
> *Colors slip away from and chide us. The human*
>   *mind*
> *Cannot retain anything except perhaps the*
>   *dismal two-note theme*
> *Of some sodden "dump" or lament.*

One can contrast the magnificent skating episode in Book I of *The Prelude,* where colors have not slipped away, and the mind has retained its power over outer sense. The contrast, though unfair to Ashbery, still shows that there is a substance in us that prevails, though Ashbery tends to know it only by knowing also his absence from it. His poem celebrates "the intensity of minor acts," including his self-conscious mode of making-by-ellipsis, or as he calls it: "this leaving-out business." Putting off (until *Three Poems*) "the costly stuff of explanation," he movingly offers a minimal apologia:

> *. . . Except to say that the carnivorous*
> *Way of these lines is to devour their own nature,*
>   *leaving*
> *Nothing but a bitter impression of absence,*
>   *which as we know*
>   *involves presence, but still.*
> *Nevertheless these are fundamental absences,*
>   *struggling to*
>   *get up and be off themselves.*

"The Skaters," admitting that: "Mild effects are the result," labors still "to hold the candle up to the album," which is Ashbery's minimalist version of Stevens': "How high that highest candle lights the dark." In the poem's second part, Ashbery sets forth on a Romantic voyage, but like Crispin sees every vision-of-the-voyage fade slowly away. The long third movement, a quasi-autobiographical panorama of this poet's various exiles, needs careful examination, which I cannot give here, for nothing else in Ashbery succeeds nearly so well at the effect of the great improviser, an excellence shared by Whitman and by the Stevens of the blue guitar. With the fourth and final section, partly spoken by the persona of a Chinese scholar-administrator, the poem circles to a serene resolution, precisely prophetic of the Ashbery to come. "The whole brilliant mass comes spattering down," and an extraordinary simplicity takes its place. After so many leavings-out, the natural particulars are seen as being wonderfully sufficient:

> *The apples are all getting tinted*
> *In the cool light of autumn.*
>
> *The constellations are rising*
> *In perfect order: Taurus, Leo, Gemini.*

Everything promised by "The Skaters," Ashbery has performed, in the very different greatnesses of *The Double Dream of Spring* (1970) and *Three Poems* (1972). The first of these is so rich a book that I will confine myself to only a handful of poems, each so wonderful as to survive close comparison with Whitman and Stevens at almost their strongest: "Soonest Mended," "Evening in the Country," "Sunrise in Suburbia," "Parergon," and the long poem "Fragment." Before ruminating on these representative poems, a general meditation on Ashbery's progress seems necessary to me, as I am going on to make very large claims for his more recent work.

Though the leap in manner between *Rivers and Mountains* and *The Double Dream of Spring* is less prodigious than the gap between *The Tennis Court Oath* and *Rivers and Mountains,* there is a more crucial change in the later transition. Ashbery at last says farewell to ellipsis, a farewell confirmed by *Three Poems,* which relies upon "putting it all in," indeed upon the discursiveness of a still-demanding prose. The abandonment of Ashbery's rhetorical evasiveness is a self-curtailment on his part, a purgation that imparts simplicity through intensity, but at the price of returning him to the rhetorical world of Stevens and of the American tradition that led to Stevens. It is rather as if Browning had gone from his grotesque power backwards to the Shelleyan phase of his work. Perhaps Browning should have, since his last decades were mostly barren. As a strong poet, Ashbery has matured almost as slowly as his master Stevens did, though unlike Stevens he has matured in public. Even as Stevens provoked a critical nonsense, only now vanishing, of somehow being a French poet writing in English, so Ashbery still provokes such nonsense. Both are massive sufferers from the anxiety-of-influence, and both developed only when they directly engaged their American precursors. In Ashbery, the struggle with influence, though more open, is also more difficult, since Ashbery desperately engages also the demon of discursiveness, as Hart Crane differently did (for the last stand of Crane's mode, see the one superb volume of Alvin Feinman, *Preambles And Other Poems,* 1964). This hopeless engagement, endemic in all Western poetries in our century, is a generalized variety of the melancholy of poetic influence.

It is not problematic form, nor repressed allusiveness, nor recondite matter, that makes much modern verse difficult. Nor, except rarely, is it conceptual profundity, or sustained mythical invention. Ellipsis, the art of omission, almost always a central device in poetry, has been abused into the dominant element rhetorically of our time. Yet no modern poet has employed it so effectively as Dickinson did, probably because for her it was a deep symptom of everything else that belonged to the male tradition that she was leaving out. I cannot involve myself here in the whole argument that I have set forth in a little book, *The Anxiety of Influence: A Theory of Poetry* (1973; see the discussion of Ashbery in the section called *"Apophrades:* or the Return of the Dead"), but I cite it as presenting evidence for the judgment that influence becomes progressively more of a burden for poets from the Enlightenment to this moment. Poets, defending poetry, are adept at idealizing their relation to one another, and the magical Idealists among critics have followed them in this saving self-deception. Here is Northrop Frye, greatest of the idealizers:

> *Once the artist thinks in terms of influence rather than of clarity of form, the effort of the imagination becomes an effort of will, and art is perverted into tyranny, the application of the principle of magic or mysterious compulsion to society.*

Against this I cite Coleridge's remark that the power of originating *is* the will, our means of escaping from nature or repetition-compulsion, and I add that no one needs to pervert art in this respect, since the Post-Enlightenment poetic imagination is necessarily quite perverse enough in the perpetual battle against influence. Wordsworth *is* a misinterpretation of Milton (as is Blake), Shelley *is* a misinterpretation of Wordsworth, Browning and Yeats *are* misinterpretations of Shelley. Or, in the native strain, Whitman perverts or twists askew Emerson, Stevens is guilty of misprision towards both, and Ashbery attempts a profound and beautiful misinterpretation of all his precursors, *in his own best poetry.* What the elliptical mode truly seeks to omit is the overt continuity with ancestors, and the mysterious compulsion operative here is a displacement of what Freud charmingly called "the family romance."

Ashbery's own family romance hovers uneasily in all-but-repressed memories of childhood; his family-romance-as-poet attains a momentarily happy resolution in *The Double Dream of Spring,* but returns darkly in *Three Poems.* Ashbery is a splendid instance of the redemptive aspect of influence-anxiety, for his best work shows how the relation to the precursor is humanized into the greater themes of all human influence-relations, which after all include lust, envy, sexual jealousy, the horror of families, friendship, and the poet's reciprocal relation to his contemporaries, ultimately to all of his readers.

I begin again, after this anxious digression, with "Soonest Mended," and begin also the litany of praise and advocacy, of what Pater called "appreciation," that the later work of Ashbery inspires in me. The promise of *Some Trees* was a long time realizing itself, but the realization came, and Ashbery is now something close to a great poet. It is inconvenient to quote all of "Soonest Mended," but I will discuss it as though my reader is staring at pages 17 through 19 of *The Double Dream of Spring.* The poem speaks for the artistic life of Ashbery's generation, but more for the general sense of awakening to the haphazardness and danger of one's marginal situation in early middle age:

> *To step free at last, minuscule on the gigantic*
> *   plateau—*
> *This was our ambition: to be small and clear*
> *   and free.*
> *Alas, the summer's energy wanes quickly,*
> *A moment and it is gone. And no longer*
> *May we make the necessary arrangements,*
> *   simple as they are.*

> *Our star was brighter perhaps when it had*
> *water in it.*
> *Now there is no question even of that, but only*
> *Of holding on to the hard earth so as not to get*
> *thrown off,*
> *With an occasional dream, a vision . . .*

Dr. Johnson, still the most useful critic in the language, taught us to value highly any original expression of common or universal experience. "Has he any fresh matter to disclose?" is the question Johnson would have us ask of any new poet whose work seems to demand our deep consideration. The Ashbery of his two most recent volumes passes this test triumphantly. "Soonest Mended," from its rightly proverbial title through every line of its evenly distributed rumination, examines freshly that bafflement of the twice-born life that has been a major theme from Rousseau and Wordsworth to Flaubert and Stevens. This is the sense of awakening, past the middle of the journey, to the truth that: *"they* were the players, and we who had struggled at the game/Were merely spectators . . ." Uniquely, Ashbery's contribution is the wisdom of a wiser passivity:

> *. . . learning to accept*
> *The charity of the hard moments as they are*
> *doled out,*
> *For this is action, this not being sure, this*
> *careless*
> *Preparing, sowing the seeds crooked in the*
> *furrow,*
> *Making ready to forget, and always coming back*
> *To the mooring of starting out, that day so long*
> *ago.*

Action, Wordsworth said, was momentary, only a step or blow, but suffering was permanent, obscure, dark and shared the nature of infinity. Ashbery's action is Wordsworth's suffering; the way through to it, Ashbery says, is "a kind of fence-sitting/Raised to the level of an esthetic ideal." If time indeed is an emulsion, as this poem asserts, then wisdom is to find the mercy of eternity in the charity of the hard moments. Shelley, forgiving his precursors, said that they had been washed in the blood of the redeemer and mediator, time. Ashbery domesticates this fierce idealism; "conforming to the rules and living/Around the home" mediate his vision, and redemption is the indefinite extension of the learning process, even if the extension depends upon conscious fantasy. The achievement of "Soonest Mended" is to have told a reductive truth, yet to have raised it out of reductiveness by a persistence masked as the commonal, an urgency made noble by art.

The implicit argument of "Soonest Mended" is adumbrated in "Evening in the Country," a reverie rising out of a kind of Orphic convalescence, as another spent seer consigns order to a vehicle of change. "I am still completely happy," Ashbery characteristically begins, having thrown out his "resolve to win further." Yet, this is not the "false happiness" that Stevens condemned, for it is being rather than consciousness, cat more than rabbit. The shadow of Stevens hovers overtly in this poem, the poet of the never-satisfied mind:

> . . . *He wanted that,*
> *To face the weather and be unable to tell*
> *How much of it was light and how much*
>   *thought,*
> *In these Elysia, these origins,*
> *This single place in which we are and stay,*
> *Except for the images we make of it,*
> *And for it, and by which we think the way,*
> *And, being unhappy, talk of happiness*
> *And, talking of happiness, know that it means*
> *That the mind is the end and must be satisfied.*

Away from this Ashbery executes what Coleridge (in *Aids to Reflection*) calls a *"lene clinamen,* the gentle bias," for

Ashbery's inclination is to yield to a realization that the mind had better be satisfied. Somewhere else, Coleridge speaks of making "a *clinamen* to the ideal," which is more in Stevens' mode, despite Stevens' qualifications. Ashbery, in his maturity, tries to be content not to originate an act or a state, though his achievement is to have done so anyway. "Evening in the Country" persuades that Ashbery has "begun to be in the context you feel," which is the context of the mind's surrender to visionary frustration. I quote at length from the poem's marvelous conclusion:

> *Light falls on your shoulders, as is its way,*
> *And the process of purification continues*
>   *happily,*
> *Unimpeded, but has the motion started*
> *That is to quiver your head, send anxious beams*
> *Into the dusty corners of the rooms*
> *Eventually shoot out over the landscape*
> *In stars and bursts? For other than this we know*
>   *nothing*
> *And space is a coffin, and the sky will put out*
>   *the light.*
> *I see you eager in your wishing it the way*
> *We may join it, if it passes close enough:*
> *This sets the seal of distinction on the success or*
>   *failure of your attempt.*
> *There is growing in that knowledge*
> *We may perhaps remain here, cautious yet free*
> *On the edge, as it rolls its unblinking chariot*
> *Into the vast open, the incredible violence and*
>   *yielding*
> *Turmoil that is to be our route.*

Purification here is a kind of Orphic *askesis,* another revisionary movement away from the fathers. The gods of Orphism, at least of that variety which is the natural religion of the native strain in American poetry, are Dionysus, Eros and Ananke. Ashbery's Dionysiac worship, in his recent work, is mostly directed to absence. Eros, always hovering in Ashbery, is more of a presence in "Fragment." Ananke, the Beautiful Necessity worshipped by the later Emerson and all his poetic children, is the governing deity of "Evening in the Country" as of "Soonest Mended" and the *Three Poems.* Purgation "continues happily," while the poet asks the open question as to whether the motion of a new transcendental influx has started. Ashbery's genuine uncertainty is no longer the choice of poetic subject, as it was in *The Tennis Court Oath*, but concerns his relation to his own subject, which is the new birth or fresh being he has discovered in himself, yet which sets its own timing for manifestation.

Nothing is more difficult for me, as a reader of poetry, than to describe *why* I am moved when a poem attains a certain intensity of quietness, when it seems to wait. Keats, very early in his work, described this as power half-slumbering on its own right arm. I find this quality in only a few contemporary poets—Ashbery, Ammons, Strand, Merwin, James Wright, among others. Recent Ashbery has more of this deep potential, this quietness that is neither quietism nor repression, than any American poet since the last poems of Stevens. Webern is the nearest musical analogue I know, but analogues are hard to find for a poem like "Evening in the Country." For, though the poem is so chastened, it remains an Orphic celebration, as much so as Hart Crane at his most ecstatic.

Ashbery's ambitions as a mature poet, rising out of this still Orphic convalescence, are subtly presented in "Sunrise in Suburbia." Ashbery, never bitter, always charged by the thrill of the sun coming up, nevertheless suggests here an initial burden too complex for the poem to bear away from him. This burden is eloquently summed up in a line from "Parergon": "That the continuity was fierce beyond all dream of enduring." Repetition is the antagonist in "Sunrise in Suburbia," which quests for discontinuity or, as the poem calls it, "nuance":

> *And then some morning there is a nuance:*
> *Suddenly in the city dirt and varied*
> *Ideas of rubbish, the blue day stands and*

A sudden interest is there:
Lying on the cot, near the tree-shadow,
Out of the thirties having news of the true
   source:
Face to kiss and the wonderful hair curling
   down
Into margins that care and are swept up again
   like branches
Into actual closeness
And the little things that lighten the day
The kindness of acts long forgotten
Which gives us history and faith
And parting at night, next to ocean, like the
   collapse of dying.

An earlier passage in the poem juxtaposes the "flatness of what remains" to the "modelling of what fled," setting the poem in the large tradition that goes from "Tintern Abbey" to "The Course of a Particular." The difficulty, for Ashbery as for his readers, is how to construct something upon which to rejoice when you are the heir of this tradition, yet reject both privileged moments of vision and any privileged heightenings of rhetoric in the deliberately subdued and even tone of your work. Stevens is difficult enough in this kind of poem, yet for him there are times of unusual excellence, and he momentarily will yield to his version of the high style in presenting them. For Ashbery, the privileged moments, like their images, are on the dump, and he wants to purify them by clearly placing them there. Say of what you see in the dark, Stevens urges, that it is this or that it is that, but do not use the rotted names. Use the rotted names, Ashbery urges, but cleanse them by seeing that you cannot be apart from them, and are partly redeemed by consciously suffering with them. Stevens worked to make the visible a little hard to see; Ashbery faces: "a blank chart of each day moving into the premise of difficult visibility." The sounds of nature on this suburban sunrise have a hard tone: "this deaf rasping of branch against branch." These too are the cries of branches that do not transcend themselves, yet they do concern us:

They are empty beyond consternation because
These are the droppings of all our lives
And they recall no past de luxe quarters
Only a last cube.
The thieves were not breaking in, the castle was
    not being stormed.
It was the holiness of the day that fed our
    notions
And released them, sly breath of Eros,
Anniversary on the woven city lament, that
    assures our arriving
In hours, seconds, breath, watching our salary
In the morning holocaust become one vast
    furnace, engaging all tears.

Where "The Course of a Particular" rejects Ruskin's Pathetic Fallacy or the imputation of life to the object world, Ashbery uncannily labors to make the fallacy more pathetic, the object world another failed version of the questing self. Yet each day, his poem nobly insists, is holy and releases an Orphic "sly breath of Eros," to be defeated, and yet "engaging all tears." If a poem like this remains difficult, its difficulty arises legitimately from the valuable complexity of its vision, and not from the partial discontinuity of its rhetoric.

The thematic diffidence of "Sunrise in Suburbia" is transformed in the superb short poem "Parergon," which gives us Ashbery's version of pure Shelleyan quest, "Alastor" rather than its parody in "The Comedian as the Letter C." As in "Evening in the Country," Ashbery begins by affirming, without irony, a kind of domestic happiness in his artist's life of sitting about, reading, being restless. In a dream-vision, he utters the prophecy of the life he has become: "we need the tether/ of entering each other's lives, eyes wide apart, crying." Having done so, he becomes "the stranger," the perpetual uncompromising quester on the model of the Poet in Shelley's "Alastor":

As one who moves forward from a dream
The stranger left that house on hastening feet

Leaving behind the woman with the face shaped
*   like an arrowhead,*
And all who gazed upon him wondered at
The strange activity around him.
How fast the faces kindled as he passed!
It was a marvel that no one spoke
To stem the river of his passing
Now grown to flood proportions, as on the sunlit
*   mall*
Or in the enclosure of some court
He took his pleasure, savage
And mild with the contemplating.
Yet each knew he saw only aspects,
That the continuity was fierce beyond all dream
*   of enduring,*
And turned his head away, and so
The lesson eddied far into the night:
Joyful its beams, and in the blackness blacker
*   still,*
Though undying joyousness, caught in that trap.

Even as the remorseless Poet of "Alastor" imperishably
caught up the element in Shelley that was to culminate in
"Adonais" and "The Triumph of Life," so "Parergon" por-
trays the doomed-poet aspect of Ashbery, of whom presumably we will hear more in his later life. One of the few ironies
in Ashbery is the title, which I assume is being used in the
sense it has in painting, something subsidiary to the main
subject. Yet the poem is anything but bywork or ornamenta-
tion. As beautiful as nearly anything in Ashbery, it is central
to his dilemma, his sorrow and his solace.

With reverence and some uneasiness, I pass to "Fragment," the crown of *The Double Dream of Spring* and,
for me, Ashbery's finest work. Enigmatically autobiographical, even if it were entirely fantasy, the poem's fifty
stately ten-line stanzas, orotundly Stevensian in their rhetoric, comment obliquely upon a story never told, a relationship never quite a courtship, and now a nostalgia.

Studying this nostalgia, in his most formal and traditional poem, more so than anything even in *Some Trees,* Ashbery presents his readers, however faithful, with his most difficult rumination. But this is a wholly Stevensian difficulty, neither elliptical nor obscure, but a ravishing simplicity that seems largely lacking in any referential quality. I have discussed the poem with excellent and sympathetic students who continue to ask: "But what is the poem *about?*" The obvious answer, that to some extent it is "about" itself, they rightly reject, since whether we are discussing Shelley, Stevens, or Ashbery, this merely distances the same question to one remove. But though repeated readings open up the referential aspect of "Fragment," the poem will continue to inspire our uneasiness, for it is profoundly evasive.

What the all-but-perfect solipsist *means* cannot be right, not until he becomes perfect in his solipsism, and so stands forth as a phantasmagoric realist (one could cite Mark Strand, a superb poet, as a recent example). "Fragment," I take it, is the elegy for the self of the imperfect solipsist, who wavered before the reality of another self, and then withdrew back into an interior world. The poem being beautifully rounded, the title evidently refers not to an aesthetic incompleteness, but to this work's design, that tells us only part of a story, and to its resigned conclusion, for the protagonist remains alone, an "anomaly" as he calls himself in the penultimate line.

The motto to "Fragment" might be from Ashbery's early "Le Livre est sur la table" where much of the enigma of the poet's mature work is prophesied. Playing against the mode of *The Man with the Blue Guitar,* Ashbery made a Stevensian parable of his own sorrows, stating a tentative poetic and a dark version of romance. The overwhelming last stanza of "Fragment" comes full circle to this:

> *The young man places a bird-house*
> *Against the blue sea. He walks away*
> *And it remains. Now other*

Men appear, but they live in boxes.
The sea protects them like a wall.
The gods worship a line-drawing

Of a woman, in the shadow of the sea
Which goes on writing. Are there
Collisions, communications on the shore

Or did all secrets vanish when
The woman left? Is the bird mentioned
In the waves' minutes, or did the land
*   advance?*

As the table supports the book, this poem tells us, so depri-
vation supports "all beauty, resonance, integrity," our poverty being our imaginative need. The young poet, deprived
of a world he can only imagine, and which he is constrained
to identify with "the woman," learns that the sea, Stevensian
emblem for all merely given reality, must triumph. Yet, if he
is to have any secrets worth learning in his womanless world,
it must come from "collisions, communications on the
shore," where his imagination and the given meet. "Collisions, communications" is a fearfully reductive way of describing whatever sustenance Eros grants him to live, and is
part of an open question. The final question can be read more
as a rhetorical one, since the poems got written, and the later
work of Ashbery proves that the land did advance.

We need to read this against the splendid final stanza of
"Fragment":

But what could I make of this? Glaze
Of many identical foreclosures wrested from
The operative hand, like a judgment but still
The atmosphere of seeing? That two people
*   could*
Collide in this dusk means that the time of
Shapelessly foraging had come undone: the
*   space was*
Magnificent and dry. On flat evenings

In the months ahead, she would remember
   that that
Anomaly had spoken to her, words like
   disjointed beaches
Brown under the advancing signs of the air.

He has learned that there are indeed "collisions, communications on the shore," but this apparently crucial or unique
instance saw two people "collide in this dusk." Yet this was
not failure; rather, the advent of a new time. The stanza's
balance is precarious, and its answer to the crucial earlier
question, "Did the land advance?" is double. The brown,
disjointed beaches seem a negative reply, and "the advancing signs of the air" a positive one.

In the context of Ashbery's development, "Fragment" is
his central poem, coming about a year after "The Skaters"
and just preceding "Clepsydra," his last major poem written
abroad. "Sunrise in Suburbia" and the powerful shorter poems in *The Double Dream of Spring* came later, after the
poet's return to this country in the autumn of 1966. My own
intoxication with the poem, when I first read it in *Poetry*
magazine, led me on to the two recent volumes, and my
sense of the enormous importance of this poet. Though I lack
space here for any extended account of "Fragment" before
I go on to *Three Poems,* I want to give an encapsulated sense
of some of its meanings, and the start of the appreciation it
deserves, as perhaps the first successful poem of its kind in
English since Swinburne's "The Triumph of Time."

The poem opens, as it will close, with the unnamed woman
of "a moment's commandment," whom Ashbery sometimes
addresses, and sometimes describes in the third person. After
a vision of April's decline, "of older/Permissiveness which
dies in the/Falling back toward recondite ends,/The sympathy of yellow flowers," the poet commences upon one of
these recondite ends, an elegy for "the suppressed lovers,"
whose ambiguous time together seems to have been only a
matter of weeks.

Much of the difficulty, and the poignance, of "Fragment"

is generated by Ashbery's quasi-metaphysical dilemma. Committed, like the later Stevens, to the belief that poetry and *materia poetica* are the same thing, and struggling always against the aesthetic of the epiphany or privileged moment, with its consequent devaluation of other experience, Ashbery nevertheless makes his poem to memorialize an intense experience, brief in deviation. This accounts probably for the vacillation and evasiveness of "Fragment," which tries to render an experience that belongs to the dialectic of gain and loss, yet insists the experience was neither. There are passages of regret, and of joy, scattered through the poem, but they do little to alter the calm, almost marmoreal beauty of the general tone of rapt meditation. Even the apparent reference to the death of a paternal figure, in the forty-seventh stanza, hardly changes Ashbery's almost Spenserian pace. The thirtieth stanza sums up Ashbery's inclination against the Stevensian tendency to move from a present intensity to a "That's it" of celebration, "to catch from that/ Irrational moment its unreasoning." The strength of Ashbery's denial of "that Irrational moment" comes from its undersong of repressed desire:

> *But why should the present seem so particularly*
>   *urgent?*
> *A time of spotted lakes and the whippoorwill*
> *Sounding over everything? To release the*
>   *importance*
> *Of what will always remain invisible?*
> *In spite of near and distant events, gladly*
> *Built? To speak the plaits of argument,*
> *Loosened? Vast shadows are pushed down*
>   *toward*
> *The hour. It is ideation, incrimination*
> *Proceeding from necessity to find it at*
> *A time of day, beside the creek, uncounted stars*
>   *and buttons.*

Of story, "Fragment" gives almost nothing, yet it finds oblique means of showing us: "the way love in short periods/

Puts everything out of focus, coming and going." Variations upon this theme constitute almost the whole of the poem's substance, and also its extraordinary strength, as Ashbery's insights in this area of perception seem endless. In its vision of love, "Fragment" hymns only the bleak truth of the triumph of absence:

> *Thus your only world is an inside one*
> *Ironically fashioned out of external phenomena*
> *Having no rhyme or reason, and yet neither*
> *An existence independent of foreboding and sly*
>   *grief.*
> *Nothing anybody says can make a difference;*
>   *inversely*
> *You are a victim of their lack of consequence*
> *Buffeted by invisible winds, or yet a flame*
>   *yourself*
> *Without meaning, yet drawing satisfaction*
> *From the crevices of that wind, living*
> *In that flame's idealized shape and duration.*

This eloquent despair, Shelleyan in its paradoxical affirmation of love yet acknowledgement of love's delusiveness, ends precisely in Shelley's image of the coming and going of the Intellectual Beauty, "like darkness to a dying flame." Uniquely Ashberyian is the emphasis on *satisfaction*, despite the transitoriness of "living" in so purely "idealized" a shape and duration. "Fragment" alternately explores the saving crevices and the shape of love's flame. Progression in this almost static poem is so subtle as to be almost indiscernible until the reader looks back at the opening from the closing stanzas, realizing then that:

> *. . . This time*
> *You get over the threshold of so much*
>   *unmeaning, so much*
> *Being, prepared for its event, the active*
>   *memorial.*

The reader's gain is an intensified sense of "time lost and won," never more strongly felt than in the poem's erotic culmination, stanzas 13–20, where Ashbery seeks "to isolate the kernel of/Our imbalance." In stanza 16, Ashbery finds no satisfaction in satisfaction anyway, in the only stanza of the poem that breaks the baroque stateliness and artful rhetorical repetitiveness of its form:

> *The volcanic entrance to an antechamber*
> *Was not what either of us meant.*
> *More outside than before, but what is worse,*
>   *outside*
> *Within the periphery, we are confronted*
> *With one another, and our meeting escapes*
>   *through the dark*
> *Like a well.*
> *Our habits ask us for instructions.*
> *The news is to return by stages*
> *Of uncertainty, too early or too late. It is the*
>   *invisible*
> *Shapes, the bed's confusion and prattling. The*
>   *late quiet,*
>   *This is how it feels.*

"The volcanic entrance to an antechamber," as a dismissal of the inadequacy of phallic heterosexuality to the love meant, is a kind of elegant younger brother to Hart Crane's bitter characterization of this means of love as: "A burnt match skating in a urinal." Ashbery wisely does not pause to argue preferences, but accomplishes his poem's most surprising yet inevitable transition by directly following: "This is how it feels" with a return to childhood visions: "The pictures were really pictures/Of loving and small things." As the interchange of interior worlds continues, Ashbery attains a point of survey in stanza 36 where he can assert: "You see, it is/Not wrong to have nothing." Four years later, writing "Soonest Mended," this joined an echo of Lear's speech to Cordelia to become: "both of us were right, though nothing/

Has somehow come to nothing." Expectation without desire is henceforth Ashbery's difficult, more-than-Keatsian attitude, not a disinterestedness nor any longer a renunciation, but a kind of visionary sublimation. This self-curtailing poetic *askesis* is performed as I think the dialectic of poetic influence compels it to be performed by a strong poet, as Ashbery has now become. That is, it is a revisionary movement in regard to the prime precursor, Stevens, who blends with what seems to be the dying figure of Ashbery's own father in the dense and exciting sequence of stanzas 38 through 49. These stanzas are Ashbery's version of Stevens' "Farewell to Florida" and recall its Spenserian image of the high ship of the poet's career being urged upon its more dangerous and mature course. Though Ashbery will back away from this ominous freedom in his final stanza (which I quoted earlier), the quest aspect of his career attains a wonderful culmination in stanza 49:

> *One swallow does not make a summer, but are*
> *What's called an opposite: a whole of raveling*
>   *discontent,*
> *The sum of all that will ever be deciphered*
> *On this side of that vast drop of water.*
> *They let you sleep without pain, having all that*
> *Not in the lesson, not in the special way of*
>   *telling*
> *But back to one side of life, not especially*
> *Immune to it, in the secret of what goes on:* ·
> *The words sung in the next room are*
>   *unavoidable*
> *But their passionate intelligence will be studied*
>   *in you.*

Here, as in so many passages having a similar quality, Ashbery reaches his own recognizable greatness, and gives us his variety of the American Sublime. The "parental concern" of Stevens' "midnight interpretation" (stanza 38) produced the grand myth of the Canon Aspirin in *Notes toward a Supreme*

Fiction, where Stevens at last, detaching himself from the Canon, could affirm: "I have not but I am and as I am, I am." Ashbery, in his moment most akin to Stevens' sublime self-revelation, affirms not the Emersonian-Whitmanian Transcendental Self, as Stevens most certainly (and heroically) does, but rather "the secret of what goes on." This is not, like Stevens' massive declaration, something that dwells in the orator's "special way of telling," but inheres painfully in Ashbery's vulnerability. As a self-declared "anomaly," Ashbery abides in the most self-revelatory and noble lines he has yet written:

> *The words sung in the next room are*
> *unavoidable*
> *But their passionate intelligence will be studied*
> *in you.*

That the pathos of "Fragment," a poem of the unlived life, of life refusing revenge upon its evaders, could lead to so lucid a realization, is a vital part of Ashbery's triumph over his earlier opacities. In the recent *Three Poems,* written in a prose apparently without precursors, this triumph expands, though again large demands are made upon the reader. But this I think is part of Ashbery's true value; only he and Ammons among poets since Stevens compel me to re-read so often, and then reward such labor.

Though "The New Spirit," first of the *Three Poems,* was begun in November 1969, most of it was written January to April, 1970. In a kind of cyclic repetition, the second prose poem "The System" was composed from January to March 1971, with the much shorter "The Recital" added as a coda in April. This double movement from winter vision to spring's re-imaginings is crucial in *Three Poems,* which is Ashbery's prose equivalent of *Notes toward a Supreme Fiction,* and which has the same relation as *Notes* to *Song of Myself.* Where Stevens reduces to the First Idea, which is "an imagined thing," and then equates the poet's act of the mind with the re-imagining of the First Idea, Ashbery reduces to a First

Idea of himself, and then re-imagines himself. I am aware that these are difficult formulae, to be explored elsewhere, and turn to a commentary upon *Three Poems*, though necessarily a brief and tentative one.

I described "Evening in the Country" as a "convalescent's" displacement of American Orphism, the natural religion of our poetry. *Three Poems* might be called the masterpiece of an invalid of the Native Strain, even a kind of invalid's version of *Song of Myself*, as though Whitman had written that poem in 1865, rather than 1855. Ashbery's work could be called *Ruminations of Myself* or *Notes toward a Saving but Subordinate Fiction*. Whitman's poem frequently is address of I, Walt Whitman, to you or my soul. Ashbery's *Three Poems* are addressed by *I*, John Ashbery writing, to *You*, Ashbery as he is in process of becoming. *I*, as in Whitman, Pater, Yeats is personality or self or the *antithetical; You*, as in the same visionaries, is character or soul or the *primary.* Ashbery's swerve away from tradition here is that his *You* is the re-imagining, while his *I* is a reduction.

"The New Spirit," the first poem's title, refers to a rebirth that takes place after the middle-of-the-journey crisis, here in one's late thirties or early forties:

> *. . . It is never too late to mend. When one*
> *is in one's late thirties, ordinary things—like a*
> *pebble or a glass of water—take on an*
> * expressive*
> *sheen. One wants to know more about them,*
> * and one*
> *is in turn lived by them . . .*

This "new time of being born" Ashbery calls also "the new casualness," and he writes of it in a prose that goes back to his old rhetorical dialectic of alternating ellipsis and the restored cliché. Indeed, "The New Spirit" opens by overtly giving "examples of leaving out," but Ashbery then mostly chooses to stand himself in place of these examples. Why does he choose prose, after "The Skaters" had shown how well he could absorb prose into verse at length? It may be a mistake, as one advantage, in my experience, of "The New Spirit" over "The System" and "The Recital," is that it crosses over to verse half-a-dozen times, while they are wholly in prose. I suppose that the desire to tell a truth that "could still put everything in" made Ashbery wary of verse now, for fear that he should not be as comprehensive as possible. Speaking again as the poet of "Fragment" he defines his predicament: "In you I fall apart, and outwardly am a single fragment, a puzzle to itself." To redress his situation, the New Spirit has come upon him, to renovate a poet who confesses he has lost all initiative:

> . . . It has been replaced by a strange kind of happiness within the limitations. The way is narrow but it is not hard, it seems almost to propel or push one along. One gets the narrowness into one's seeing, which also seems an inducement to moving forward into what one has already caught a glimpse of and which quickly becomes vision, in the visionary sense, except that in place of the panorama that used to be our customary setting and which we never made much use of, a limited but infinitely free space has established itself, useful as everyday life but transfigured so that its signs of wear no longer appear as a reproach but as indications of how beautiful a thing must have been to have been so much prized, and its noble aspect which must have been irksome before has now become interesting, you are fascinated and keep on studying it. . . .

This, despite its diffidence, declares what Emerson called Newness or Influx, following Sampson Reed and other Swedenborgians. Sometimes the *Three Poems,* particularly "The System," sound like a heightened version of the senior Henry James. But mostly Ashbery, particularly in "The New Spirit," adds his own kind of newness to his American tradition. At first reading of "The New Spirit," I felt considerable bafflement, not at the subject-matter, immediately clear to any exegete aged forty-two, but at the procedure, for it was difficult to see how Ashbery got from point to point, or even to determine if there were points. But repeated reading uncovers a beautiful and simple design: first, self-acceptance of the minimal anomalies we have become, "the color of the filter of the opinions and ideas everyone has ever entertained about us. And in this form we must prepare, now, to try to live." Second, the wintry reduction of that conferred self is necessary: "And you lacerate yourself so as to say, These wounds are me." Next, a movement to the *you* and to reimagining of the *I*, with a realization that the *you* has been transformed already, through the soul's experience as a builder of the art of love. With this realization, the consciousness of the New Spirit comes upon the *I*, and self and soul begin to draw closer in a fine lyric beginning: "Little by little/You are the mascot of that time" (pp. 33–34). An event of love, perhaps the one elegized in "Fragment," intervenes, illuminates, and then recedes, but in its afterglow the New Spirit gives a deeper significance to the object-world. After this seeing into the life of things, the growth of the mind quickens. But the transparency attained through the new sense of wholeness "was the same as emptiness," and the sense of individual culmination serves only to alienate the poet further from the whole of mankind, which "lay stupefied in dreams of toil and drudgery." It is at this point of realization that the long and beautiful final paragraph comes (pp. 50–51), ending "The New Spirit" with a deliberate reminiscence of the end of "The Skaters." Two visions come to Ashbery, to make him understand that there is still freedom, still the wildness of time that may allow the highest form of love to come. One is "the completed Tower of Babel," of all busyness, a terror that could be shut out just by turning away from it. The other is of the constellations that the tower threatened, but only seemed to threaten. They beckon now to "a new journey" certain to be benign, to answer "the major question that revolves around you, your being here." The journey is a choice of forms for answering, which means both Ashbery's quest for poetic form, and his continued acceptance of an "impassive grammar of cosmic unravelings of all kinds, to be proposed but never formulated."

I think that is an accurate account of the design of "The New Spirit," but I am aware such an account gives little sense of how Ashbery has added strangeness to beauty in thus finding himself there more truly and more strange. The transcendental re-awakening of anyone, even of an excellent poet, hardly seems *materia poetica* anymore, and perhaps only Ashbery would attempt to make a poem of it at this time, since his aesthetic follows Stevens by discovering the poem already formed in the world. His true and large achievement in "The New Spirit" is to have taken the theme of "Le Monocle de Mon Oncle," already developed in "Fragment," and to have extended this theme to larger problems of the aging and widening consciousness. Men at forty, Stevens says, can go on painting lakes only if they can apprehend "the universal hue." They must cease to be dark rabbis, and yield up their lordly studies of the nature of man. "The New Spirit" is Ashbery's exorcism of the dark rabbi in his own nature. Its achievement is the rare one of having found a radiant way of describing a process that goes on in many of us, the crisis of vision in an imaginative person's middle age, without resorting to psychosexual or social reductiveness.

"The System" is Ashbery's venture into quest-romance, his pursuit as rose rabbi, of "the origin and course/Of love," the origin and course together making up the System, which is thus a purposive wandering. Since the poem opens with the statement that "The system was breaking down," the reader is prepared for the prose-poem's penultimate paragraph, that tells us "we are rescued by what we cannot imagine: it is what finally takes us up and shuts our story."

The account of the System begins in a charming vision too genial for irony, as though Aristophanes had mellowed wholly:

> From the outset it was apparent that someone had
> played a colossal trick on something. The switches had
> been tripped, as it were; the entire world or one's lim-

> ited but accurate idea of it was bathed in glowing love,
> of a sort that need never have come into being but was
> now indispensable as air is to living creatures . . . if only,
> as Pascal says, we had the sense to stay in our room, but
> the individual will condemns this notion and sallies
> forth full of ardor and *hubris*, bent on self-discovery in
> the guise of an attractive partner who is *the* heaven-sent
> one, the convex one with whom he has had the urge to
> mate all these seasons without realizing it. . . .

This "glowing love" inevitably is soon enough seen as "muddle," and the first phase of quest fails: "Thus it was that a kind of blight fell on these early forms of going forth and being together, an anarchy of the affections sprung from too much universal cohesion." Rather than despair, or yield to apocalyptic yearnings, Ashbery consolidates upon his curious and effective passivity, his own kind of negative capability, becoming "a pillar of waiting," but Quixotic waiting upon a dream. As he waits, he meditates on "twin notions of growth" and on two kinds of happiness. One growth theory is of the great career: "a slow burst that narrows to a final release, pointed but not acute, a life of suffering redeemed and annihilated at the end, and for what?" This High Romanticism moves Ashbery, but he rejects it. Yet the alternative way, a Paterian "life-as-ritual" concept, the *locus classicus* of which we could find in the magnificent "Conclusion" to *The Renaissance*, he also turns from, or asserts he does, though I think he is more a part of this vision than he realizes. He fears the speed with which the soul moves away from others: "This very speed becomes a source of intoxication and of more gradually accruing speed; in the end the soul cannot recognize itself and is as one lost, though it imagines it has found eternal rest."

By evading both notions of growth, Ashbery rather desperately evades growth itself. Confronting two kinds of happiness, "the frontal and the latent," he is again more evasive than he may intend to be. The first is a sudden glory, related to the epiphany or Paterian "privileged moment," and Ashbery backs away from it, as by now we must expect, because of its elitism, he says, but rather, we can surmise, for defensive reasons, involving both the anxiety of influence and more primordial Oedipal anxieties. The latent and dormant kind he seeks to possess, but his long espousal of it (pp. 73–86) seems to me the weakest sequence in *Three Poems*, despite a poignant culmination in the great question: "When will you realize that your dreams have eternal life?" I suspect that these are, *for Ashbery*, the most important pages in his book, but except for the lovely pathos of a dreamer's defense, they are too much the work of a poet who wishes to be more of an anomaly than he is, rather than the "central" kind of a poet he is fated to become, in the line of Emerson, Whitman, Stevens.

This "central" quality returns wonderfully in the last twenty pages of "The System," as the quest for love begins again. A passage of exquisite personal comedy, Chaplinesque in its profundity, climaxes in the poet's defense of his mask: "your pitiable waif's stance, that inquiring look that darts uneasily from side to side as though to ward off a blow—." Ashbery assimilates himself to the crucial Late Romantic image of the failed quester, Browning's Childe Roland, for the author of *Three Poems* now approaches his own Dark Tower, to be confronted there by every anxiety, as human and as poet, that he has evaded:

> ... It is only that you happened to be wearing this look as you arrived at the end of your perusal of the way left open to you, and it "froze" on you, just as your mother warned you it would when you were little. And now it is the face you show to the world, the face of expectancy, strange as it seems. Perhaps Childe Roland wore such a look as he drew nearer to the Dark Tower, every energy concentrated toward the encounter with the King of Elfland, reasonably certain of the victorious outcome, yet not so much as to erase the premature lines of care from his pale and tear-stained face. Maybe it is just that you don't want to outrage anyone, especially now that the moment of your own encounter seems to be getting closer.

This version of Childe Roland's ordeal is an Ashberyian transformation or wish-fullfillment, as we can be reasonably certain that Browning's quester neither wants nor expects a "victorious outcome." But Ashbery feels raised from a first death, unlike Childe Roland, who longs for any end, and lacks a "quiet acceptance of experience in its revitalizing tide." Very gently, Ashbery accomplishes a Transcendental and open ending to "The System," complete with an Emersonian "transparent axle" and even an equivalent to the closing chant of Emerson's Orphic Poet in *Nature,* though Ashbery's guardian bard speaks to him in a "dry but deep accent," promising mastery (p. 99). Insisting that he has healed the sadness of childhood, Ashbery declares his System-wanderings are completed, the right balance attained in "what we have carefully put in and kept out," though a lyric "crash" may impend in which all this will be lost again. But, for now:

> The allegory is ended, its coils absorbed into the past, and this afternoon is as wide as an ocean. It is the time we have now, and all our wasted time sinks into the sea and is swallowed up without a trace. The past is dust and ashes, and this incommensurably wide way leads to the pragmatic and kinetic future.

This Shelleyan conclusion, akin to Demogorgon's dialectical vision, offers hope in "the pragmatic" yet menaces a return of the serpent-allegory (whose name is Ananke, in Ashbery as in Stevens or Shelley) in the still "kinetic" future.

The Coda of "The Recital" is a wholly personal apologia, with many Whitmanian and Stevensian echoes, some of them involuntary. "We cannot interpret everything, we must be selective," Ashbery protests, "nor can we leave off singing" which would return the poet to the living death of an unhappy childhood. Against the enemy (p. 111), who is an amalgam of time and selfishness, Ashbery struggles to get beyond his own solipsism, and the limits of his art. On the final page, an Emersonian-Stevensian image of saving transparence serves to amalgamate the new changes Ashbery meets and welcomes. This transparence movingly is provided by a Whitmanian vision of an audience for Ashbery's art: "There were new people watching and waiting, conjugating in this way the distance and emptiness, transforming the scarcely noticeable bleakness into something both intimate and noble." So they have and will, judging by the response of my students and other friends, with whom I've discussed Ashbery's work. By more than fifteen years of high vision and persistence he has clarified the initial prophecy of his work, until peering into it we can say: "We see us as we truly behave" and, as we see, we can think: "These accents seem their own defense."

IO

A. R. Ammons

THE BREAKING OF THE VESSELS

Paul Valéry, in defining an artist as someone who compelled others to create in response to *his* creation, went on to speak of "creative misunderstanding" as being the artistic mode of interpretation. If there is any validity to my own belief that canon-formation, the general acceptance of a poet into a tradition, is itself necessarily the strongest mode of creative misunderstanding, then there would be a particular value in examining a poet whose work is in the actual, contemporary, on-going process of being raised high into the hierarchy of poetic tradition. No contemporary poet, in America, is likelier to become a classic than A. R. Ammons, and so I intend here to re-visit some of his major poems, in that kind of re-reading I am trying to teach myself, in which one tries, however vainly, to guard against or compensate for the strong mis-readings that are created by the rigors of canon-formation.

Ammons is a dangerous poet to read in the context of hierarchy, because hierarchy is one of his overt and obsessive concerns, particularly in his new, long poem, "Sphere: The Form of a Motion," which may be his most remarkable achievement to date. "Hierarchy" as a word goes back to the Greeks, where it meant the "rule of a priest," but our dictionaries define it as a body of persons or entities graded by authority, by rank or, surely most crucially, by capacity. Ammons once told an interviewer that, in his view, poetic influence is only a sub-branch of the larger subject of hierarchy, and I suspect that for Ammons, as for Milton's Satan, hierarchy actually serves as what Satan called "quickening power," or what Nietzsche called the Will to Power. Nietzsche thought that the Will to Power, in an artist, resulted in the willful misinterpretation of all reality, which I find a refreshing de-mystification of what the publicists of poetry always assert to be the true relationship between poetry and reality. Yeats, a fierce Nietzschean when most himself, was merely fibbing when he said that art was but a vision of reality. Ammons fibs a lot about art also, but when most himself Ammons is a fierce Emersonian, and a fierce Emersonian is about as dangerous a visionary misinterpreter of "reality" as you can find. Ammons, like Whitman, has inherited from Emerson a wild ambition for the poet, which involves some very dark hierarchical obsessions, as in "Sphere: The Form of a Motion":

> . . . *the gods have come and gone*
> *(or we have made them come and go) so long*
>   *among us that*
> *they have communicated something of the sky*
>   *to us making us*
>
> *feel that at the division of the roads our true*
>   *way, too,*
> *is to the sky where with unborn gods we may*
>   *know no*
> *further death and need no further visitations:*
>   *what may have*
>
> *changed is that in the future we can have the*
>   *force to keep*
> *the changes secular: the one: many problem, set*
>   *theory, and*
> *symbolic signifier, the pyramid, the pantheon*
>   *(of gods and*
>
> *men), the pecking order, baboon troop, old man*
>   *of the tribe,*
> *the hierarchy of family, hamlet, military,*
>   *church, corporation,*

civil service, of wealth, talent—everywhere the
scramble for

place, power, privilege, safety, honor, the
representative
notch above the undistinguished numbers:
second is as good
as last: pyramidal hierarchies and solitary
persons: the

hierarchies having to do with knowledge and
law, the solitaries
with magic, conjuration, enchantment: the loser
or apostate
turns on the structure and melts it with vision,
with

summoning, clean, verbal burning: or the man
at the top may
turn the hierarchy down and walk off in a
private direction:
meanwhile, back at the hierarchy, the chippers
and filers

hone rocks to skid together . . .

The passage, like most of "Sphere," is extravagantly pell-mell, and by its implications substitutes "hierarchy," as a trope, for mental order of any kind, for those intellectual demarcations that Ammons is always telling us have no kin in nature, where the hierarchies flow together, where there are no sharp lines. Of the multitude of intense struggles that never abandon the poetry of Ammons, the most violent is the war between two visions of the mind, one that believes it can take nature up into itself, and the other that believes nature can never be adequate to it. Even the first of these visions has a transcendental strain in it, but the second is almost unmatched in our century in its exaltation and high sorrow. I say "almost" because of Hart Crane, a poet who also stemmed from Whitman, as Ammons does, but who seems not to have affected Ammons. But only Crane rivals the extraordinary poignance of prophetic self-presentation that Ammons sometimes allows himself, as here in the dedicatory verses to "Sphere":

> *I went to the summit and stood in the high*
>   *nakedness:*
> *the wind tore about this*
> *way and that in confusion and its speech could*
>   *not*
> *get through to me nor could I address it:*
> *still I said as if to the alien in myself*
>   *I do not speak to the wind now:*
> *for having been brought this far by nature I*
>   *have been*
> *brought out of nature*
> *and nothing here shows me the image of myself:*

What was the mode of his speech when he still addressed the wind? I go back to the earliest Ammons, to the ephebe who walked "the bleached and broken fields" near the North Carolina shore, listening to the wind yet not being inspirited by it, but rather punished into song: "the wind whipped my throat." He "swayed as if the wind were taking me away," but knew already that: "unlike wind/that dies and/never dies I said/I must go on/consigned to/form that will not/let me loose/except to death." Except for an occasional chat with a mountain, the young Ammons seems to have relied upon the wind for most of his conversational company. The most poignant of these early encounters is called "The Wide Land":

> *Having split up the chaparral*
> *blasting my sight*
> *the wind said*
>   *You know I'm*
>   *the result of*
> *forces beyond my control*

I don't hold it against you
I said
It's all right I understand

Those pressure bowls and cones
the wind said
are giants in their continental gaits
I know I said I know
they're blind giants
Actually the wind said I'm
  if anything beneficial
     resolving extremes
filling up lows with highs
No I said you don't have
to explain
It's just the way things are

Blind in the wide land I
turned and risked my feet
to loose stones and sudden

alterations of height

The wind is apologetic because of its particular relation to Ammons, being his guide, yet here the guide is blinding its seer. We can say that the wind, throughout his poetry, serves as Virgil to Ammons' Dante. As the emblem of the composite precursor, the wind subsumes those aspects of the Emersonian-Whitmanian tradition that most deeply have found and touched Ammons. Emerson said: "We cannot write the order of the variable winds," and Whitman sang of "the impalpable breezes that set in upon me" as he confronted the ebbing of his own poethood. Ammons, always affectionate towards the wind, confronts it more directly than any poet since Shelley, as here in the early "Joshua Tree":

> *unlike wind*
> *that dies and*
> *never dies I said*

I must go on
consigned to
form that will not
let me loose
except to death
till some
syllable's rain
anoints my tongue
to strangers:

This is not yet what Ammons now calls "the form of a motion." In one of the early Ezra-poems, "The Wind Coming Down From," the wind identifying itself with the Emersonian law of Compensation: "pushed, pushing/not air or motion/but the motion of air." "Nothing is got for nothing" is Emerson's motto, and is the Law of Compensation for Ammons also. Excerpts from Emerson's essay, "Compensation," are the proper context for Ammons' encounters with the wind:

> . . . An inevitable dualism bisects nature, so that each thing is a half, and suggests another thing to make it whole. . . .
>
> Whilst the world is thus dual, so is every one of its parts. . . .
>
> The same dualism underlies the nature and condition of man. Every excess causes a defect; every defect an excess. . . . For every thing you have missed, you have gained something else; and for every thing you gain, you lose something. . . . Or do men desire the more substantial and permanent grandeur of genius? Neither has this an immunity. . . . With every influx of light comes new danger. Has he light? He must bear witness to the light, and always outrun that sympathy which gives him such keen satisfaction, by his fidelity to new revelations of the incessant soul. . . .

It is this obsession with the *Ananke* of Compensation that seems to have motivated the greatest experience of Ammons' life and poetry, the savage will-to-transcendence that marked him with an ecstasy he had to abandon, all too quickly, in order for life and poetry to go on. I don't find it possible to over-praise those poems in which Ammons violently first found and first lost himself: "Hymn," "Gravelly Run," "Bourn," "Mansion," "Prodigal," "Guide," "Terrain," "Bridge," "Raft," ending in the double culminations of this phase, "Corsons Inlet" and "Saliences." In these dozen or so poems, Ammons tried the impossible task, beyond a limit of art, in which language seeks its own end to the one:many problem. Whitman wisely took this impossibility as a given of his art, and began *Song of Myself* as though the great experience of union were accomplished already, and subsequently could be celebrated. But the young Ammons was a purer and wilder Emersonian, akin really to the young Thoreau or to Jones Very, and so attempted the incredible. He gave himself up to the wind of Compensation, as here in "Mansion":

> *So it came time*
> > *for me to cede myself*
> *and I chose*
> *the wind*
> > *to be delivered to*
>
> *The wind was glad*
> > *and said it needed all*
> *the body*
> *it could get*
> > *to show its motions with*

The magnificent compensation comes in one of Ammons' masterpieces, "Guide," and here I want to subject this poem to a full-scale antithetical critique, for this is one of those texts in which Ammons clarifies the way in which a poem is for him as much an act of breaking as of making, as much a blinding as a seeing. "Guide" is a revisionist poem in relation to Ammons' American tradition, and its meaning needs to be developed in the interplay between it and major precursor texts in Emerson and Whitman. The dialectic of revisionism, as I have explained elsewhere, is perfectly applicable to Ammons. His characteristic poem moves back and forth from tropes, defenses, images of limitation to those of representation, and always through an extraordinary agility in rhetorical and psychic *substitution*. For Ammons, as for all revisionists since the Gnostics and Kabbalists, every act of creation is also a catastrophe, a breaking-of-the-vessels, to use the great image of the Lurianic Kabbalah. Ammons' way of saying this is admirably instanced in the poem "Guide":

> *You cannot come to unity and remain*
>   *material:*
> *in that perception is no perceiver:*
>   *when you arrive*
> *you have gone too far:*
>   *at the Source you are in the mouth of*
>   *Death:*
> *you cannot*
>   *turn around in*
> *the Absolute: there are no entrances or exits*
>   *no precipitations of forms*
> *to use like tongs against the formless:*
>   *no freedom to choose:*
> *to be*
>   *you have to stop not-being and break*
> *off from is to flowing and*
>   *this is the sin you weep and praise:*
> *origin is your original sin:*
>   *the return you long for will ease your*
>   *guilt*
> *and you will have your longing:*
>   *the wind that is my guide said this: it*
> *should know having*
>   *given up everything to eternal being*
>   *but*
> *direction:*
> *how I said can I be glad and sad: but a man goes*

> *from one foot to the other:*
> *wisdom wisdom:*
> > *to be glad and sad at once is also*
> *unity*
> *and death:*
> > *wisdom wisdom: a peachblossom blooms on*
> > *a particular*
> *tree on a particular day:*
> > *unity cannot do anything in*
> *particular:*
> *are these the thoughts you want me to think I*
> *said but*
> > *the wind was gone and there was no more*
> *knowledge then.*

Breaking off from *is* to *flowing* is the Ammonsian Breaking-of-the-Vessels. I find that Ammons reminds me (without, I think, his knowing anything, overtly, about Kabbalah) of the origin or original sin of the image of the vessels breaking. The Kabbalists say that it was the strength of the Divine Light, the influx of transcendental power, that broke the vessels that ought to have received the radiance. In his private experience, which hardly benefits by being termed "mysticism," the young Ammons seems to have taught himself this paradox of all belated creativity.

Ammons begins "Guide" with his own version of a dialectic of images of presence and absence. Neither unity nor materiality is present, and a rhetorical irony offers us a perception without a perceiver, an arrival that has gone a station too far, and then by synecdoche is converted into a Source that is Death's mouth, every origin suddenly being seen as a mutilated part of the whole unity that is Death.

With the negative image of a reified Absolute, without direction or openings, the language of the poem moves into the psychic defenses of undoing and isolation, but only in order to recoil from this limitation so as to mount up into a daemonic Sublime, itself based upon a repression of this poet's deepest longings. With this, the wind ceases to speak, and the poem moves into a psychic area that alternates sublimating metaphor with a sad, final projection of the wind, in which the possibility of future knowledge is lost.

In Ammons, the Breaking of the Vessels is what another great poem, "Prodigal," calls "the mental/blaze and gleam,/ the mind in both motions building and tearing down." But the wind in "Guide," though it represents Compensation, is less balanced and hopeful than the Emersonian law of our nature and of all nature. What does it mean to have "given up everything to eternal being but/direction," which is to say, what would it mean if we were speaking of the poet and not of the wind? The answer is not just that "unity cannot do anything in particular" except presumably move in one direction at a time, but is more largely involved in this poem's transumptive stance at its close. Transumption, as I've indicated in other contexts, is a trope upon a trope that undoes time. Here, it undoes the future, which is projected with the wind, leaving Ammons with no present moment, but alone with a past ecstasy, a guide evidently no longer a guide.

In one of his most visionary poems, "Bridge," Ammons achieved a momentary tone of acceptance in regard to his central dilemma:

> *when the spirit comes to the bridge of*
> *   consciousness*
> *and climbs higher and higher*
> *   toward the peak no one reaches live*
>
> *but where ascension*
> *   and descension meet*
> *completing the idea of a bridge*
>
> *think where the body is,*
> *   that going too deep*
>
> *it may lose touch,*
> *   wander a ghost in hell*
> *   sing irretrievably in gloom,*
> *and think*

how the spirit silvery with vision may
break loose in high wind

   and go off weightless

body never to rise or spirit fall again to unity,

      . . .

But the costs of such acceptance are too high, even for Ammons. His version of the High Romantic quest for oblivion, his equivalent of Shelley's "Alastor," is the darkly beautiful poem, "Raft," where he surrenders even direction and goes with the tide, only at last to be rescued again, however equivocally, by the wind. Motion for motion, I think it fair to say that Ammons was losing his battle against himself until he wrote his most famous poem, "Corsons Inlet," and its more remarkable sequel, "Saliences." One of his most distinguished and sympathetic critics, Geoffrey Hartman, insists that Ammons, as opposed to Wordsworth, is trapped perpetually in the difficulty of nature-poetry, which is the "loss of self and voice to nature." I think myself that Hartman beautifully and canonically misreads when he says of Ammons that "he subdues himself totally to *love of perception,* refusing all higher adventure." For Hartman, even the later Ammons of the long poems, including *Hibernaculum* and presumably even "Sphere," is giving us "a massively playful nature-thinking" in which adequate form is partly evaded. The danger, as again Hartman wisely observes, is that a longer poem by Ammons can seem "all periphery and no center." The dangers of pastoral, on this critical view, become constant in Ammons. Every poetic phrase becomes casual rather than causal, and the poem becomes less an instrument against entropy, and more a part of entropy itself. Ammons of course defends his procedure by comparing the energy of his poems to that of nature, so that the movement of a poem becomes more sexual in its rhythm and less compensatory. Yet Hartman, despite his admiration for Ammons, implies a very dangerous critique; the Ammonsian poem begins to show rather more in common with nature's entropy than with nature's energy.

I myself would say that both Hartman and Ammons are strong mis-readers of Ammons, for at least from "Saliences" on he does not write nature-poetry, and indeed I would go back to origins and say truly that he never did write nature-poetry. What Ammons calls "nature," whether he celebrates it or says goodbye to it, is no more natural than Emerson's *Nature* was, or Whitman's either. Unfortunately Ammons wants it both ways, as Emerson did, and so he indulges himself in such wasted postures of the spirit as section 38 of "Sphere," where the hard-pressed writers of New York City (who have troubles enough) are urged out into the woods to watch the redwing. But this is a quirkiness that we have to accept, reading Ammons. He seems to need it, because he cannot bear always to concede the truth, which is that he is as foreign in nature as if he had landed, a visitor. His image, as he admits, is of desire or the will-to-power, what he calls *longing,* and such an image can never be fulfilled by or in nature. Ammons, like Wordsworth, and like Whitman, was and is a poet of the Romantic Sublime.

The best account of the Romantic Sublime is by Thomas Weiskel, who emphasizes transcendence as being central:

> The essential claim of the Sublime is that men can, in feeling and in speech, transcend the human. . . . An "humanistic Sublime" is an oxymoron. Yet . . . the Sublime revives as God withdraws. . . . The Romantic Sublime was an attempt to revise the meaning of transcendence precisely as the traditional apparatus of sublimation . . . was failing to be exercised or understood.

Let us trace the Sublime backwards in Ammons, from "Sphere" to the early Ezra-chants that began his work. In "Sphere" there is no daemonic Sublime, as there is in earlier Ammons, but we are given instead a curiously discursive Sublime:

> ... *so to look to the*
> *moment of consciousness as to find there,*
> *beyond all the*
> *individual casts and horrors, perplexing pains*
> *and seizures,*
>
> *joy's surviving radiance: I ask because I am*
> *terrified of my*
> *arrogance and do not know and do not know if*
> *the point in the*
> *mind can be established to last beyond the*
> *falling away*
>
> *of the world and the dreams of the world . . .*

This is very much the poetry of our moment, of an economy and a culture undergoing catastrophe. As a seer, Ammons shies away from prophecy, but "Sphere: The Form of a Motion" allows itself to end in a difficult joy:

> *to float the orb or suggest the orb is floating:*
> *and, with the*
> *mind thereto attached, to float free: the orb*
> *floats, a blue green*
> *wonder: so to touch the structures as to free*
> *them into rafts*
>
> *that reveal the tide: many rafts to ride and the*
> *tides make a*
> *place to go: let's go and regard the structures,*
> *the six-starred*
> *easter lily, the beans feeling up the stakes: we're*
> *gliding: we*
>
> are *gliding: ask the astronomer, if you don't*
> *believe it: but*
> *motion as a summary of time and space is*
> *gliding us: for a while,*
> *we may ride such forces: then, we must get off:*
> *but now this*

> beats any amusement park by the shore: our
>   Ferris wheel, what a
> wheel: our roller coaster, what mathematics of
>   stoop and climb: sew
> my name on my cap: we're clear: we're ourselves:
>   we're sailing.

Partly this is a transumption of the earlier poem, "Raft," as Ammons attempts to carry his past alive into his own future. Partly it is a fine desperation, again too appropriate to the present moment. But mostly it is a revision of Whitman, who haunts all of "Sphere," and whose presence is pervasive in the last third of the poem. Here is Whitman, in the last section of *Song of Myself,* clear, himself and sailing:

> *The last scud of day holds back for me,*
> *It flings my likeness after the rest and true, as*
>   *any on the shadow'd wilds,*
> *It coaxes me to the vapor and the dusk.*
>
> *I depart as air, I shake my white locks at the*
>   *runaway sun*
> *I effuse my flesh in eddies, and drift it in lacy*
>   *jags.*

Whitman projects and so casts away the past, and introjects and so identifies himself with the future, at the price of the present moment. So, in the poem's final lines, the floating Walt is no place in no time, but we must quest for him:

> *Failing to fetch me at first keep encouraged,*
> *Missing me one place search another,*
> *I stop somewhere waiting for you.*

Part of Ammons' meaning is his loss of this Sublime sense that as the bard he is up ahead of us somewhere, waiting for us like Whitman. No, he says, he is sailing *with* us, floating along, and he also is going to lose his cap. His poem has no center, because *he* is its center, as Walt was earlier, but the Emersonian self once wavered a touch less than now, though it was always rather unstable. There is an illuminating comment by a great allegorist, Angus Fletcher:

> For what is a center, in human terms? Surely the body, and surely within the body some part of the body regarded as *its* center, whether head, heart or loins. By giving so much value to such a frail temple the critic has been forced to measure the bleakness of the hostile world of nature. Nothing could be more striking than those obsessively emptied scenes represented by so many of the quotations in this book. Shelley is the master of the bleak Antonioni vista, but there are sand-dunes and deserts here from Whitman, from Stevens, and above all from . . . Ammons. Ammons particularly emerges as the poet of earth's intransigent geometrical control over men. *Corsons Inlet* and the other Ammons poems are sublime in their emptiness and their adherence to the magic of pure line, absolute boundary and border.

A sublime emptiness: this parallels Hartman's praise of Ammons at his best, when the poet addresses "the empty place that threatens his power of speech." Certainly Fletcher and Hartman are correct in finding that Ammons attains the Sublime in a context of the void. His power touches the heights in one passage of *Hibernaculum* that comes near to the Stevens of "The Auroras of Autumn" as a major example of the American Sublime, in our age:

>   *. . . to lean belief the lean*
> *word comes,*
> *each scope adjusted to the plausible: to the*
>   *heart*
> *emptied of, by elimination, the world, comes*
>   *the small*
>
> *cry domesticating the night: if the night is to be*

*habitable, if dawn is to come out of it, if day is
   ever
to grow brilliant on delivered populations, the
   word*

*must have its way by the brook, lie out cold all
   night
along the snow limb, spell by yearning's wilted
   weed till
the wilted weed rises, know the patience and
   smallness*

*of stones: I address the empty place where the
   god
that has been deposed lived: it is the godhead:
   the
yearnings that have been addressed to it bear
   antiquity's*

*sanction: for the god is ever re-created as
emptiness, till force and ritual fill up and
   strangle
his life, and then he must be born again:*

Though the patterning of images here depends upon a
sexual reductiveness (since for Ammons the center is loins,
not head or heart), the larger reduction comes from Ammons' characteristic metonymic defense of isolation, his version of *kenosis*. One sees now why his earlier guide was the
wind, not because of its traditional identity with spirit, but
because it was already a metonymy for the lean word, and
then for the empty word. Whitman's word located all direc-
tions in Whitman himself, a location inherited by Stevens
Hoon, when that Paterian grandly said: "I was myself the
compass of that sea." Ammons' word began by locating direction only in the wind, a metonymic limitation that prepared
for a perpetually possible Sublime representation, for all
those daemonic and repressive hyperboles through which
the young Ammons touched the Sublime.

Moving backward from *Hibernaculum*, I want now to center upon three lyrics by Ammons, all of them justly famous: "Plunder," "Peak," and "Moment," the first later Ammons, the other two middle, and all of them poems about the precariousness and the expense of the Ammonsian Sublime. "Plunder" is so complete a lyric that very nearly the whole of Ammons is in it:

I have appropriated the windy twittering of
  aspen leaves
into language, stealing something from reality
  like a
silverness: drop-scapes of ice from peak sheers:

much of the rise in brooks over slow-rolled
  glacial stones:
the loop of reeds over the shallow's edge when
  birds
feed on the rafts of algae: I have taken right
  out of the

air the clear streaks of bird music and held
  them in my
head like shifts of sculpture glint: I have sent
  language
through the mud roils of a raccoon's paws like
  a net,

netting the roils: made my own uses of a
  downwind's
urgency on a downward stream: held with a
  large scape
of numbness the black distance upstream to the
  mountains

flashing and bursting: meanwhile, everything
  else, frog,
fish, bear, gnat has turned in its provinces and
  made off
with its uses: my mind's indicted by all I've
  taken.

The poem's crucial word is "indicted" which does not so much mean "accused" or "charged" here as it does "proclaimed" or even perhaps "dictated," both of them significations held back in the pre-history of the word. Ammons accuses himself of a misprision of nature, a mis-taking or mis-apprehending, by all the tropes of limitation: dialectical irony of presence and absence, metonymic reduction, metaphoric displacement. What this lyric powerfully refuses is the full burden of representation; it excludes tropes of representation, and so willfully negates the Sublime. "Plunder," as a word, goes back to the Middle Dutch for household goods or clothes, and thus Ammons indicts his mind for having been a thieving guest of the natural world, betraying hospitality. Nature proclaims the poet's mind as its despoiler, and Ammons, despite his pride, manifests anxiety as to the dictation involved. Yet whatever kind of a poem we want to call this, it is no version of pastoral, for implicitly the poet tells us that nature was never his home.

Contrast this to Ammons, briefly but poignantly caught up in the Sublime, in the perfectly entitled "Peak":

> *Everything begins at the tip-end, the dying-out*
> *of mind:*
> *the dazed eyes set and light*
> *dissolves actual trees:*
>
> *the world beyond: tongueless,*
> *unexampled*
> *burns dimension out of shape,*
> *opacity out of stone:*
>
> *come: though the world ends and cannot*
> *end,*
> *the apple falls sharp*
> *to the heart starved with time.*

This brief lyric, one of Ammons' most astonishing artistries, is both a total, Sublime epiphany, and a complete, revisionist act of misprision in relation to the American tradition of

Romantic sublimity. It does all that a short poem can do, as a complete pattern of images, both as a structure of tropes and as a network of psychic defenses against the burden of anteriority. "Peak" begins with a dialectic of presence and absence, things present and mind absent, conveyed through the rhetorical trope of irony, since Ammons says "everything" and means "nothing." This is his *clinamen* or reaction-formation against Emersonian perception, against the dark and solipsistic adage: "That which we are, that only can we see." The poetic compensation for this initial contraction or withdrawal of meaning begins with the synecdoche of "the world beyond" replacing "actual trees." The antithetical completion of Emerson represents psychically a turning of Ammons against himself, a fresh realization that *his* poetic self is at last only part of a mutilated whole.

With the metonymy of "tongueless" for that world, Ammons goes on to a *kenosis*, an ebbing-away of the poetic self that is defensively an undoing, emptying out the imagery by moving from examples to the "unexampled," burning shape away. Yet, with almost incredible economy, the characteristic Sublime representation of Emersonian tradition, the repressive force Emerson called "transparency," is immediately invoked as opacity is burned out of stone, so that even stone becomes transparent. "Come," the poem tells us, urging us to enter its final movement with it, where the external world re-enters with the dualizing perspectivism of an apocalyptic metaphor. This sublimation or *askesis* is a fearful one for Ammons to suffer, whether as visionary or as naturalist, but is miraculously and all-but-immediately restituted by the poem's closing transumption: "the apple falls sharp/to the heart starved with time." Time, necessarily meaning past time, has been introjected here, and there seems no more future than there is a present at this peak-moment. Yet the moment *is* a moment of vision or of what Emerson called Influx or Reason. The apple falls sharp because the angle of vision is sharp, and momentarily the axis of vision is indeed one with the axis of things. In just fifty words, Ammons has extended an intolerably wealthy tradition, and compelled anteriority to yield him some room. There are not many poets, in any generation, who can edge a mountain of meaning over, even if just a notch, by the use of fifty very plain words.

As I am exhibiting Ammons in his most drastic mode of economy, I turn now to an even more remarkable act of poetic compression, "Moment," where Ammons needs only about twenty-five words:

> *He turned and*
> *stood*
>
> *in the moment's*
> *height,*
>
> *exhilaration*
> *sucking him up,*
>
> *shuddering and*
> *lifting*
>
> *him*
> *jaw and bone*
>
> *and he said*
> *what*
>
> *destruction am I*
> *blessed by?*

Rather than comment on this, I want to juxtapose it to one of the greatest of entries in Emerson's vast journal, this one being March 24, 1838, one of the seeds of the essay "Self-Reliance":

> In the highest moments, we are a vision. There is nothing that can be called gratitude nor properly joy. The soul is raised over passion. It seeth nothing so much as Identity. It is a Perceiving that Truth and Right ARE. Hence it becomes a perfect Peace out of the knowing that all things will go well. Vast spaces of nature the

Atlantic Ocean, the South Seas; vast intervals of time
years, centuries, are annihilated to it; this which I think
and feel underlay that former state of life and circumstances, as it does underlie my present, and will always
all circumstances, and what is called life and what is
called death.

Ammons speaks of an exhilaration that is a destruction,
and of a blessing that might as well be a wound. Emerson
too speaks of a heightening that is an annihilation, but
characteristically he emphasizes only the gain of the exalted moment, and not its compensating loss. For Ammons, the transcendental moment is a Purgatory, and not
the Edenic state it was for Emerson. Yet even this distinction is only part of a complex difference that Ammons'
quest for autonomy has enforced. Here, in the clarity and
maturity of *Sphere*, sections 32–33, is Ammons tolling up
the cost of a purgatorial wisdom:

> *poor assessments, it's hard to draw a line, the*
>   *careful,*
> *arrogant, arbitrary imposition, the divider that*
>   *blocks off*
> *and sets apart, the arising of difference and*
>   *distinction:*
>
> *the discrete a bolus of slowed flux, a locus of*
>   *depressed*
> *reaction rates, a boned and fibered replication:*
>   *slowed*
> *but not stopped (heightened within its slows):*
>   *on the instant*
>
> *of cessation, disintegration's bacteria flare:*
>   *bloom, puff,*
> *and blow with change: much energy devoted to*
>   *staving off*
> *insweeps of alteration: to slow, defer, to chew*
>   *up change*

into the materials of slowing: until the body,
　increasingly
owed, is paid: take the mind's radiant works,
　the ground
changes under them: they lift off into
　distraction: one

needs clarities to know what one is baffled by,
　the small
left- and righthandedness: suppose one saw the
　nonsupportive
clearly: how could the mind, lit up and
　possessed, find

energy for salvation's befuddlement: to confront
　nothingness
the best baffler, is to disengage monsters and
　prevent
lofty identifications: to be saved is here, local
　and mortal:

everything else is a glassworks of flight: a
　crystal
hankering after the unlikely: futures on the
　next illusion:
order is the boat we step into for the crossing:
　when we

step out, nothingness welcomes us: inspiration
　spends through:
by the snowroad the boulder floats afire:
　fir-bark,
skittering under a startled squirrel, falls in
　flames

This is wisdom, and it is also defeat. I do not mean personal defeat, nor do I mean poetic defeat, but a purely transcendental surrender, akin to Wordsworth's in the last stanza of the "Intimations" Ode, or to Whitman's in "As I Ebb'd," or Stevens' in *The Rock*. Ammons has got to learn to be a different kind of poet than he was, and he is still in the process of learning that this different kind will return him to origins again, though with a more exacting music than he set out to bring into being. The canon of American poetry will read him more deeply into his tradition than he cares to read himself, but this characteristic misreading need not be deplored, as it too is part of the poetic process. Let us return him to origins by going back to one of the early Whitmanian chants that began his poetry nearly a quarter of a century ago. This is chant 27 of the "Ommateum" poems, excluded by Ammons from the *Collected Poems* (as well as the *Selected* volume), yet it is a poem I, as one reader, cannot get out of my memory:

> *I should have stayed longer idle*
> *and done reverence*
> *to it*
> > *waterfalls*
> > *humbling in silent slide*
> *the precipice of my effrontery*
> > *poured libations of arms*
> *like waterwheels*
> *toward the ground but*
> *knowing the fate of sunset things*
> *I grew desperate and entertained it*
> > *with sudden sprints*
> > *somersaults*
> *and cartwheels figuring eight*
>
> *It would not stay*
> > *Ring of cloud I said*
> *high pale ringcloud*
> *ellipsis off evening moment's miracle*
> *where will I go looking for your return*
> *and rushing to the rim*
> *I looked down into the deep dissolution*
>
> *I should have held still*
> *before it*
> > *and been mute*

cancelled by an oak's trunk
and done honors unseen
and taken the beauty sparingly
as one who fears to move and
shatter vision from his eyes

Patricia Parker, in what I judge to be the best essay yet written upon the poetry of Ammons, observes the curious centrality of this rejected poem in the geometry of the Ammonsian heterocosm:

> . . . it takes us, both in image and concern, all the way forward [in Ammons]. . . . The poet who knows the fate of sunset things and from the western rim looks down into the deep dissolution is, of course, simply reminding us of the obvious visual extensions of the first sentence of Emerson's remarkable essay *Circles*—"the eye is the first circle; the horizon which it forms is the second."

I think that Ammons is warning us now, in "Sphere," against "rushing to the rim," out of his prophetic fear that to know us, and himself, is to find oneself "knowing the fate of sunset things." By one of the ironies of canon-formation, a self-proclaimed "spent seer" finds himself in the unsought position of opposing a transcendental stance, that he himself has forsaken, to his own and our conscious belatedness. The necessity of misreading will make of Ammons what he ceased to be when he was a young man, a monist attempting to hold mind and nature together in a single vision. Ammons, as a man, must be rueful about so misprized a critical destiny, but as a poet he prophesied it, darkly, in the closing lines of his first volume:

Sometimes the price of my content
consumes its purchase
and martyrs' cries, echoing my peace,
rise sinuously like smoke
out of my ashen soul.

But I will not end on such a tone, for this great poet demands more. Though for him "the apple falls sharp/to the heart stoned with time," for him also the last word is more central. Like Whitman, he ends with the sun, and with the fruit of existence uniquely radiant at each fresh encounter. Here are the lines that he chose to end his *Collected Poems:*

> . . . *neither way to go's to stay, stay*
> *here, the apple an apple with its own hue*
> *or streak, the drink of water, the drink,*
>
> *the falling into sleep, restfully ever the*
> *falling into sleep, dream, dream, and*
> *every morning the sun comes, the sun.*

II

Geoffrey Hill

THE SURVIVAL OF STRONG POETRY

Strong poetry is always difficult, and Geoffrey Hill is the strongest British poet now alive, though his reputation in the English-speaking world is somewhat less advanced than that of several of his contemporaries. He should be read and studied for many generations after they have blent together, just as he should survive all but a handful (or fewer) of American poets now active. Such canonic prophecy is founded on the authority of his best work, as I have experienced it in the fifteen years since the publication of *For The Unfallen*, his first book. From his first poem, appropriately "Genesis," on through the *Mercian Hymns*, Hill has been the most Blakean of modern poets. But this is deep or true influence, or Blake's Mental Warfare, rather than the easy transmission of image, idea, diction and metric that superficially is judged to be poetic influence. The merely extrinsic influences on Hill's early verse are mostly American; I can detect the fierce rhetoric of Allen Tate, and the visionary intensities of Richard Eberhart, in some places. Yet the true precursor is always Blake, and the War in Heaven that the strong poet must conduct is fought by Hill against Blake, and against Blake's tradition, and so against Hill himself.

As a war of poetry against poetry, Hill's work testifies to the repressive power of tradition, but also to an immensely individual and deeply moving moral protest against tradition. Like the hero he celebrates in his masterpiece, the *Mercian Hymns*, Hill is a martyrologist. His subject is human pain, the suffering of those who both do and sustain violence, and more exactly the daemonic relationship between cultural tradition and human pain. Confronted by Hill's best poems, a reader is at first tempted to turn away, for the intellectual difficulty of the rugged, compressed verse is more than matched by the emotional painfulness and directness of Hill's vision. Hill does not comfort nor console, and offers no dialectic of gain through loss. His subject, like his style, is difficulty; the difficulty of apprehending and accepting moral guilt, and the difficulty of being a poet when the burden of history, including poetic history, makes any prophetic stance inauthentic. In more than twenty years of writing, Hill has given us three very slim volumes, not because his gift is sparse, but because he is too scrupulous to have allowed himself a less organized or less weighted utterance. There are no bad poems in Hill's three books, and so much is demanded of the reader, in concentration and in the dignity of a desperate humanism, that more productive poets are likely to seem too indulgent, by comparison. Hill does not indulge his reader, or himself, and just this remorseless concentration is Hill's assured greatness. The reader who persists will learn to read not only Hill, but other difficult and wholly indispensable poets as well, for only a poet as strong as Hill compels each of us to test his own strength as a reader, and so to test and clarify also our own relation to tradition.

Tradition, Freud surmised, was the cultural equivalent of repressed material in the consciousness of the individual. The role of repression in poetry was misunderstood by Freud and has been misunderstood by most of his followers. Freud thought that sublimation was the psychic defense that *worked*, whether in life or in literature, while repression invariably failed, since repression augmented the unconscious. But poetry *is* figurative language, and in poetry sublimation is accomplished through the self-limiting trope of metaphor, while repression is represented by the expansive trope of hyperbole, with all of its Sublime glories and Grotesque dangers. From the viewpoint of poetry, the "unconscious mind" is an oxymoron, since repressed material in poetry has no place to go but up, onto the heights of what Romanticism called the Imagination. Romantic Imagination, whether in Blake or Coleridge, does not represent a return of the repressed, but is identical with the process of repression itself.

An individual poetic imagination can defend itself against the force of another imagination only by troping, so that a successful defense against poetic tradition always answers repression by an increase in repression. The return of the repressed is only an utopian or apocalyptic dream much indulged in by Marxist speculation, and by assorted contemporary shamans who inspire what is still being termed a counter-culture. Authentic poets show us that Emersonian Compensation is always at work in poetry as in life: nothing is got for nothing. What returns in authentic poetry is never the repressed, but rather the daemonic or uncanny element within repression, which poetic tradition has called by various names, including the Sublime, and the Imagination, both of them hyperbolical figurations for something that has no referential aspect or literal meaning, but that nevertheless guarantees the survival and continuity of poetic tradition. Poets and readers go on questing for one another in order to give a voice to this daemonic impulse that informs and purifies repression. "Purifies" here has no moral or spiritual meaning but refers rather to a process by which the daemonic is reconciled with the writing of poetry.

"Daemonic," in this sense, refers to a realm of power that invades the human world yet seems apart from human origins or human ends. In a very early poem, a visionary lyric in the mode of Eberhart, but like Eberhart reaching back to Blake's "Tyger," Hill laments the inadequacy of poetic language to tell his own experience of daemonic influx:

> *I waited for the word that was not given,*
>
> *Pent up into a region of pure force,*
> *Made subject to the pressure of the stars;*
> *I saw the angels lifted like pale straws;*
> *I could not stand before those winnowing eyes*
>
> *And fell, until I found the world again.*

Hill dislikes his early poems, yet they are not only permanent achievements but also quite essential for understanding
all that comes after. "Genesis," for which he has a particular
dislike, is superb in itself, a perfect "first" poem, and also a
clear intimation of his largest debt to Blake's vision, which is
the conviction that the Creation and the Fall were the same
event. Another fine early poem, "In Memory of Jane Fraser"
(which Hill evidently dislikes most, of all his work), speaks of
a single, particular death as uncreating all of nature. For Hill,
the natural world is, at best, "a stunned repose," a judgment
that allies him to Blake rather than to Wordsworth, Shelley
rather than to Keats. Hill's poem on the death of Shelley
emphasizes the survival of the animal world, even as Shelley,
the Modern Poet proper, or New Perseus, quests aimlessly,
"clogged sword, clear, aimless mirror—/With nothing to
strike at or blind/in the frothed shallows."

The themes and procedures of both Hill's books of short
poems are summed up in what I judge to be his best single
poem, the double-sonnet called "Annunciations." Though
Hill transcends his own earlier mode in *Mercian Hymns* (as
will be seen), "Annunciations" is so important a poem that I
will discuss it at some length. A reader who can interpret
"Annunciations" can learn to interpret the rest of Hill, and
also acquire many insights that will aid in reading any truly
difficult poetry of the Post-Romantic tradition. For, in "Annunciations," Hill wrote what later tradition may judge to
have been the central shorter poem of his own generation,
a poem that is itself a despairing poetics, and a total vision
both of natural existence, and of the necessary limitations of
what we have learned to call imagination.

An "annunciation" can be any proclamation, but despite
Hill's plural title, the reverberation here depends upon the
Annunciation proper, the announcement of the Incarnation
by the Angel Gabriel in Luke 1:26–38. In some grim sense,
Hill's starting-point is the festival (25 March) celebrating Gabriel's announcement. But "the Word" here is not the Logos,
nor simply the words of poetry, all poetry, but the idealization of poetry that is so pervasive in Western tradition:

> *The Word has been abroad; is back, with a*
> *   tanned look*
> *From its subsistence in the stiffening-mire.*
> *Cleansing has become killing, the reward*
> *More touchable, overt, clean to the touch.*

This Word seems more a tourist than an Eliotic explorer; indeed a hygienic tourist-hunter. Returned, the questers sit together at a literary feast with their scholarly and critical admirers:

> *Now, at a distance from the steam of beasts,*
> *The loathly neckings and fat shook spawn*
> *(Each specimen-jar fed with delicate spawn)*
> *The searchers with the curers sit at meat*
> *And are satisfied.*

I do not know how to interpret this except as an attack upon everyone who has to do with poetry: poets, critics, teachers, students, readers. It is as though Yeats, after observing in vision his nymphs and satyrs copulating in the foam, his Innocents re-living their pain and having their wounds opened again, then attended a banquet in honor of his "News for the Delphic Oracle." The poem becomes a "specimen-jar," holding an aesthetic reduction of copulation and bleeding wounds. Is such an attack as Hill's legitimate, since it would apply as much to Homer as to any other poet? Is Hill attacking a false idealization of poetry or the *Ananke* that governs all poetry? The remainder of the first part of "Annunciations" will not answer these questions:

> *   Such precious things put down*
> *And the flesh eased through turbulence, the soul*
> *Purples itself; each eye squats full and mild*
> *While all who attend to fiddle or to harp*
> *For betterment, flavour their decent mouths*
> *With gobbets of the sweetest sacrifice.*

Primarily this is Hill's uncompromising attack upon himself, for more even than Yeats, or even his contemporary Ted Hughes, he writes a poetry whose subject is violence and pain, thus accepting the danger of easing the flesh through a vision of turbulence. Much of the success with readers, particularly British readers, of the later Yeats and of Hughes is surely based upon feeding the reader's eye with imaginary lust and suffering until that eye "squats full and mild." Hill's attack upon "all who attend to fiddle or to harp/For betterment" is therefore an attack upon the most traditional, Aristotelian defense of poetry, an attack upon the supposed function of catharsis. Poems are "gobbets of the sweetest sacrifice," and readers flavor their mouths decently even as decent Christians swallow the bread of communion. It becomes clear that Hill is attacking, ultimately, neither poetry nor religion, but the inescapable element that always darkens tradition, which is that the living, feeding upon the repressions of the dead, repress further and so become the sustenance of the dead. Hill's "sacrifice" is what Nietzsche and Freud would have termed an Antithetical Primal Word, for it is debatable whether the victims commemorated by the poem, or the readers, are the "sacrifice."

The Antithetical Primal Word of the second part of "Annunciations" is of course "love," and here the majestic bitterness of the Sublime triumphs in and over Hill:

> *O Love, subject of the mere diurnal grind,*
> *Forever being pledged to be redeemed,*
> *Expose yourself for charity; be assured*
> *The body is but husk and excrement.*
> *Enter these deaths according to the law,*
> *O visited women, possessed sons! Foreign lusts*
> *Infringe our restraints; the changeable*
> *Soldiery have their goings-out and comings-in*
> *Dying in abundance. Choicest beasts*
> *Suffuse the gutters with their colourful blood.*
> *Our God scatters corruption. Priests, martyrs,*
> *Parade to this imperious theme: 'O Love,*

You know what pains succeed; be vigilant; strive
To recognize the damned among your friends.'

If I could cite only one stanza by Hill as being wholly representative of him, it would be this, for here is his power, his despair and (in spite of himself) his Word, not in the sense of Logos but in the Hebraic sense of *davhar,* a word that is also an act, a bringing-forward of something previously held back in the self. This Word that rejects being a Word is a knowing misprision or mis-taking of tradition, but even the most revisionary of Words remains a Word, as Hill doubtless knows. Being willing to go on writing poems, however sparsely, is to believe that one possesses a Word of one's own to bring forward. When Hill says, "Our God scatters corruption," he means that the God of lovers (and of poets) is antithetical to Himself, that this God is the ambivalent deity of all Gnostics. I take it that "scatters" does not mean "drives away" but rather "increases" corruption by dispersal, which implies that "corruption" takes something of its root-meaning of "broken-to-pieces." Hill's subject then is the Gnostic or Kabbalistic "Breaking of the Vessels," the Fall that is simultaneously a Creation, as in his first, Blakean, chant-poem "Genesis."

Part II of "Annunciations" is thus more of a proclamation against Love than a prayer to Love. Love, addressed under its aspect of repetition, is urged to more honesty, and to a reductive awareness of the body. Corporeal passion lives and dies according to the old dispensation, or law, but Hill comes to proclaim a new Incarnation, which is only a Gnostic dying into yet more sexual abundance. As an incessant martyrologist, Hill grimly announces the imperious as against the imperial or Shakespearean theme. Love, who knows that pains only succeed or follow one another (but are never successful), is urged at least to distinguish its true martyrs among the panoply of its worshippers, and so recognize accurately its valid theme.

Repeated readings of "Annunciations" should clarify and justify Hill's densely impacted style, with its reliance upon figurations of hyperbole. Hill's mode is a negative or counter-Sublime, and his characteristic defense against the tradition he beautifully sustains and extends is an almost primal repression:

> *Not as we are but as we must appear,*
> *Contractual ghosts of pity; not as we*
> *Desire life but as they would have us live,*
> *Set apart in timeless colloquy:*
> *So it is required; so we bear witness,*
> *Despite ourselves, to what is beyond us,*
> *Each distant sphere of harmony forever*
> *Poised, unanswerable . . .*

This is again a Gnostic sublimity. Blake could still insist that pity survived only because we kept on rendering others piteous, but Hill comes later, and for him the intoxication of belatedness is to know that our reality and our desire are both negated by our appearance as legatees. It is tradition that makes us into "contractual ghosts of pity." A Beautiful Necessity represses us, and makes us bear witness to a dead but still powerful transcendence. Hill characterizes one of his sequences as "a florid grim music" or an "ornate and heartless music punctuated by mutterings, blasphemies and cries for help." A baroque pathos seems to be Hill's goal, with the ornateness his tribute to tradition, and the punctuation of pathos his outcry against tradition. Hill's is clearly a poetics of pain, in which all the calamities of history become so many poetic salutes, so many baroque meditations, always trapped in a single repetition of realization. Man is trapped "between the stones and the void," without majesty and without justice except for the errors of rhetoric, the illusions of poetic language. Like his own Sebastian Arrurruz, Hill's task is "to find value/In a bleak skill," the poet's craft of establishing true rather than false "sequences of pain."

"It must give pleasure," Stevens rightly insisted, and any critic responding to Hill should be prepared to say how and why Hill's poetry can give pleasure, and in what sense Hill's reader can defend himself from being only another decent mouth opened wide for the poetry-banquet. How is the reader to evade becoming "the (supposed) Patron" so bitterly invoked in the final poem of Hill's first book? The Gnostic answer, which is always a latecomer's answer, is that the reader must become not a patron but one of those unfallen who gave Hill's first book its title:

> *For the unfallen—the firstborn, or wise*
> *Councillor—prepared vistas extend*
> *As far as harvest; and idyllic death*
> *Where fish at dawn ignite the powdery lake.*

The final trope here is perhaps too Yeatsian, but the previous trope that gives back priority to the unfallen has a more High Romantic tenor, looking back to Keats' vision of Autumn. Hill cannot celebrate natural completion, but he always finds himself turning again "to flesh and blood and the blood's pain" despite his Gnostic desire to renounce for good "this fierce and unregenerate clay." Of his incessant ambivalence, Hill has made a strong poetry, one that battles tradition on tradition's own terms, and that attempts to make of its conscious belatedness an earliness. The accomplished reader responds to Hill's work as to any really strong poetry, for the reader too needs to put off his own belatedness, which is surely why we go on searching for strong poetry. We cannot live with tradition, and we cannot live without it, and so we turn to the strong poet to see how he acts out this ambivalence for us, and to see also if he can get beyond such ambivalence.

Hill begins to break through his own dialectics of tradition in *Mercian Hymns,* the sequence of prose-poems he published on the threshold of turning forty. His hero is Offa, an eighth century Midlands "king," who merges both into a spirit of place and into the poet celebrating him, particularly the poet-as-schoolboy, for *Mercian Hymns* is a kind of *Prelude*-in-little. Yet here the growth of a poet's mind is not stimulated by nature's teachings, but only by history and by dreams. Transcendence, for Hill, returned or re-entered the sublunary world in old tapestries, sculpture, and metal-work, but mostly in historicizing reverie, which is the substance of these hymns. With *Mercian Hymns*, Hill rather triumphantly "makes it new," and though the obsession with tradition is as strong, much of the ambivalence towards tradition is miraculously diminished. Indeed, certain passages in *Mercian Hymns* would approach sentimentality if the poet did not remain characteristically condensed and gnomic, with the familiar spectre of pain hovering uncannily close:

> *We have a kitchen-garden riddled with*
>   *toy-shards,*
> *with splinters of habitation. The children*
>   *shriek*
> *and scavenge, play havoc. They incinerate*
>   *boxes,*
> *rags and old tyres. They haul a sodden log,*
>   *hung*
> *with soft shields of fungus, and launch it*
>   *upon*
> *the flames.*

Difficult as Hill was earlier, *Mercian Hymns*, despite the limpidity of its individual sections, is the subtlest and most oblique of his works. It is not only hard to hold together, but there is some question as to what it is "about," though the necessary answer is akin to *The Prelude* again; Hill has at last no subject but his own complex subjectivity, and so the poem is "about" himself, which turns out to be his exchange of gifts with the Muse of History (section X). I suggest that the structure and meaning of *Mercian Hymns* is best approached through its rhetoric, which as before in Hill is largely that of metaleptic reversal or transumption, the dominant trope of Post-Romantic poetry in English. For a full analysis of the trope and its poetic history, I must refer to my book, *A Map of Misreading* and give only a brief account here. Transumption is the trope of a trope, or technically the metonymy of a metonymy. That is, it tends to be a figure that substitutes an aspect of a previous figure for that figure. Imagistically, transumption from Milton through the Romantics to the present tends to present itself in terms of earliness substituting for lateness, and more often than not to be the figure that concludes poems. Translated into psychoanalytic terms, transumption is either the psychic defense of introjection (identification) or of projection (refusal of identity), just as metaphor translates into the defense of sublimation, or hyperbole into that of repression. The advantage of transumption as a concluding trope for belated poems is that it achieves a kind of fresh priority or earliness, but always at the expense of the presentness of the present or living moment. Hill is as transumptive a poet, rhetorically, as Milton or Wordsworth or Wallace Stevens, and so he too is unable to celebrate a present joy.

There is no present time, indeed there is no self-presence in *Mercian Hymns*. Though Hill's own note on the sequence betrays some anxiety about what he calls anachronisms, the genius of his work excludes such anxiety. Nothing can be anachronistic when there is no present:

> *King of the perennial holly-groves, the riven*
>   *sand-*
> *stone: overlord of the M5: architect of the his-*
> *toric rampart and ditch, the citadel at*
>   *Tamworth,*
> *the summer hermitage in Holy Cross: guardian*
>   *of*
> *the Welsh Bridge and the Iron Bridge:*
>   *contractor*
> *to the desirable new estates: saltmaster:*
>   *money-*
> *changer: commissioner for oaths:*
>   *martyrologist:*
> *the friend of Charlemagne.*

'I liked that,' said Offa, 'sing it again.'

It is not that Offa has returned to merge with the poet, or that Hill has gone back to Offa. Hill and Offa stand together in a figuration that has introjected the past and the future, while projecting the present. Hill's epigraph, from the neglected poet and essayist, C. H. Sisson, analogizes his own conduct as private person and Offa's conduct of government, in all aspects of conduct having to do with "object and justification." Hill's struggle, as person and as poet, is with the repressive power of tradition, with the anxieties of history. Offa is seen by Hill as "the starting-cry of a race," as the master of a Primal Scene of Instruction, an imposition of order that fixates subsequent repression in others, which means to start an inescapable tradition. By reconciling himself with Offa, Hill comes close to accepting the necessary violence of tradition that earlier had induced enormous ambivalences in his poetry.

This acceptance, still somber but no longer grim, produces the dominant tone of *Mercian Hymns*, which is a kind of Wordsworthian "sober coloring" or "still sad music of humanity." But the sequence's vision remains Blakean rather than Wordsworthian, for the world it pictures is still one in which Creation and Fall cannot be distinguished, and at the end Offa is fallen Adam or every man: "he left behind coins, for his lodging, and traces of red mud." The reader sees that each hymn is like the inscription on one of Offa's hammered coins, and that these coins are literally and figuratively the price of a living tradition, its perpetual balance of Creation and Fall. Hill has succeeded, obliquely, in solving his aesthetic-moral problem as a poet, but the success is as equivocal and momentary as the pun on "succeed" in "Annunciations." Hill now knows better "what pains succeed," and his moving sequence helps his readers to the same knowledge.

No critical introduction to a poet only just past forty in age can hope to prophesy his future development. I have seen no poems written by Hill since *Mercian Hymns*, but would be surprised if he did not return to the tighter mode of *For The Unfallen* and *King Log*, though in a finer tone. His achievement to date, as gathered in his volume, seems to me to transcend the more copious work of his contemporary rivals: Hughes, Gunn, Kinsella, Tomlinson, Silkin. Good as they are, they lack poetic strength when compared with Hill. He has the persistence to go on wrestling with the mighty dead—Blake, Wordsworth, Shelley, Yeats—and to make of this ghostly struggle a fresh sublimity. He is indeed a poet of the Sublime, a mode wholly archaic yet always available to us again, provided a survivor of the old line comes to us:

> *Against the burly air I strode,*
> *Where the tight ocean heaves its load,*
> *Crying the miracles of God.*

12

The Sorrows of American-Jewish Poetry

American-Jewish literature, in English, began most inauspiciously with the verse of Emma Lazarus, whose intentions were noble, but who rarely rose even to the level of the English Romantic poet, Mrs. Felicia Hemans (whose much-mourned early loss, popularity, and general badness might inspire us to term her the Sylvia Plath of her age). Unfortunately, Emma Lazarus was an involuntary prophet, for though it causes me real grief to say this, the achievement of American-Jewish poets down to the present moment remains a modest and mixed one. There are no Bellows or Malamuds among them, though there are a few signs that this melancholy estimate some day may need to be revised upward.

I wish to be precise about this; there are a number of good poets, in several generations, with a particularly thick concentration of those now in their late thirties or early forties. As a broad grouping they compare favorably enough with most of what is now going. But no poet with the high individuality of the major sequence of modern American poets —E. A. Robinson, Robert Frost, Wallace Stevens, William Carlos Williams, Ezra Pound, Marianne Moore, T. S. Eliot, John Crowe Ransom, R. P. Warren, E. E. Cummings, Hart Crane, Theodore Roethke, Elizabeth Bishop—seems likely to emerge from among them, any more than a single American-Jewish poet of undoubted major status has established himself in a century now more than two-thirds gone. I would find it irrational to suppose that this is accidental (though I would be pleased to believe that) and I turn to the process of critical surmise so as to attempt to account for so melancholy a phenomenon.

A comparison with Yiddish poetry, so much of the best of which has been written in America, seems to me an inevitable starting point. Moshe Leib Halpern and Mani Leib at the least—probably also H. Leivick and Jacob Glatstein—are more impressive poets, in my experience as a reader, than any American-Jewish poet who has written in English. This is not to sentimentalize the legitimate if strictly limited achievement of even the best Yiddish poets, but only to recognize the self-truncation, the uneasiness, the inhibiting and poetically destructive excessive self-consciousness of American-Jewish poetry. Admirers of Charles Reznikoff, Louis Zukofsky, Delmore Schwartz, Howard Nemerov, and the many Jewish poets of the generation after would dissent from my general judgment, but a dispassionate view of the matter will sustain my sorrowful conclusion. There have been, and go on being, very good minor poets aplenty, but the more deeply one reads in them the more they do tend to merge into one another. Those who stand out, like the mock-bardic Allen Ginsberg, are distinctive primarily by being egregious, like Norman Mailer in his prose and his public manifestations.

In his book on American-Jewish literature, Allen Gutt-mann, sensitively and accurately perplexed, asks: "But where are the poets?" and comes up with Karl Shapiro and two poets of my own generation, Irving Feldman and John Hollander, all of whom he discusses quite usefully.* I will consider these, and add a number besides, but am compelled still to stay a while longer with the problem: Why haven't the poets been better?

The most distinguished Jewish poet writing in English in this century was clearly the Londoner Isaac Rosenberg, killed in World War I at the age of twenty-seven. Rosenberg's strength is not in the famous "Trench Poems," but in a handful of quasi-biblical fragments, such as this:

---

*Allen Guttmann, *The Jewish Writer in America: Assimilation and the Crisis of Identity* (New York: Oxford University Press, 1971).

A worm fed on the heart of Corinth,
Babylon and Rome:
Not Paris raped tall Helen,
But this incestuous worm,
Who lured her vivid beauty
To his amorphous sleep.
England! famous as Helen
Is thy betrothal sung
To him the shadowless,
More amorous than Solomon.

It isn't often one can call a prophetic fragment Blake-like, and be observing with accuracy, yet here Rosenberg deserves the comparison. The poem turns on the fine play between "amorphous" and "amorous," the gently sinister introduction of the shadowless Satan, and the evocation of sexual excess in a continuum from Corinth to Solomon. Taken together with the subtle indirection of the prophetic warning to turn now, before the betrothal is consummated, these moral insights fuse into a powerful Hebraic pattern. Where, in his non-biblical poems, Rosenberg rarely could arrive at mature terms with his English literary influences, his biblical fragments do show the achievement of a poetry firmly Jewish.

The closest American equivalent to Rosenberg was the even more tragic Samuel Greenberg, brought to the United States from Vienna in 1900, at the age of seven, to endure the Lower East Side and to die of tuberculosis at twenty-three. Greenberg is remembered today only because Hart Crane read his poems in manuscript, and reworked some of them in the lyric "Emblems of Conduct" and in the "Voyages." Educated only through the seventh grade, Greenberg found his precursor by reading Emerson, whose essays and poems are echoed all through Greenberg's work. Amazingly, Greenberg was a true prophet of the direction the best American-Jewish writing would take, for it seems clear today that Bellow, Malamud, and the better poets maturing now, constitute a variety of American Romanticism, an amalgama-

tion of Emerson's "optative mood" with the moral pressures
of Jewish tradition. Sometimes in Greenberg the amalgama-
tion results, not surprisingly, in moving parallels to Emily
Dickinson, as in "Regret at Parting":

> *"Our God!" in prayer is said;*
> *"Our child!" announced so, too—*
> *And its senses that grasp your heart*
> *That travels through speechless awe.*
> *Beware of the intellectual, changing mood*
> *That trembles a universe afar:*
> *Deep in thy shadowed soul*
> *Immortal creatings are!*
>
> . . . .
>
> *O friend, a pardon in a reviewed past,*
> *That inner selfish brand*
> *The Almighty has deemed to brush our path;*
> *Soon we part—I grasp thy hand!*

The formal inadequacy is clear enough, but so is the subtle
probing of a profound and desperate religious temperament.
When, in a double handful of Emersonian lyrics, Greenberg
overcomes his formal limitations, something close to greatness in the visionary mode is given to us. Here is "The Glass
Bubbles," Greenberg's version of the "transparent eyeball"
of Emerson's *Nature:*

> *The motion of gathering loops of water*
> *Must either burst or remain in a moment.*
> *The violet colors through the glass*
> *Throw up little swellings that appear*
> *And spatter as soon as another strikes*
> *And is born; so pure are they of colored*
> *Hues, that we feel the absent strength*
> *Of its power. When they begin they gather*
> *Like sand on the beach: each bubble*
> *Contains a complete eye of water.*

The immense sorrow of the transitoriness, the ebb answering the flow, of Emersonian vision and inspiration, has never been set down so gently or so persuasively. Elsewhere, anticipating Crane, Greenberg found inevitable expression for the fate of Emerson's Orphic Bard when fallen upon evil days:

> *I live in an age where the age lives alone,*
> *And lonesome doth it rage*
> *Where the Bard dare not come.*

But what is Jewish about the poetry of the Emersonian Greenberg? The God he addresses, who is not a Person in whom a believer has faith, but the God of the Torah, beyond personality, in Whose Way Greenberg must try to walk. In his many plangent, unfinished, frequently incoherent hymns to this God, Greenberg sought to win acceptance of poverty, illness, early death, but achieved only the brave pathos of a tempered anguish.

Greenberg died just after the fashions of literary modernism had begun to inundate America and Britain, and he was strangely fortunate in his self-education, for the writers who moved him—Keats, Shelley, Thoreau, Emerson above all—were none of them inimical to the relative naturalism and humanism of Jewish tradition. American-Jewish poets from the Twenties down to the present day have found themselves, more often than not, in the dilemma of Hart Crane: how can one accommodate one's vision to the metric and rhetoric of Eliot, Pound, Williams, and their followers? Poets as various as Charles Reznikoff and Delmore Schwartz, despite all their gifts, failed finally as poets for lacking a language appropriate to their desired stance. Reznikoff, whose selected volume, *By The Waters of Manhattan*, is nevertheless an impressive testament, should have been the American-Jewish poet in whom younger writers could find a precursor of real strength. A few writers of talent have found aid in Reznikoff, but prolonged reading in him depresses me with the sense of unnecessary loss. Why attempt to translate

Yehudah Halevi into the idiom of Pound and William Carlos Williams? Is the form of this in any way appropriate to its burden?

> *My heart in the East*
> *and I at the farthest West:*
> *how can I taste what I eat or find it sweet*
> *while Zion*
> *is in the cords of Edom and I*
> *bound by the Arab?*
> *Beside the dust of Zion*
> *all the good of Spain is light;*
> *and a light thing to leave it.*

In one poem, Reznikoff sadly and accurately remarks that he has "married the speech of strangers," and he tends to be most moving when he studies the nostalgias:

> *My grandfathers were living streams*
> *in the channel of a broad river;*
> *but I am a stream that must find its way*
> *among blocking rock*
> *and through sands and sand.*

The principal name among American-Jewish poets in the generation after Reznikoff is clearly that of Delmore Schwartz, where the inherited idiom is Eliot's, rather than Pound's or Williams'. But, like so many poets of his generation (Stanley Kunitz, Howard Nemerov, Ben Belitt), Schwartz curiously evaded whatever Jewish concerns existed in his consciousness. The exception in Schwartz is the patriarchal figure of Abraham, who enters the early poem, "For the One Who Would Not Take His Life in His Hands," is oddly invoked in tandem with Orpheus in another poem, and then makes one of a trilogy of three late poems, together with "Sarah" and "Jacob." Schwartz's "Abraham" is impressive work, except that the irrelevance of the precursor who found Schwartz makes again, as in the Jewish poems of Reznikoff and Louis Zukofsky, for a disturbing incongruity between style and imaginative attitude. With Isaac restored to him, Abraham sums up his life in the accents of the late T. S. Eliot:

> *And I am not gratified*
> *Nor astonished. It has never been otherwise:*
> *Exiled, wandering, dumbfounded by riches,*
> *Estranged among strangers, dismayed by the*
> *   infinite sky,*
> *An alien to myself until at last the caste of*
> *   the last alienation*
> *The angel of death comes to make the alienated*
> *   and indestructible one a part of his famous*
> *   society.*

Clearly there is a peculiar problem of poetic influence at work among American-Jewish poets. Strong poets tend to achieve an individualized voice by first all-but-merging with a precursor and then by pulling away from him, usually by way of a complex process of fault-finding and actual misinterpretation of the precursor. All post-Enlightenment poetry in English tends to be a displaced Protestantism anyway, so that the faith in a Person easily enough is displaced into an initial devotion to the god-like precursor poet. This, to understate it, is hardly a very Jewish process, and yet something like it seems necessary if poets are to continue to be incarnated. However far from Jewish tradition they may be, something recalcitrant in the spirit of young Jewish poets prevents them from so initially wholehearted a surrender to a Gentile precursor, and indeed makes them nervous about the process itself. Displaced Judaism tends to become one or another kind of a moralism, but not the pragmatic religion-of-poetry that young poets, for a time, must accept.

A glance at two poetical Shapiros—Karl and the less-well-known but more interesting Harvey—can begin to test my speculations, before I move on to my own generation of poets —Irving Feldman, John Hollander, Richard Howard, Allen

Grossman, Edward Field, Robert Mezey, and a few others, including the celebrated Ginsberg.

Mr. Guttmann sensibly points out that Karl Shapiro, who has been so fierce against modernist literary criticism, nevertheless "offered a metaphoric defense of peoplehood." The defense in fact, as John Hollander noted in a 1958 review of Shapiro's *Poems of a Jew*, just barely dodged "a stereotyped Gentile intellectual's view of Jew as victor-victim." Right now, Shapiro's defense seems to me to have been merely absurd. In justice to Shapiro, I quote from his Preface:

> . . . the modern Jew, insofar as he is a Jew, remains intransigent and thankless, man in all his raw potentiality. . . . He is man left over, after everything that can happen has happened.

Nothing is more self-deceptive for any Jewish writer than the notion that he can define the Jew. Whatever else is possible for him, it is hardly given to him that he may forge the uncreated conscience of his people, the people of the Book and of the *halakhah*. When Saul Bellow, with his customary and invariable wisdom, wished to create a hero with "raw potentiality" or "man left over," he gave us Henderson, a pure Emersonian and Gentile American. Whatever else it is that a Jew may be, his tradition cannot allow him to be Natural Man alone.

The best of Karl Shapiro's overtly Jewish poems is probably "The Synagogue," yet even here the reader confronts a curious mixture of sentimentalism, misinformation about Judaism, and the by now too-familiar incongruity of an overtly Jewish stance being rendered in an alien idiom, here that of W. H. Auden and Louis MacNeice. Even more bothersome is the technique of defining what is Jewish by seeing it only as the negation of the Catholic:

> *Our wine is wine, our bread is harvest bread*
> *That feeds the body and is not the body.*
> *Our blessing is to wine but not the blood*

Nor to sangreal the sacred dish. We bless
The whiteness of the dish and bless the water
And are not anthropaphagous to him.

Harvey Shapiro's poetry, so much of which turns upon Jewish themes, lacks only a language adequate to its genuine and accurate apprehensions of Jewish dilemmas. Its style goes back to Williams, by way of the school of Reznikoff, Zukofsky, George Oppen, and the spareness of this style is rarely adequate to Harvey Shapiro's own intensities. I read this poet's major collections *(Battle Report: Selected Poems* and *This World)* with continuous sympathy, but longing also to hear him speak out in a more expressionistic, highly colored, biblicizing idiom than he can bear to allow himself. Take as a characteristic poem by him, "The Way," from *This World:*

Why are you crying in Israel,
Brother, I ask as I switch over
To the emergency oxygen.
Do we have to dig up all
The Freudian plumbing
To reconstruct our lives?
If I had clean air like you
I think I could breathe.
As it is my mouthpiece keeps
Clogging and my eyes blur.
I can barely make it
Between the desks.
And you, walking
Between orange trees
Among the companions,
And still so far from the way.

With its fine economy, this parable conveys rather more than the climactic Israeli scenes of Philip Roth's *Portnoy's Complaint.* The "Way" is *halakhah* or right conduct, based on a Mishnaic word meaning "to walk." As a poet, knowing that "my mouthpiece keeps/Clogging," Shapiro laments the universality of the departure from *halakhah,* as far away in Israel as in America. Spare and moving as the poem is, the deep reader in me wants more, and laments the attachment of Shapiro to so minimal a modernist tradition, so sadly lacking in the rhetorical resources that his insights desperately require.

Richard Howard, taking a retrospective view of his own book *Alone With America* ("essays on the art of poetry in the United States since 1950") notes that fifteen out of the forty-one poets surveyed are Jews, and concludes that they have "a certain ease within the alienation of poetry" and that they move "upon the Word naturally, by tradition, as it were." This is handsomely said, and completely untrue, as I have been trying to demonstrate. The Jewish poets Howard studies fall into the two patterns described above. Either they evade or ignore their Jewishness (for many, of course, it hardly exists) or they confront the fearful problem of expressing their cultural diversity in the essentially hostile idiom bequeathed them by the various modernist or post-modernist masters. Howard himself, who has emerged in the dramatic monologues of *Untitled Subjects* and *Findings* as the best modern continuator of Browning, has only one poem on a Jewish theme, the remarkable "A Montefiore Memorandum," an urbanely bitter meditation on Wagner's hatred for Meyerbeer.

As I contemplate the poets of my own generation, I find it difficult to avoid the conclusion that the Jews among them work on under peculiarly internalized disadvantages. The clearest achievements of the poetic generation already seem to center elsewhere, in A. R. Ammons, John Ashbery, W. S. Merwin, Mark Strand, James Wright, among others. When Sidney Hook lucidly protested Sartre's notion that Jewish authenticity was dependent upon the self-acceptance of ancestral identity, he movingly spoke of giving all individuals "the right to freely determine themselves as Jews or Gentiles, as citizens of one country or another, as cultural heirs of Socrates or Aquinas. . . ." But poets are not citizens or cultural heirs in any philosophic sense; they do not choose their tradition but must be chosen by it. Most directly, they require *to be found by* the inevitable, the liberating precursor, if ever they are to be capable of finding themselves at all.

Of the poets of his generation, Irving Feldman has been the most directly Jewish in his thematic concerns. His first book, *Works and Days*, all but drowns in the turbulence of these concerns, while his second, *The Pripet Marshes*, does drown, engulfed by his temerity in taking the Holocaust as subject. Elie Wiesel, Paul Celan, Nelly Sachs can touch the horror with authority, but British and American writers need to avoid it, as we have no warrant for imagination in that most terrible of areas. Feldman becomes both a serious and a vitally Jewish poet only in his recent volume, *Magic Papers*, which Mr. Guttmann finds "almost entirely without reference to Jewishness." The long title-poem, as well as "The Word" and "The Father," are extraordinary efforts to recapture a lost relation to living tradition. Necessarily, Feldman quests for an appropriate voice ("My voice/is thick, is mud,/my depth of anguish is/my depth of reservation./I detest the wryness of my voice,/its ulteriority, its suffering/—what is not lived only/can suffer so.") The quest is answered in "Psalm," Feldman's best poem, where a massive and disciplined anguish mounts from its initial recognition: "There is no singing without God" to a final stanza in which the poet does stand at the turning:

> *But if I enter, vanished bones*
> *of the broken temple, lost people,*
> *and go in the sanctum of the scattered*
> *house, saying words like these,*
> *forgive—my profaneness is*
> *insufferable to me—and bless, make fertile*
> *my words, give them a radiant burden!*
> *Do not deny your blessing, speak to us.*

Feldman is evidently in the midst of the difficult process of becoming a genuinely devotional poet, within the immense grandeur of his tradition, now rendered all but inaccessible by the circumstances of history. John Hollander, a skeptical polymath, has no way back to Judaism, but is ruggedly and constantly aware of the burdens of his almost-lost tradition. His autobiographical long poem of 1965, *Visions from the Ramble*, attains one of its visionary climaxes on Tisha B'av, mingling the Lamentation of Jeremiah with the prophecy of ruin for New York as the Newer Jerusalem:

> *But here in this room, when the last*
> *Touches of red in the sky have sunk, these few*
>   *men, lumped*
> *Toward the end away from the windows, some*
>   *with bleachy white*
> *Handkerchiefs comically knotted at each corner,*
>   *worn*
> *In place of black skullcaps, read what was*
>   *wailed at a wall*
> *In the most ruined of cities. Only the City is*
>   *missing.*

It is in *The Night Mirror,* his recent volume, that Hollander emerges as a fully integrated poet, who can deal with the very diverse elements of his own consciousness, including his Jewish heritage. "At The New Year" is a powerful secularization of that celebration, and an extraordinary poem addressed to Borges on the Golem vividly recreates the world of "my ancestor, the Rabbi Loew of Prague." The almost-Yiddish lyric, "The Long and the Short of It," ends in the mode of Ecclesiastes: "They who look out of/The windows are darkened," and the same plangency is conveyed by the immensely somber closing lyric, "As the Sparks Fly Upward." The operative influence upon so many of the poems in *The Night Mirror* is Yiddish poetry, particularly the work of M. L. Halpern and of Mani Leib. Included in the volume are versions of two of Halpern's most mordant pieces, "The Will" and "The Bird" and Mani Leib's poignant "I Am." Readers consulting *A Treasury of Yiddish Poetry,* edited by Irving Howe and Eliezer Greenberg, will discover that Hollander's translations are one of the staples of the volume. Abraham Reisen, Leib, Halpern, Itzik Feffer, Jacob Sternberg, A. Glanz-Leyeles, Eliezer Steinberg, Eliezer Greenberg, Aaron Zeitlin—Hollander renders all of them with remarkable diversity, vividness, and particularity. I am reminded of the vigor and sense of release that Rossetti attained in his translations of Italian poetry. It is no insult to Rossetti to see that his version of Dante's strong sestina, "To the Dim Light and the Large Circle of Shade," is his strongest poem, and similarly I do not dispraise Hollander in judging his version of Halpern's "The Bird" to be his best work so far. I give only the first two stanzas of this superb phantasmagoria:

> *Well, this bird comes, and under his wing is a*
> > *crutch*
> *And he asks why I keep my door on the latch;*
> *So I tell him that right outside the gate*
> *Many robbers watch and wait*
> *To get at the hidden bit of cheese,*
> *Under my ass, behind my knees.*
>
> *Then through the keyhole and the crack in the*
> > *jamb*
> *The bird bawls out he's my brother Sam,*
> *And tells me I'll never begin to believe*
> *How sorely he was made to grieve*
> *On shipboard, where he had to ride*
> *Out on deck, he says, from the other side.*

In the grotesque power of Halpern's mode, as in the very different poignance of Mani Leib, Hollander has begun to be discovered by precursors wholly available to his imaginative needs. For Halpern and Leib, in the full context of American literature, are minor but authentic late Romantics, desperately defrauded seers of a transcendental vision. Hollander's own subsequent development is likely to come somewhere in the broad currents of American Romantic tradition.

Though no other poets of their generation seem to have progressed as far as Feldman and Hollander in solving the Jewish-American apparent dichotomy, several deserve consideration as working at the problem. Edward Field's astonishing "Mark Twain and Sholem Aleichem," a brilliant invention, takes the two writers to Coney Island, where "pretty soon they were both floundering in the sea." Field's closing vision is precariously balanced between affection and despair:

> *They had both spent their lives trying to make*
> *the world a better place*
> *And both had gently faced their failure.*
> *If humor and love had failed, what next?*
> *They were both drowning and enjoying it now,*
> *Two old men of the two worlds, the old and the*
> *new,*
> *Splashing about in the sea like crazy monks.*

So memorable an extinction of two literary fathers can be balanced against Allen Ginsberg's many lame invocations of his own literary fathers as the ever-living. The chanter of *Howl, Kaddish,* and many lesser litanies is as much beyond the reach of criticism as Norman Mailer; both have been raised to that bad eminence where every fresh failure is certain of acclaim as an event, something that has happened and so is news, like floods, fires, and other stimulating disasters. The genuine painfulness of reading through *Kaddish* is not an *imaginative* suffering for the reader, but is precisely akin to the agony we sustain when we are compelled to watch the hysteria of strangers. Still, time will judge against us on Ginsberg as, I believe, on Mailer; for here and now, it is sufficient firmly to note Ginsberg's irrelevance to the achievement I seek to sketch.

It seems clear to me that American-Jewish poetry as it moves into maturity will become more and more overtly a blend of a devotional strain and a late Romantic visionary intensity. These are representative excerpts, all of considerable distinction:

You will awaken with the dignity
Of beauty still upon you, and go forth
Like one who has not long since worshipped.
It will be like some mysterious Sabbath
When the Book was taken from the Ark,
The crown, the breastplate with its wreath of
*   bells,*
And all the royalty that hides the Law
Opened and laid aside, and you knew the
*   words,*
As a man knows a woman who is raven haired
*   and odorous,*
You will be as infinite as your desire
Knowing the Law is young and beautiful
When you awake one morning in your cold
*   hotel*
After a night of vision.
      ALLEN GROSSMAN, "The Law"

Some other side of memory
And nothing still to think;
The soul consumed a heaviness
Of thirst it couldn't drink. . . .
      ALVIN FEINMAN, "Covenant"

How rarely your mercy visits me,
My king, my father;
And so, most of my days, I am your wandering
*   son*
Who has cast his lot like a prophet
In the desert of his days.

And your deliverance that comes to me then,
My father, my king,
Is like a well that the wanderer came on at last,
When he had almost prayed for death from
*   thirst*
And the heat that shrivels the body.
     ROBERT MEZEY, "On the Equator"

After he had maimed the dragon deep
and throned us in new limbs of everlasting
opening to fable the mortal stars
we wept praises and harped the flood of his
    word.
Our tears might have filled an ocean
our blood a sea.
We followed or wantoned before him,
He was our serpent, flexible and brazen,
on his broad back we crossed the seas
or stood precipitously between worlds.
Come now, with a staunch heart, a steady love,
redeem his river-bones from Egypt,
fetch home his visions, and out of his grave
make a vineyard to plant the voice of the dove.
    GEOFFREY HARTMAN, "Mariner's Song"

For all their differences, particularly in style, these passages move toward a common thematic center, which they share with Feldman's "Psalm." There is no recovery of covenant, of the Law, without confronting again, in all deep tribulation, the God of the Fathers, Who is beyond image as He is beyond personality, and Who can be met only by somehow again walking His Way. For all our mutual deep skepticisms, the increasing enterprise of American-Jewish poetry is what it must be: persistence in seeking to recover what once our ancestors had. The motto for that poetry's future can be taken from Rabbi Tarphon: "You are not required to complete the work, but neither are you free to desist from it."

13

Nebuchadnezzar's Dream

HOLLANDER'S *THE HEAD OF THE BED*

*Thy dream, and the visions of thy head upon thy
bed, are these;*
DANIEL 2:28

*   *   *

Lilith, bride of Sammael as she became, nevertheless began as Adam's first wife. Perhaps she is due for some worship
in these days of Liberation, and for all I know she currently
may have her overt following, in one coven or another. But
John Hollander is a traditionalist, and particularly in his
nightmares. The *Zohar* tells us that, after being supplanted
by Eve, Lilith "flew to the cities of the sea coast," thus explaining her manifestations to the poet in New York City.
The demoness is immortal, and I would be surprised that so
few poems have been devoted to her, except that I assume
she is widely celebrated under the disguise of many names,
not all of them mythological. Hollander names her only in
the fourth and fifth sections of his dark sequence, but she
lurks in or near every tercet of every part.

The "two countries" of Hollander's prose prelude are life
and the dream, and the Trumpeter of a prophecy belongs to
both. At the poem's conclusion, the dreamer wakes "to a
trumpet of light" only to discover that the demarcations have
become ghostlier, the sound keener, and the nightmare has
been assimilated to life. Whether the poet is like the Nebuchadnezzar of the prophets Daniel and Blake, a Nebuchadnezzar who would not learn from the visions of the
night, or hopefully more like the Nebuchadnezzar of Kierke-

gaard, who surmounted being a natural man, the close of this sequence does not tell us. In Babylon, early in the sixth century B.C., Nebuchadnezzar II, the High King, set down the public prayer: "May I attain eternal age." The Hebrew prophets who hated him gave him that age. It was Kierkegaard, following them, who gave the King of Babylon a true latecomer's chant, as the sufferer of seven transformations brooded obsessively on the Hebrew Lord, murmuring as refrain: "No one knows where he dwells." In so brooding, Kierkegaard's dreamer approached, not redemption, but the recognition of what was needful for redemption. Blake's Nebuchadnezzar, in his bestial crouch depicted on the last plate of *The Marriage of Heaven and Hell,* remains a less fanciful emblem of the relation of any natural selfhood to the world of its dream-work.

As I brood on *The Head of the Bed,* I am haunted by the truth Hollander begins to express as well as suffer: that the true muse of all poets necessarily afflicted with a sense of latecoming is Lilith. How does the tradition that speaks through Hollander's sequence call upon us to interpret her?

Begin with the assumption that the vision men call Lilith is formed primarily by their anxiety at what they perceive to be the beauty of a woman's body, a beauty they believe to be, at once, far greater and far less than their own. Lilith becomes the threat to male narcissism, and so the true muse, not the false idealization of a muse that crowds through poetic history. For what is the function of a muse? To make the poet remember. But what has he forgotten? That he is, as the Emersonian poet Christopher Cranch wrote, only a column left alone of a temple once complete. Lilith, "body's beauty" as Rossetti called her, reminds the poet that he is bound to origins and not to ends, that his autonomy is (at best) a saving fiction.

Hollander's triadic melodies, unlike the Trumpeter's, are knowingly unclear, and break out only through the swirling mists of the Fuseli-like phantasmagoria of nightmare that rides with her ninefold of anxieties all through this Kabbalistic sequence. The mythic world giving context to *The Head of the Bed* is the over-determined thicket of meanings that made up the theosophical universe of the Great Rabbi, Isaac Luria, Lion of Safed, and of the copious redactor, Moses de Leon, who compiled the *Zohar.*

Kabbalah, in its root, is another word meaning tradition, that which was not only given but was joyously received. Always in Kabbalistic literature what moves and repels me are the stigmata of a psychology of latecoming. No latecomer is capable of explaining that which forever possesses priority over him, and no latecomer is capable of wholly fresh creation. The Kabbalistic interpreter is neither an explainer nor a poet; he is necessarily a revisionist. And this must be his working principle (which I render from the *Zohar* III, 152a):

> As wine in a jar, if it is to keep, so is the Torah, contained within the outer garment. Such a garment is constituted of many stories; but we, we are required to pierce the garment.

The Head of the Bed, however Hollander came to it, is a Kabbalistic text, haunted by an implicit psychology of belatedness. As its interpreter, I swerve from it, strive to complete it antithetically, empty myself out in relation to its self-emptying, raise myself to a Sublime that will counter its afflatus, purge myself as it purges itself into solitude, and seek finally to make it return from its death in the colors as much my own as any of Hollander's. Wilde, visionary critic who greatly deplored the Decay of Lying, would bless my quest to see this text as in itself it really is not, which is to say, as to me truly it is. For the sequence is Hollander's version of a Nebuchadnezzar's dream, and I come to it as its Daniel.

The dreamer in canto 1 creates his images out of rhymes and consonances, a process sporadic but incessant throughout the sequence. *Heard, wind, birds, perched, wood, bird, hurting, words;* the movement indeed is from "broken aspirates" to "where, fluttering, first words/Emerge," according to a dream-equation: *words* = *birds.* What the sleeper dreams is the poet's origins *qua* poet, the primal scene of

Poetic Incarnation being here not the Whitmanian "ebbs and throbs . . . with a shore rhythm" near a maternal ocean, but the "pulsing of dark groves," a sacred wood paternal and sacrificial. When, at the start of canto 2, the sleeper is awakened prematurely by his own hair, "Herr Haar," he confronts an ancestral skull in the night-wall, and again we overhear a faint, unmistakable Oedipal guilt. In canto 3 the sleeper associates the New York night with the memory of a watchful crone out of childhood, forerunner of darker mysteries, as these three introductory cantos close.

With the dense, Pre-Raphaelite canto 4, the sequence proper begins. Though the influence of Rossetti is direct (his version of Villon, and his "Body's Beauty" from *The House of Life*), the verbal style is precisely that of the American Pre-Raphaelitism of Trumbull Stickney and Conrad Aiken:

> *Now in the palace gardens warm with age,*
> *On lawn and flower-bed this afternoon*
> *The thin November-coloured foliage*
> *Just as last year unfastens lilting down.*
> S T I C K N E Y , *Eride, v*

> *And in the hanging gardens there is rain*
> *From midnight until one, striking the leaves*
> *And bells of flowers, and stroking bales of*
>   *planes*
> *And drawing slow arpeggios over pools.*
> A I K E N , "And in the Hanging Gardens"

Hollander's erotic dream studies the nostalgias with an American belatedness, identifying the poet with sad Biblical heroines of rejection and exile, yet distinguishing between the passive outcasts and the self-reliant (Orpah and Martha, in preference to Vashti and Hagar; see the second poem, "Orpah Returns to Her People," in Hollander's first book of poems, *A Crackling of Thorns*, 1958). This distinction vanishes with the enthrallment to Lilith, a night-girl about whom we cannot learn too much. As the Adversary Female of Kabbalah, she presides over many visionary fantasies, but they can be fitted to a single pattern: she is the muse of self-gratification, of dark secret love, of Narcissus encountering himself in the vegetable glass of nature. Mother of imps, Lilith is a perpetually self-replenishing daemoness, and truly the eternal goddess of all latecomers. For Hollander, descendant of the Kabbalistic Rabbi Loew of Prague, she is, remarkably, a being of light, and a vegetation goddess, in a scene that seems drawn by Blake's disciple, Edward Calvert. Compare his remarkable wood engraving, "The Ploughman" *(Victoria and Albert Museum)* to this:

> *. . . where faces blossomed*
> *Out of the darkness, where creepers mingled*
> *With long, low-lying trunks, humming among*
> *Damp hollows, herding and gathering there,*
> *But unheard by him undreaming . . .*

Hollander's vision also is of a secondary paradise, but for so guilty a sensibility every paradise belongs to Lilith, or to her surrogate, "Madam Cataplasma, her anointment/Vast," whose name means "poultice" (see Tourneur's *The Revenger's Tragedy*). Lilith's origins are properly hidden in mythology, but the name seems vaguely Sumerian, and most Midrashic tradition insists on her priority over our mother Eve. Hollander speaks of 'a filthy myth of Lilith,' filling the mouth with almost too much luxury of sound, because of the tradition that God formed Lilith neither from pure red clay and dust, like Adam, nor from Adam's rib, like Eve, but from sediment and various filth.

Tradition holds also that Lilith abandoned Adam because of a quarrel over sexual dominance, particularly related to the problem of position in intercourse, with Adam insisting upon the missionary posture, and Lilith refusing to lie beneath him, as she would not yield priority to clay over sediment, dust over filth. If Lilith's name *was* of Hebrew origin, presumably it derived from the word for "night" (hence Hollander's "nightgirl"), but more likely she began as a Babylonian wind-demon (hence the 'coarse breath fanning the closed air' in Hollander's fifth canto). For nearly all subsequent tradition, our filthy myths of Lilith stem from the *Zohar*, where she is the female of the Leviathan, and many other dark manifestations. But this is her central epiphany, which I translate from *Zohar, Vayikra,* 19a:

> In the Great Abyss, down in the depth, there is that spirit called Lilith, a hot and burning female, who first had intercourse with Adam. When Adam was created and his body finished, the spirits of the Left Side, a thousand in number, congregated around the completed body, each one attempting to penetrate it, until finally God drove them away by a descending cloud, that came down when God said: "Let the earth bring forth the living creature" [Genesis 1:24]. Then it brought forth a spirit to breathe into Adam, who thus became complete, with two sides, as it says: "And God breathed into his nostrils the breath of life; and man became a living soul" [Genesis 2:7]. When Adam arose, Eve was fixed to his side, and the Holy Spirit spread in him to each side, and so perfected itself. Afterwards, God sawed Adam in two and fashioned Eve, and brought her to him as a bride is brought to the canopy. When Lilith saw this, she fled to the cities of the sea coast, where she is still, attempting to catch men in her snares. Only when the Almighty destroys wicked Rome, will He then settle Lilith among its ruins, for she is the ruin of the world, as it is written: "Yea. the night-hag shall repose there, and shall find her a place of rest" [Isaiah 34:14, where the word *lilith* is used for the only time in the text of the Hebrew Bible].

As the *Zohar* goes on to note, Lilith flees Adam when the *neshamah* or soul is placed in him. She has not fled many poets since, and rather seems to have the power of driving their souls from them, as she does to Hollander when he emulates the dying Hadrian in a dream of death at the close of canto 6, "like something bland and vague deserting them."

The vision of a saving "sudden lady, tall, fair and distant," rises in canto 7, but Hollander's version of the *Shekhinah* is not the Kabbalistic "beautiful woman without eyes" but a cripple more out of the European Decadence, one-legged and on crutches. This displacement of Geza Roheim's mythological "woman with a penis," Aphrodite as phallic girl, is an equivocal emblem anywhere, but particularly negative in a Kabbalistic context, where it ends as the obsessive Narcissistic revelation of the closing lines of canto 7. Recoiling from this horrified nadir of vision, the poet begins a triad of cantos that will culminate in the relative serenity of canto 10, the turning-place of the sequence, where nightmare at last begins to be vanquished by peace.

Cantos 8–10 rely upon the myth of the Hyperboreans, dwellers "beyond the mountains" and "beyond the North wind," whose earthly paradise in the far North was sacred to Apollo. In Hollander's dream-allegory, the Hyperboreans represent simply his escape route from the world of Lilith into the world of peace, a route identical with the process of becoming a poet, and echoing many poets and poems. Canto 8 echoes, sometimes deliberately, Spenser's "Gardens of Adonis," Lovelace's "The Grasshopper," Tuckerman's "The Cricket," Stevens' "A Discovery of Thought," and Hart Crane's "The Broken Tower." In the next canto, other sources of vision are invoked, including the older version of the film, *Lost Horizon*, and the Hemingway story, "The Snows of Kilimanjaro," to help suggest a menacing rite-of-passage between realms of being. The beautiful canto 10, with its traditional emblems of achieved poetic peace, echoes Stevens' characteristic mode of resolution:

> *There will have been room*
> *To come upon the end of summer where*
> *Clustered, blue grapes hang in a shattered bell.*

With the modulation into the final third of his sequence, the poet begins to pass judgment upon himself. The opening of Canto 11 deliberately echoes a great passage of Sir Thomas Browne, from his *Notebooks:*

> Half our days we pass in the shadow of the earth; and
> the brother of death exacteth a third part of our lives.
> A good part of our sleep is peered out with visions and
> fantastical objects, wherein we are confessedly de-
> ceived. The day supplieth us with truths; the night with
> fictions and falsehoods.

For these unsaving fictions and falsehoods, the poet chastises
himself, echoing the Rossetti translation of Dante's stony sestina, "To the Dim Light and the Large Circle of Shade." The
greatest of precursors, Milton, is invoked in the following
canto, which relies upon the legend attached to the Jewish
festival of Simchas Torah, that the skies open in response to
the congregants' rejoicing in the Law. With canto 13, something closer to self-acceptance is achieved. Lilith's body,
which terminated in a serpent's tail, is transformed into the
constellation Scorpio, the poet's birth-sign, with its "unsting-
ing tail." This canto attempts a sky-scape, on the model of
Stevens' "Auroras of Autumn," with Jupiter passing at night
like the Haroun Al-Rashid of Tennyson's beautiful early
poem. The Orphic lyre appears as "the diamond Harp,/By
crossbow Swan," identified with Orpheus as archetypal poet.
"The pale stream" of the Milky Way illuminates a lost epiphany, "the moment that was" hinting at a kind of deferred
Gnostic salvation: "the time of this dark/Light beyond, that
seemed to be light above."

As the snow descends in the pre-dawn gloom of canto 14,
transcending the grotesque enlargements of children's stories (Chicken Little "now grown huge and old") the sleeper
finally wakens, uncertain whether the snow itself is a visionary experience ("fictions taking/Place *in vitro*"), a Lucretian
swerving of particles in a flask or test tube, or an actual
precipitate in the animal body, *in vivo*, in a greasy rain col-
lapsing on streets incapable of further givings-back of the
light. The final canto juxtaposes Lady Evening, a realized
apocalypse or actual *Shekhinah*, to the final appearance of
Lilith as "lilting Miss Noctae, witch/Of windless darknesses."
Images of a Last Judgment—the plucking out of the Roman-

tic moon as presiding but offending Eye, the seals, whirl-
winds, a last trumpet of light—herald a clarification that the
poem's final tercet lacks the revelation to assert for itself. The
poet has dreamed Nebuchadnezzar's dream, and at the close
of the cycle knows that he tells us implicitly he must dream
it over and over again.

Following Wilde, we turn to the Highest Criticism, our
own version of this Nebuchadnezzar's dream, the filthy
myths of our own visions of Lilith. In Heraclitus, Death is
Earth, Sleep is Water, Waking is Air. Fragment 77 reads:

> *Man kindles a light for himself in the*
>   *night-time,*
> *when he has died but is alive. The sleeper, whose*
> *vision has been put out, lights up from the dead;*
> *he that is awake lights up from the sleeping.*

Take this as motto, and by its light read Lilith for what she
is and must be, a myth of Earth masking as Water and Air.
Kabbalists and Gnostics, like latecomer poets, confound
Lilith with the Muse of Nihilism, the Lower Sophia, who
must suffer grief, fear, bewilderment, and ignorance, the
"affections" of all strong sensibilities afflicted by a psychology
of belatedness. The fifth "affection" in the Valentinian
Speculation, most poetic of all Gnosticisms, was the "turning
back," a conversion towards the lost Light. *The Head of the
Bed* nears greatness as a Kabbalist and Gnostic text by its
authentic and vivid portrayal of the four dark "affections"
and its poignant approach to the fifth "affection" of a "turning back."

The Gnostic Lower Sophia is akin to the Kabbalistic metaphor of the *Shekhinah*-in-exile. But even the *Shekhinah*
still-at-home, within *En Soph*, the Infinite Godhood, possesses an ambivalence unknown in the unfallen Higher
Sophia within the Valentinian Pleroma or original Fullness.
Hollander's version of the *Shekhinah*, the "Lady Evening"
of his final canto, is not wholly distinguishable from the last
appearance of his Lilith, "lilting Miss Noctae," since they

never exist simultaneously, but only in continuity with one another. Each has her terrible aspect, as in Kabbalah, where the *Shekhinah* stands as much for the divine power of "stern judgment" as for the divine quality of "mercy." To cite the *Zohar* again: "Sometimes the *Shekhinah* tastes the other side, the bitter side, and then her countenance is darkened."

Filthy myths of Lilith actually are filthy myths of the male dread of female otherness, and of what the male envies as female proximity to origins. Primal scenes, for poets, are less the scenes where they were begotten than those where they were instructed. Every poet, as he aspires towards strength, wants to be the universe, to be the whole of which all those others are parts:

> *And all the world lies well before you*
> *And in denial you glimpse the truth*
> *Whose recognition will restore you*
> *To the cool savagery of youth.*

> JAN SCHREIBER, "Camelot"

No poet, alas, can be so restored. Hollander's sequence, like all his work, is incurably elegiac, and in that quality possesses a peculiar *clinamen,* a swerve or twist away from British and European study of the nostalgias, that has distinguished American poetry at least since the Age of Emerson. American psychopoetics are dominated by an American difference from European patterns of the imagination's struggle with its own origins. The literary psychology of America is necessarily a psychology of belatedness, in which the characteristic anxiety is not so much an expectation of being flooded by poetic ancestors, as already *having been* flooded before one could even begin. Emerson's insistence upon Self-Reliance made Whitman and Dickinson and Thoreau possible, and doubtless benefited Hawthorne and Melville despite themselves. But the Scene of Instruction that Emerson sought to void glows with a more and more vivid intensity for contemporary American poets, who enter upon a legacy that paradoxically has accumulated wealth while continuing to insist that it has remained poverty-stricken.

Piaget, in studying the child's cognitive development, has posited a dynamic in which the egocentric infant develops by a progressive decentering until (usually in adolescence) the decentering is complete. The child's space then yields to universal space, and the child's time to history. Having assimilated much of the Not-Me, the child at last accommodates his vision to the vision of others. Poets, we can assume, are children who have *assimilated* more than the rest of us, and yet somehow have *accommodated* less, and so have won through the crisis of adolescence without totally decentering. Faced by the primal scene of Instruction, even in its poetic variant (where the Idea of poetry first came to them), they managed to achieve a curious detachment towards crisis that made them capable of a greater attachment to their own wavering centers. In American poets, I surmise, the detachment must be more extreme, and the consequent resistance to decentering greater, for American poets are the most conscious latecomers in the history of poetry.

All men are belated in their stance towards all women. All Kabbalists and Gnostics are latecomers in their stance towards divinity. Combine the Gnostic or Kabbalistic temperament with a male American desperately intelligent about his own origins, and you get a series of latecomer bards from the Melville of *Timoleon* through the Crane of *The Bridge* on to a large group of greatly talented and greatly handicapped contemporary Americans. Hollander's remarkable achievement is to have so dreamed his own nightmares as to have joined, if not quite the universal, at least the national predicament of our poetry. Seven times passed over Nebuchadnezzar, and did not suffice to save him. No contemporary Nebuchadnezzar can dream to save himself, or us. It is enough to take from the dream-work of Instruction a style fit for our despair.